soul survivors

Published by *Black Classics*
An imprint of The X Press
6 Hoxton Square, London N1 6NU
Tel: 0171 729 1199
Fax: 0171 729 1771
E-mail: vibes@xpress.co.uk
Website: www. xpress.co.uk

Printed by LEGO of Italy

Distributed in US by INBOOK, 1436 West Randolph Street, Chicago, Illinois 60607, USA Orders 1-800 626 4330 Fax orders 1-800 334 3892

Distributed in UK by Turnaround Distribution, Unit 3, Olympia Trading Estate, Coburg Road, London N22 6TZ
Tel: 0181 829 3000
Fax: 0181 881 5088

ISBN 1-874509-90-5

Introduction

This compilation is the record of the experience of displacement by exiled women in their own words.

The day the first of the African captives overcame the initial desperation of his new and wretched condition, flouted the viciously enforced ban of the plantation owner and slowly learned, night after night in his miserable shack, at the feeble glow of a dying candle, to decipher the first few words of, presumably, the Bible, the motion had started that would finally bring the end of over four centuries of the abomination known as slavery.

IT MUST HAVE BEEN A HELL OF A SHOCK FOR THE OVERSEER WHEN HE REALISED THAT NOT ONE BUT SEVERAL OF THE CAPTIVES HE HAD UNDER HIS WHIP COULD ACTUALLY READ.

The man himself was most probably half-illiterate; his only skill in life being the applied 'psychology' of how to keep the slaves working. Whether he knew the actual reason behind the prohibition of educating the slaves or whether he remained ignorant, he had realised they were not quite what he had expected.

Sheer brutality and terror was dispensed to those first generations of young men and women straight from the slave ship out of distant Africa. A small number managed to actually run away and set up their own communities but the majority, those who actually started to toil on the plantations of the West Indies and America were the ones who, having witnessed the carnage that open rebellion to the Europeans meant, decided there was no other way to stay alive but to submit and try to survive, one terrible day at a time. The trauma they went through is impossible to imagine. Many were but children of ten or eleven, most just teenagers, none above thirty. It is a measure of the inner strength of these first African survivors that they managed not only to hang on to their sanity, but actually started aspiring to intellectual goals. Amongst these captives were people who had been students, sons and daughters of scholars, some from Muslim societies of West Africa who knew the Koran by heart.

Within a relatively short time of their dramatic arrival in that hellish environment that the plantation was, some of these Africans not only learned to speak their tormentors' language but also achieved the illegal feat of reading and writing it well enough to express their point of view on their condition. In 1773, a young black woman called Phillys Wheatley, kidnapped as a child of 13 on the coast of Senegal years earlier, was brought to England from Boston by her owners' son. Her collection of poems was the first book by a black woman ever published. *Letters* by Ignatius Sancho, an African born on a slave ship in mid-Atlantic who had taught himself to read and write while growing up in England, was an immediate bestseller on its publication in London in 1782. By the time Ottobah Cugoano and Olaudah Equiano, both kidnapped as children from the coasts of West Africa and sold into slavery, surfaced in London a few years later and started campaigning actively against the iniquities of the slave trade, the exiles had found their voices.

While the men told of their enslavement in published volumes, rarely was the voice of the slave mother/daughter/sister/wife/aunt/niece/grandmother heard. In this unique 'no holds barred' collection, women who were there reveal the full horror of the sexual exploitation of the black female in slavery.

Marcia Williams
London, September 1999

BURY ME IN A FREE LAND

Make me a grave where'er you will,
In a lowly plain, or a lofty hill;
Make it among earth's humblest graves,
But not in a land where men are slaves.

I could not rest if around my grave
I heard the steps of a trembling slave;
His shadow above my silent tomb
Would make it a place of fearful gloom.

I could not rest if I heard the tread
Of a coffle gang to the shambles led,
And the mother's shriek of wild despair
Rise like a curse on the trembling air.

I could not sleep if I saw the lash
Drinking her blood at each fearful gash,
And I saw her babes torn from her breast,
Like trembling doves torn from their parent nest.

I'd shudder and start if I heard the bay
Of bloodhounds seizing their human prey,
And I heard the captive plead in vain
As they bound afresh his galling chain.

If I saw young girls from their mothers' arms
Bartered and sold for their youthful charms,
My eye would flash with a mournful flame,
My death-paled cheek grow red with shame.

I would sleep, dear friends, where bloated might
Can rob no man of his dearest right
My rest shall be calm in any grave
Where none can call his brother a slave.

I ask no monument, proud and high
To arrest the gaze of the passers-by,
All that my yearning spirit craves,
Is bury me not in a land of slaves.

FRANCES E.W. HARPER

CONTENT

MATTIE'S STORY

My ancestors were transported from Africa to America at the time the slave trade flourished in the Eastern States. I cannot give dates, as my progenitors, being slaves, had no means of keeping them.

By all accounts my great-grandfather was captured and brought from Africa. His original name I never learned. His master's name was Jackson and he resided in the State of New York.

My grandfather was born in the same State and also remained a slave for some length of time before being emancipated, his master presenting him with quite an amount of property. He was true, honest and responsible and this present was given him as a reward. He was much encouraged by the cheering prospect of better days. A better condition of things now presented itself.

As he possessed a large share of confidence, he came to the conclusion, as he was free, that he was capable of selecting his own residence and manage his own affairs with prudence and economy. But, alas, his hopes were soon blighted. More heart-rending sorrow and degradation awaited him.

He was earnestly invited by a white man to relinquish his former design and accompany him to Missouri and join him in speculation and become wealthy. As partners, they embarked on board a schooner for St. Charles, Mo. On the passage, my grandfather was seized with a fever and, for a while, was totally unconscious.

When he regained his reason he found himself near his journey's end, divested of his free papers and all others. On his arrival at St. Charles he was seized by a huge, surly-looking slaveholder who claimed him as his property. The contract had previously been concluded by his Judas-like friend, who had received the bounty.

Oh, what a sad disappointment. After serving for thirty years to be thrust again into bondage where a deeper degradation and sorrow and hopeless toil were to be his portion for the remaining years of his existence.

In deep despair and overwhelmed with grief, he made his escape to the woods, determined to put an end to his sorrows by perishing with cold and hunger. His master immediately pursued him and, in twenty-four hours, found him with hands and feet frost-bitten, in consequence of which he lost the use of his fingers and toes and was thenceforth of little use to his new master.

He remained with him, however, and married a woman in the same station in life. They lived as happily as their circumstances would permit.

As Providence alloted, they only had one son, which was my father, Westly Jackson. He had a deep affection for his family, which the slave ever cherishes for his dear ones. He had no other link to fasten him to the human family but his fervent love for those who were bound to him by love and sympathy in their wrongs and sufferings.

My grandfather remained in the same family until his death. My father, Westly Jackson, married, at the age of twenty-two, a girl owned by James Harris, named Ellen Turner. Nothing of importance occurred until three years after their marriage when her master, Harris, became bankrupt through the extravagance and mismanagement of his wife, who was a great spendthrift and a dreaded terror to the poor slaves and all others with whom she associated in common circumstances. Consequently the entire stock was sold by the sheriff to a trader residing in Virginia.

On account of the good reputation my mother sustained as a worthy servant and excellent cook, a tyrannical and much dreaded slaveholder watched for an opportunity to purchase her, but fortunately arrived a few moments too late and she was bid off in too poor a condition of health to remain long a subject of banter and speculation. Her husband was allowed to carefully lift her down from the block and accompany her to her new master's, Charles Canory, who treated her very kindly while she remained in his family.

Mr. Canory resided in St. Charles County for five years after he purchased my mother. During that time my father and mother were in the same neighborhood, but a short distance from each other.

But another trial awaited them.

Her master moved twenty miles away to a village called Bremen, near St. Louis, Mo. My father, thereafter, visited my mother once a week, walking the distance every Saturday evening and returning on Sunday evening.

Through all her trials and deprivations, her trust and confidence was in Him who rescued his faithful followers from the fiery furnace and the lion's den and led Moses through the Red Sea. Her trust and confidence was in Jesus. She relied on His precious promises and ever found Him a present help in every time of need.

Two years later my father was sold and separated from us. But previous to his delivery to his new master he made his escape to a free State. My mother was then left with two children. She had three during the time they were permitted to remain together, and buried one. Their names were Sarah Ann, Mattie Jane and Esther J.

When my father left I was about three years of age, yet I can well remember the little kindness he used to bestow upon us and the deep affection and fondness he manifested for us. I shall never forget the bitter anguish of my parents' hearts, the sighs they uttered or the profusion of tears which coursed down their sable cheeks.

Oh, what a horrid scene, but he was not her's, for cruel

hands had separated them.

> *The strongest tie of earthly joy that bound the aching heart*
> *His love was e'er a joyous light that o'er the pathway shone*
> *A fountain gushing ever new amid life's desert wild*
> *His slightest word was a sweet tone of music round her heart*
> *Their lives a streamlet blended in one. Oh, Father, must they part?*
> *They tore him from her circling arms, her last and fond embrace*
> *Never again can her sad eyes gaze upon his mournful face*
> *It is not strange these bitter sighs are constant bursting forth*
> *Amid mirth and glee and revelry she never took a part*
> *She was a mother left alone with sorrow in her heart.*

My mother was conscious some time previous of the change that was to take place with my father and if he was sold in the immediate vicinity he would be likely to be sold again at their will. She concluded to assist him to make his escape from bondage. Though the parting was painful, it afforded her solace in the contemplation of her husband becoming a free man and cherishing a hope that her little family, through the aid of some angel of mercy, might be enabled to make their escape also and meet to part no more on earth.

My father came to spend the night with us, according to his usual custom. It was the last time, and sadness brooded upon his brow. It was the only opportunity he had to make his escape without suspicion and detection, as he was immediately to fall into the hands of a new master. He had never been sold from the place of his birth before and was determined never to be sold again if God would verify his promise.

My father was not educated, but was a preacher and administered the word of God according to the dictation and revelation of the Spirit. His former master had allowed him the privilege of holding meetings in the village within the limits of his pass on the Sundays when he visited my mother. But on this

Saturday evening he arrived and gave us all his farewell kiss and hurried away.

His master called a number of times and enquired for him and strongly pressed my mother to give him an account of my father, but she never gave it. We waited patiently, hoping to learn if he succeeded in gaining his freedom.

Many anxious weeks and months passed before we could get any tidings from him, until at length my mother heard that he was in Chicago, a free man and preaching the Gospel.

He made every effort to get his family, but all in vain. The spirit of slavery so strongly existed that letters could not reach her; they were all destroyed. My parents had never learned the rescuing scheme of the underground railroad which had borne so many thousands to the standard of freedom and victories. They knew no other resource than to depend upon their own chance in running away. If caught, they were in a worse condition than before.

Two years after my father's departure, my mother, with my sister and myself, attempted to make her escape. After traveling two days we reached Illinois. We slept in the woods at night. I believe my mother had food to supply us but fasted herself. But the alarm had reached there before us and loafers were already in search of us. As soon as we were seen on the riverbank, one of the spies made enquiries respecting my mother's suspicious appearance. She was aware that she was arrested, consequently she gave a true account of herself — that she was in search of her husband. We were then destitute of any articles of clothing excepting our wearing apparel. Mother had become so weary that she was compelled to abandon our package of clothing on the way.

We were taken back to St. Louis and committed to prison and remained there one week, after which they put us in Linch's trader's yard, where we remained about four weeks. We were then sold to William Lewis.

Mr. Lewis was a very severe master and inflicted such punishment upon us as he thought proper. However, I only remember one severe contest Mr. Lewis had with my mother.

For some slight offence Mrs. Lewis became offended and was tartly and loudly reprimanding her, when Mr. L. came in and rashly felled mother to the floor with his fist.

His wife was constantly pulling our ears, snapping us with her thimble and rapping us on the head. It appeared impossible to please her. They had a cowhide which she used to inflict on a little slave girl she previously owned, nearly every night. This was done to teach the little girl to wake early enough to wait on her children.

My mother was a cook, as I before stated, and was in the habit of roasting meats and toasting bread. As they stinted us for food my mother roasted the cowhide. It was rather poor picking, but it was the last cowhide my mother ever had an opportunity to cook while we remained in that family.

Mr. L. soon moved about six miles from the city and entered in partnership with his brother-in-law. The servants were then divided and distributed in both families. It unfortunately fell to my lot to live with Mrs. Larry, my mistress' sister, which rendered my condition worse than the first. My master even disapproved of my ill-treatment and took me to where my mother resided before my father's escape.

After six years absence of my father, my mother married again, a man by the name of George Brown with whom she lived for about four years and had two children, before he was sold for requesting enough food. His master considered it a great insult and declared he would sell him. Previous to this insult, as he called it, my step-father was foreman in Mr. L.'s tobacco factory. He was trusty and of good moral habits and was calculated to bring the highest price in the human market; therefore the excuse to sell him for the above offence was only a plot.

The morning this offence occurred, Mr. L. bid my father to remain in the kitchen 'til he had eaten his breakfast. After pulling his ears and slapping his face, bade him come to the factory. Instead of going to the factory my step-father went to Canada.

Thus my poor mother was again left alone with two more children added to her misery and sorrow to toil on her weary pilgrimage.

Racked with agony and pain, with a purpose nought could move and the zeal of woman's love, down she knelt in agony to ask the Lord to clear the way.

Though nine long years had passed without one glimmering light of day, she never did forget to pray And has not yet, though whips and chains are cast away.

For thus said the blessed Lord:

> *I will verify my word.*
> *By the faith that has not failed*
> *Thou hast asked and shall prevail.*

We remained but a short time at the same residence when Mr. Lewis moved again to the country. Soon after, my little brother was taken sick in consequence of being confined in a box in which my mother was obliged to keep him. If permitted to creep around the floor her mistress thought it would take too much time to attend to him. As a consequence, he was two years old and had never walked. His limbs were perfectly paralyzed for want of exercise. We now saw him gradually failing, but were not allowed to render assistance. Mother watched over him for three months by night and attended to her domestic affairs by day. Even the morning he died, she was compelled to attend to her usual work.

The night previous to his death we were aware he could not survive through the approaching day, but it made no impression on my mistress until she came into the kitchen and saw his life fast ebbing away, then she put on a sad countenance for fear of being exposed and told my mother to take the child to her room, where he only lived one hour. When she found he was dead she ordered grave clothes to be brought and gave my mother time to bury him that morning, that solemn morning.

It appears to me that when that little spirit departed as though all heaven rejoiced and angels veiled their faces, my mother too in concert joined her mingled praise with them combined. Her little saint had gone to God, who saved him with his precious blood. Who said, "Suffer little children to come unto me and forbid them not."

Soon after the war commenced the rebel soldiers encamped near Mr. Lewis' residence and remained there one week. They were then ordered by General Lyons to surrender, but they refused. There were seven thousand Union and seven, hundred rebel soldiers. The Union soldiers surrounded the camp and took them and exhibited them through the city and then confined them in prison.

I told my mistress that the Union soldiers were coming to take the camp. She replied that it was false, that it was General Kelly coming to re-enforce Gen. Frost. In a few moments the alarm was heard. I told Mrs. L. the Unionists had fired upon the rebels. She replied it was only the salute of Gen. Kelley.

At night her husband came home with the news that Camp Jackson was taken and all the soldiers prisoners. Mrs. Lewis asked how the Union soldiers could take seven hundred men when they only numbered the same. Mr. L. replied they had seven thousand. She was much astonished and cast her eye around to us for fear we might hear her.

Her suspicion was correct; there was not a word passed that escaped our listening ears. My mother and myself could read enough to make out the news in the papers. The Union soldiers took much delight in tossing a newspaper over the fence to us. It aggravated my mistress very much.

My mother used to sit up nights and read to keep posted about the war. The days of sadness for mistress were days of joy for us. We shouted and laughed to the top of our voices. My mistress was more enraged than ever, nothing pleased her.

One evening, after I had attended to my usual duties and I supposed all was complete, she, in a terrible rage, declared I should be punished that night. I did not know the cause, neither did she. She went immediately and selected a switch. She placed it in the corner of the room to await the return of her husband at night for him to whip me.

As I was not pleased with the idea of a whipping I bent the switch in the shape of 'W', which was the first letter of his name and, after I had attended to the dining room, my fellow servant and myself walked away and stayed with an aunt of mine during the night.

In the morning we made our way to the arsenal, but could gain no admission. While we were wandering about seeking protection, the girl's father overtook us and persuaded us to return home.

We finally complied.

All was quiet. Not a word was spoken respecting our sudden departure. All went on as usual. I was permitted to attend to my work without interruption for the next three weeks.

One morning I entered Mrs. Lewis' room. She was inside, complaining of something I had neglected. Mr. L. then enquired if I had done my work. I told him I had. She then flew into a rage and told him I was saucy and to strike me. He immediately gave me a severe blow with a stick, which inflicted a deep wound upon my head and has left a mark which will ever remind me of my treatment while in slavery. The blood ran over my clothing, which gave me a frightful appearance.

Mr. Lewis then ordered me to change my clothing immediately. As I did not obey, he became more enraged and pulled me into another room and threw me on the floor, then placed his knee on my stomach, slapped me on the face and beat me with his fist. I struggled mightily and stood him a good test for a while, but he was fast conquering me, and would have punished me more had not my mother interfered. He told her to go away or he would compel her to, but she remained until he left me. He was aware my mother could usually defend herself against one man and that together we would overpower him, so after giving his wife strict orders to take me upstairs and keep me there, he took his carriage and drove away. But she forgot it, as usual. She was highly gratified with my appropriate treatment, as she called it and retired to her room, leaving me to myself.

I then went to my mother and told her I was going away. She bid me go and added "May the Lord help you."

I started for the arsenal again and succeeded in gaining admittance and seeing the adjutant. He ordered me to go to another tent where there was a woman in similar circumstances, cooking. When the General found I was there he sent me to the boarding house. I remained there three weeks, wearing the same stained clothing as when I was so severely punished.

Thanks be to God, though tortured by wrong and goaded by oppression, the hearts that would madden with misery have broken the iron yoke.

At the expiration of three weeks Mr. Lewis called at my boarding house, accompanied by his brother-in-law and enquired of me. The General informed him where I was.

Mr. Lewis told me my mother was very anxious for me to come home, so I returned.

The General had ordered Mr. Lewis to call at headquarters,

where he told him if he had treated me right I would not have been compelled to seek protection of him; that my first appearance was sufficient proof of his cruelty.

Mr. L. promised to take me home and treat me kindly.

Instead of fulfilling his promise, he carried me to the trader's yard, where, to my great surprise, I found my mother. She had been there during my absence, where she was kept for fear she would find me and take my brother and sister and make her escape. There was so much excitement at that time (1861) by Union soldiers rendering fugitive slaves shelter and protection, he was aware that if she applied to them, as he did not fulfill his promise in my case, he would stand a poor chance. If my mother made application to them for protection they would learn that he did not return me home and immediately detect the intrigue.

After I was safely secured in the trader's yard, Mr. L. took my mother home. I remained in the yard three months. Near the termination of the time of my confinement, I was passing by the office when the cook of the arsenal saw and recognized me and informed the General that Mr. L. had disobeyed his orders and had put me in the trader's yard instead of taking me home.

The General immediately arrested Mr. L. and gave him one hundred lashes with the cow-hide, so that they might identify him by a scarred back, as well as his slaves.

My mother had the pleasure of washing his stained clothes, otherwise it would not have been known. My master was compelled to pay three thousand dollars and let me out. He then put me to service, where I remained seven months, after which he came in great haste and took me into the city and put me into the trader's yard again.

After he received the punishment, he treated my mother and the children worse than ever, which caused her to take her children and hide themselves in the city. She would have remained undetected, had it not been for a traitor who pledged himself to keep the secret. But King Whiskey fired up his brain one evening, and out popped the secret. My mother and sister were consequently taken and committed to the trader's yard. My little brother was then eight years of age, my sister sixteen, and myself eighteen. We remained there two weeks, when a rough-looking man called Capt. Tirrell came to the yard and enquired for our family. After he had examined us, he remarked that we were a fine-looking family and bid us retire.

In about two hours he returned, at the edge of the evening, with a covered wagon and took my mother, brother and sister and left me. My mother refused to go without me and told him she would raise an alarm. He advised her to remain as quiet as possible. At length she was compelled to go. When she entered the wagon there was a man standing behind with his hands on each side of the wagon to prevent her from making her escape. She sprang to her feet and gave this man a desperate blow and, leaping to the ground, she made an alarm.

This was before the emancipation proclamation was issued and there were quite a number of Union policemen guarding the city at that time. The watchmen came to her assistance immediately and rendered her due justice as far as possible.

After she leaped from the wagon, Capt. Tirrell drove on, taking her children to the boat. The police questioned my mother. She told them that Capt. Tirrell had put her children on board the boat and was going to take them to Memphis and sell them into hard slavery. They accompanied her to the boat and arrived just as they were casting off. The police ordered them to stop and immediately deliver up the children, who had been hidden in the Captain's private apartment. They were brought forth and returned.

Slave speculation was forbidden in St. Louis at that time. The Union soldiers had possession of the city, but their power was limited to the suppression of the selling of slaves outside the city. Considerable smuggling was done, however, by pretending Unionism, which was the case with our family.

Immediately after dinner my mother called for me to accompany her to our new home, the residence of the Captain. We fared very well while we were there.

Mrs. Tirrell was insane and my mother had charge of the house. We remained there four months. The Captain came home only once a week and he never troubled us for fear we might desert him.

His intention was to smuggle us away before the State became free. That was the understanding when he bought us from Mr. Lewis, as there was not much point in purchasing slaves while the proclamation was pending and there was the likelihood of losing all your property. But they would, for a trifle, purchase a whole family of four or five persons to send out of the State. Kentucky paid as much, or more than ever, for slaves. As they pretended to take no part in the rebellion, they supposed they would be allowed to keep them without interference. Consequently the Captain's intention was to keep as quiet as possible until the excitement concerning us was over and he could get us off without detection.

Mr. Lewis would rather have disposed of us for nothing than have seen us free. He hated my mother in consequence of her desire for freedom and her endeavors to teach her children the right way as far as her ability would allow. He also held a charge against her for reading the papers and understanding political affairs. When he found he was to lose his slaves he could not bear the idea of her being free. He thought it too hard, as she had raised so many tempests for him, to see her free and under her own control. He had tantalized her in every possible way to humiliate and annoy her, yet while he could demand her services he appreciated and placed perfect confidence in mother and family. None but a fiendish slaveholder could have rended an honest Christian heart in such a manner as this.

Though it was her sad and weary lot to toil in slavery, but one thing cheered mother's weary soul when almost in despair — that she could gain a sure relief in prayer.

One day the Captain commenced complaining of the expense of so large a family, and proposed to my mother that we become engaged to Mr. Adams. He had bought himself previously for a large price.

After they became acquainted, the Captain had an excellent opportunity of carrying out his stratagem. He commenced bestowing charity upon Mr. Adams.

As he had purchased himself, and Capt. T. had agreed not to sell my mother, they had decided to marry at an early day. They hired a house in the city and were to commence housekeeping immediately. The Captain made him a number of presents and seemed much pleased with the arrangement.

The day previous to the one set for the marriage, while they were setting their house in order, a man called and enquired for a nurse, pretending he wanted one of us. Mother was absent; he said he would call again, but he never came. On Wednesday evening we attended a protracted meeting. After we had returned home and retired, a loud rap was heard at the door. My Aunt enquired who was there. The reply was, "Open the door or I will break it down."

In a moment, in rushed seven men, four watchmen and three traders, and ordered mother to take my brother and me and follow them, which she hastened to do as fast as possible, but we were not allowed time to put on our usual attire. They thrust us into a closed carriage. For fear of my mother alarming the citizens they threw her to the ground and choked her until she was nearly strangled, then pushed her into a coach.

The night was dark and dreary, the stars refused to shine, the moon to shed her light.

We were hurried along the streets. The inhabitants heard our cries and rushed to their doors, but our carriage being perfectly tight and the alarm so sudden, we were at the jail before they could give us any relief.

There were strong Union men and officers in the city and if they could have been informed of the human smuggling they would have released us. But oh, that horrid, dilapidated prison, with its dim lights and dingy walls, again presented itself to our view.

My sister was there first and we were thrust in and remained there until three o'clock the following afternoon. Could we have notified the police we should have been released, but no opportunity was given us.

It appears that this kidnapping had been in contemplation from the time we were before taken and returned; and Captain Tirrell's kindness to mother, his benevolence towards Mr. Adams in assisting him to furnish his house, his generosity in letting us work for ourselves, his approbation in regard to the contemplated marriage, was only a trap. Thus, instead of a wedding Thursday evening, we were hurled across the ferry to Albany Court House and to Kentucky, through the rain and without our outer garments. My mother had lost her bonnet and shawl in the struggle while being thrust in the coach, consequently she had no protection from the storm and the rest of us were in similar circumstances.

I believe we passed through Springfield. I think it was the first stopping place after we left East St. Louis and we were put on board a train and hidden in the gentlemen's smoking car, in which there were a few rebels.

We arrived in Springfield about twelve o'clock at night. When we took the train it was dark, bleak and cold. It was the 18th of March and, as we were without bonnets and clothing to shield us from the sleet and wind, we suffered intensely. The old trader, for fear that mother might make her escape, carried my brother, nine years of age, from one train to the other.

We took the train for Albany and arrived at eight o'clock in the morning. We were then carried on the ferry in a wagon. There was another family in the wagon, in the same condition.

We landed at Portland, from thence to Louisville and were put into John Clark's trader's yard and sold out separately, except my mother and little brother, who were sold together. Mother remained in the trader's yard two weeks, my sister six, myself four.

Mother was sold to Captain Plasio. My sister to Benj. Board, and myself to Capt. Ephraim Frisbee.

The man who bought my mother was a Spaniard. After she had been there a short time he tried to have my mother let my brother stop at his saloon, a very dissipated place, to wait upon his miserable crew, but my mother objected. In spite of her objections he took my brother down to try him, but some Union soldiers called at the saloon and, noticing that he was very small, questioned him. My brother, child-like, divulged the whole matter. The Captain, fearful of being betrayed and losing his property, let him continue with my mother.

We were all sold for extravagant prices. The Captain paid eight hundred dollars for my mother and brother. My sister, aged sixteen, was sold for eight hundred and fifty dollars. I was sold for nine hundred dollars. This was in 1863.

My mother was a cook and fared very well. My sister was sold to a single gentleman, whose intended took charge of her until they were married, after which they took her to her home. She was their waiting-maid and fared as well as could be expected.

I fared worse than either of the family. I was not allowed enough to eat, exposed to the cold and not allowed through the cold winter to thoroughly warm myself. The house was very large and I could gain no access to the fire. I was kept constantly at work of the heaviest kind — moving heavy trunks and boxes, washing 'til ten and twelve o'clock at night. There were three deaths in the family while I remained there, and the entire burden was put upon me.

I often felt to exclaim as the Children of Israel did: *O Lord, my burden is greater than I can bear.*

I was then seventeen years of age. My health has been impaired from that time to the present. I have a severe pain in my side by the slightest over-exertion. In the winter I suffer intensely with cold and cannot get warm unless in a room heated to eighty degrees. I am infirm and burdened with the influence of slavery, whose mark will ever remain on my mind and body.

For six months I tried to make my escape. I used to rise at four o'clock in the morning to find someone to assist me and, at last, I succeeded.

I was allowed two hours once in every two weeks to go and return three miles. I could contrive no other way than to improve one of these opportunities, in which I was finally successful. I became acquainted with some persons who assisted slaves to escape by the underground railroad. They were colored people.

I was to pretend that I was going to church. The man who was to assist and introduce me to the proper parties was to linger on the street opposite the house and I was to follow at a short distance.

On Sunday evening I begged leave to attend church, which was reluctantly granted if I completed all my work, which was no easy task. It appeared as if my mistress used every possible exertion to delay me from church and I concluded that her old cloven-footed companion had impressed my intentions on her mind.

Finally, when I was ready to start, my mistress took a notion to go out to ride and desired me to dress her little boy before getting ready for church. In those days women used to wear extensive hoops, and as I had attached my whole wardrobe under mine by a cord around my waist, it required considerable dexterity and no small amount of maneuvering to hide the fact from my mistress. While attending to the child I had managed to stand in one corner of the room, for fear she might come in contact with me and thus discover that my hoops were not so elastic as they usually are. I endeavored to conceal my excitement by backing and edging very genteelly out of the door. I had nine pieces of clothing thus concealed on my person and, as the string which fastened them was small, it caused me considerable discomfort.

To my great satisfaction I at last made it out into the street and watched my master and mistress drive off in great haste.

They were soon out of sight.

I saw my guide patiently awaiting me. I followed him at a distance until we arrived at the church and there met two young ladies, one of whom handed me a pass and told me to follow them at a square's distance.

It was now twilight. There was a company of soldiers about to take passage across the ferry and I followed. I showed my pass and proceeded up the stairs on the boat. While thus ascending the stairs, the cord which held my bundle of clothing broke, and my feet became entangled in my wardrobe. By proceeding, the first step released one foot and the next the other. This was observed only by a few soldiers, who were too deeply engaged in their own affairs to interfere with mine.

I seated myself in a remote corner of the boat and, shortly after, landed on free soil for the first time in my life.

I was now under my own control!

The train was waiting in Jefferson City for passengers to Indianapolis, where we arrived about nine o'clock.

My first business, after my arrival at Indianapolis, was to find a boarding place, in which I at once succeeded.

A few hours thereafter I was at a place of service of my own choice. I had always been under the yoke of oppression, compelled to submit to its laws and not allowed to advance a rod from the house, or even out of call, without a severe punishment. Now this constant fear and restless yearning was over. It appeared as though I had emerged into a new world, or had never lived in the old one before. The people I lived with were Unionists and became immediately interested in teaching and encouraging me in my literary advancement and all other important improvements, which precisely met the natural desires for which my soul had ever yearned since my earliest recollection. I could read a little, but was not allowed to learn in slavery. Instead, I was obliged to pay twenty-five cents for every letter written for me.

I now began to feel that, as I was free, I could learn to write as well as others. Consequently Mrs. Harris, the lady with whom I lived, volunteered to assist me. I was soon enabled to write quite a legible hand, which I find a great convenience. I would advise all — young, middle aged or old — in a free country to learn to read and write. If this little book should fall into the hands of one deficient of the important knowledge of writing, I hope they will remember the old maxim: *Never too old to learn.*

Manage your own secrets and divulge them by the silent language of your pen. Had our blessed President considered it too humiliating to learn in advanced years, our race would yet have remained under the galling yoke of oppression.

After I had been with Mrs. Harris seven months, the joyful news came of the surrender of Lee's army and the capture of Richmond.

> *Whilst the country's hearts were throbbing*
> *Filled with joy for victories won*
> *Whilst the stars and stripes were waving*
> *O'er each cottage, ship and dome*

Came upon like winged lightning
Words that turned each joy to dread,
Froze with horror as we listened:
Our beloved chieftain, Lincoln's dead

War's dark clouds has long held o'er us
They have rolled their gloomy folds away
And all the world is anxious, waiting
For that promised peaceful day.
But that fearful blow inflicted
Fell on his devoted head
And from every town and hamlet
Came the cry our Chieftain's dead.

Weep, weep, O bleeding nation
For the patriot spirit fled,
All untold our country's future
Buried with the silent dead.

We mourn as a nation has never yet mourned
The foe to our freedom more deeply has scorned.
In the height of his glory in manhood's full prime
Our country's preserver through darkest of time
A merciful being, whose kindness all shared
Shown mercy to others. Why was he not spared?

The lover of Justice, the friend of the slave
He struck at oppression and made it a grave
He spoke for our bond-men and chains from them fell
By making them soldiers they served our land well.

Because he had spoken from sea unto sea
Glad tidings go heavenward, our country is free
And angels I'm thinking looked down from above

With sweet smiles approving his great works of love.

His name with the honor forever will live
Time to his laurels new lustre will give
He lived so unselfish, so loyal and true
That his deeds will shine brighter at every view.

Then honor and cherish the name of the brave
The champion of freedom, the friend to the slave
The far-sighted statesman who saw a fair end
When north land and south land one flag shall defend.

Rest, rest, fallen chieftain, thy labors are o'er
For thee mourns a nation as never before
Farewell honored chieftain whom millions adore
Farewell gentle spirit, whom heaven has won.

In two or three weeks after the body of the President was carried through, my sister made her escape, but by some means we entirely lost trace of her. We heard she was in a free State.

In three months my mother also escaped. She rose quite early in the morning, took my little brother and arrived at my place of service in the afternoon. I was much surprised, and asked my mother how she came there. She could scarcely tell me for weeping, but I soon found out the mystery.

After so many long years and so many attempts, for this was her seventh, she at last succeeded and we were now all free. My mother had been a slave for more than forty-three years and liberty was very sweet to her. The sound of freedom was music in our ears; the air was pure and fragrant; the genial rays of the glorious sun burst forth with a new lustre upon us, and all creation resounded in responses of praise to the author and creator of him who proclaimed life and freedom to the slave.

I was overjoyed with my personal freedom, but the joy at my mother's escape was greater than anything I had ever known. It was a joy that reaches beyond the tide and anchors in the harbor of eternal rest. While in oppression, this eternal life-preserver had continually wafted her toward the land of freedom, which she was confident of gaining, whatever might betide.

Our joy that we were permitted to mingle together our earthly bliss in glorious strains of freedom was indescribable. My mother responded with the children of Israel: *The Lord is my strength and my song. The Lord is a man of war and the Lord is his name.*

We left Indianapolis the day after my mother arrived and took the train at eleven o'clock the following evening for St. Louis, my native State. We were then free and, instead of being hurried along bare-headed and half-naked through train wagons and boats by a brutal master with a bill of sale in his pocket, we were our own, comfortably clothed and having the true emblems of freedom.

> *Soon is the echo and the shadow o'er*
> *Soon, soon we lie with lid-encumbered eyes*
> *And the great fabrics that we reared before*
> *Crumble to make a dust to hide who dies.*

SYLVIA DUBOIS: THE SLAVE WHO WHIPPED HER MISTRESS

Most folks think that niggers ain't no account, but if you think what I tell you is worth publishing, I will be glad if you do it. It won't do me no good, but maybe it will somebody else. I've lived a good while, and have seen a good deal, and if I should tell you all I've seen, it would make the hair stand up all over your head.

I was born on this mountain in an old tavern that used to stand near the Rock Mills. My parents were slaves, and when my master moved down to Neshanic, I went along with them; and when my master went to Great Bend, on the Susquchanna, I went with him there. Afterwards I lived in New Brunswick and in Princeton and other places. Then I inherited a house and a lot of land at my grandfather's death, that's what brought me back here to the mountain.

My father was Cuffy Baird, a slave to John Baird. He was a fifer in the Battle of Princeton. He used to be a fifer for the minutemen in the days of the Revolution. My mother was Dorcas Compton, a slave to Richard Compton, the proprietor of the hotel at Rock Mills.

They didn't used to keep a record of the birth of niggers; they hardly kept a record of the birth of white children; none but the grand folks kept a record of the birth of their children — they didn't no more keep the date of a young nigger than they did of a calf or a colt; the young niggers were born in the Fall or in the Spring, in the Summer or in the Winter, in cabbage time or when the cherries were ripe, when they were planting corn or when they were husking corn, and that's all the way they talked about a nigger's age.

There's only one way to tell my age, to be sure, and that's what makes folks say that I am a hundred and fifteen years old.

They tell this by the record of the birth of Richard Compton.

Many other old folks used to tell me that, when my mother was a slave to Richard Compton, there was born to him a son, whom they called Richard after his father. When this son Richard was two days old, I was born; so there is but two days difference between the date of Richard Compton's birth and my birth.

In an old Bible which is now in the possession of Mr. Richard Gomo who lives near Rock Mills, is the record of the Compton family. By referring to this record they tell how old I am. I can't read, but I expect they tell me right. I know that I am older than anybody else around here — older than their parents were; and in most cases I knew their great-grandparents.

I remember that while we were small children, I and Richard Compton were about of a size, and that we used to play together. My mother and his mother used to tell me that we both nursed the same breast, alternately, the same day. As we were so near the same age, when his mother wished to go away to visit, or upon business, Richard was left in the care of my mother. Once, Mrs. Compton and one of the neighbors was gone to the city a whole week; and while gone, Richard was left in charge of my mother. Then she used to take us both upon her lap and, while he was nursing one breast, I was nursing the other. They used to say that this was the reason Richard and I got along so well together. As long as he lived, he always claimed to be about my age.

When I was two years old, my mother bought her time off Richard Compton, Minical Dubois going her security for the payment of the money. As my mother failed to make payment at the time appointed, she became the property of Minical Dubois. With this failure to make payment, Dubois was greatly disappointed and much displeased, as he did not wish to fall heir to my mother and her children, as slaves to him. So he treated mother badly — oftentimes cruelly. On one occasion, when her babe was but three days old, he whipped her with an ox-goad, because she didn't hold a hog while he yoked it. It was in March, the ground was wet and slippery and the hog proved too strong for her under the circumstances. From the exposure and the whipping she became severely sick with fever. It took her a long while to recover.

Under the slave laws of New Jersey, when the slave thought the master too severe and the slave and the master did not get along harmoniously, the slave had a right to find a new master. Accordingly my mother Dorcas went in quest of a new master, and as Mr. William Baird used to send things for her and her children to eat when Dubois neglected or refused to furnish enough to satisfy their craving stomachs, she asked him to buy her. This he did. And she liked him well, but she was ambitious to be free. Accordingly, she bought her time off Baird but, again, failed to make payment and returned to him his slave.

She was then sold to Miles Smith, who was a kind master and a good man. But she yearned to be free, so off Smith she bought her time and went away to work and to live with strangers. Once more, she failed to make payment at the appointed time. She was taken back a slave and spent the remainder of her days with Smith, and was buried about 45 years ago upon his homestead.

I remained a slave to Minical Dubois. He did not treat me cruelly. I tried to please him and he tried to please me and we got along together pretty well — except sometimes I would be a little obstinate, and then he would give me a severe flogging.

When I was about five years old, he moved to a farm near the village of Flagtown. While there I had good times — plenty to eat, plenty of clothes and plenty of fun — only my mistress was terribly emotional and terribly cross to me. I did not like her and she did not like me, so she used to beat me badly. On one occasion, I did something that did not suit her. As usual she scolded me. Then I was saucy. Hereupon she whipped me until she marked me so badly I will never lose the scars. You can see them here upon my head today, and I will never lose them if I live another hundred years.

They gave us Indian dumplings, samp porridge, corn bread, potatoes, pork, beef, mush and milk, and nigger butter; and we didn't get a bellyful of these sometimes. I've often gone to bed hungry, but it was no use to complain — you had your measure and you got no more. That's the way they fed young niggers in old times, but they made 'em grow.

To make Indian dumplings, scald the Indian meal, work it into a ball, and then boil until done in the liquor that meat — pork or beef — has been boiled in. These were eaten without any dip, butter, or sauce.

To make samp porridge: boil equal parts of beef and pork together until done; remove the meat and stir into the liquor in which the meat was boiled.

Corn bread was made by mixing equal measures of Indian meal and rye meal together, and baking it in an oven.

Nigger butter was made by mixing two parts of lard with one part of molasses. This nigger butter was what we had to use on our bread; and we did well if we didn't have to spread, it deuced thin. The bread was so hard that it needed greasing, and this was all that we had to grease it with — we had no gravy.

We used to have pies occasionally. Sometimes they were made out of sweet apples, sometimes out of sour ones without any sugar or molasses — they didn't feed niggers sugar and molasses much in those days. The white folks didn't get much of 'em — their pies were almost as sour as ours, and there was very little sugar in their coffee, and the sugar that they used was as black as my hide.

We never drank coffee or tea. Sometimes we got some cider. The white folks only drank tea and coffee on Sunday, or when they had company.

They used to boil or roast our potatoes with the skins on, and then we didn't take the skins off — we ate 'em skins and all. And the white folks ate theirs just so; but they had gravy or butter to put on theirs.

I expect folks nowadays think that this was hard fare, but it was good enough when we had enough of it. But sometimes we didn't get a bellyfull — that went a little hard. If the folks nowadays would live as we used to, they'd be a good deal stronger, more healthy, and wouldn't die so soon. They eat too many dainties — too much sugar, too many sweet puddings and pies, too much rich cake and too much fresh bread; and they drink too much coffee and tea; and they don't dress warm enough — that calico ain't the thing for health. We used to wear woollen underclothes, and our skirts were always made of linsey-woolsey. Our stockings were woollen and our shoes were made of good thick leather, so heavy that you could kick a man's tripe out with 'em. J

This is the way we used to dress, and it was a good way, too. The old masters knew how to take care of their niggers.

We had good beds to sleep in; the ticks were filled with straw and we had plenty of woollen blankets and coverlets, as they used to call 'em. The fires were all made of wood, and usually they were big. The fire places usually extended entirely across one end of the kitchen — 15 to 20 feet wide, with large stone jambs that made 'em three or more feet deep, provided with a chimney that two or three could climb up and stand in, side by side. In the back part of this huge fireplace a large back-log — as much as two or three could carry — was placed, and upon the handirons another log called a fore-stick, as much as a man could carry, was placed; and then between this back-log and fore-stick was piled smaller wood, until it made a fire that would scare the young folks of this generation out of their wits. This big fire not only warmed, but it also lighted the room. As a rule, the niggers had no other light and no other fire than this. So they had to stay in the kitchen — this was their part of the house, and here they had good times, too. The white folks were in another part of the house where the fireplace was not quite so big. Sometimes the white folks had stoves, and then they lighted their room with candles. There was no kerosene then, nor any coal; they didn't know how to use such things.

When I was about ten years old, the Battle of Monmouth occurred. I remember very well when my master came home from that battle. Cherries were ripe and we were gathering harvest. He was an officer, but I do not know his rank. He told great stories about the battle and of the bravery of the New Jersey Militia, and about the conduct of General Washington. He said they whipped the British badly, but it was a desperate fight. He told us that the battle occurred on the hottest day he ever saw and that he came near to perishing from the excess of heat and from thirst and that a great many died for want of water.

I also remember when my father and others returned from the battles of Trenton and Princeton — but I was younger then and only remember that it was winter, and that they complained that they had suffered much from cold and exposure.

Before the Battle of Princeton my master had been a prisoner of war. He had been captured while fighting on the water, somewhere near New York. I used to hear him tell how he and several others were crowded into a very small room in the hold of a vessel — the trap door securely fastened down and the supply of fresh air so completely shut off that almost all who were imprisoned died in a few hours. In this place they were kept two days. Dubois, by breathing with his mouth in close contact with a nail hole, held out until he was removed. Two or three others were fortunate enough to find some other defects in the woodwork, through which a scanty supply of air came.

When I was in my fourteenth year, my master moved from Flagtown to his farm along the Susquehanna River. This farm is the land on which the village called Great Bend has been built. When we moved to the farm, there was but one other house in the settlement for the distance of several miles. These two houses were built of logs. The one upon my master's farm had been kept as a tavern, and when he moved into it he kept it as a tavern.

Even then the place was known as Great Bend. It was an important stopping place for travelers on their way to the Lake Countries and to other places westward. Also, it was a place much visited by boatmen going down and up the river. Here, too, came great numbers of hunters and drovers.

In moving to Great Bend, we went in two wagons. We took with us two cows; these I drove all the way there. After we crossed the Delaware at Easton, the road extended through a great forest, with only here and there a cleared patch and a small log hut. Even the taverns were log huts, sometimes with but one room downstairs and one upstairs. Then there would be two or three beds in the room upstairs, and one in the room downstairs.

The great forest was called the Beech Woods. It was so big that we was six days in going through it. Sometimes we would go a half day without passing a house or meeting a person. The woods was full of bears, panthers, wildcats, and the like. About these I had heard a great many wild stories. So I made sure to keep my cows pretty close to the wagons.

Usually we stopped overnight at a hotel. But, as the houses were small, often it would happen that others had stopped before we arrived and the lodging rooms would all be occupied. Then we would sleep in our wagons, or in the outbuildings. In those days travelers had to get along the best way they could.

As my master saw that the site upon which he lived was favorable to business, during the third summer after our arrival he erected a large new frame house — the first house, not built of logs, in Great Bend. Then he began to do business and became a very prominent man there, as he was while he lived in New Jersey.

Already several people had moved to the neighborhood, had erected log houses, cleared the lands and begun to cultivate fields and raise stock. Very soon, storehouses and mills were built in the village. Indeed, Great Bend began to be the center of a large and thriving settlement.

At this time hunters used to come to this point to trade — to sell deer meat, bear meat, wild turkeys and the like, and to exchange the skins of wild animals for such commodities as they wished. They used to stay at our tavern and were a jolly set of fellows. I liked to see them come; there was fun then.

There was a ferry across the Susquehanna at Great Bend. The boat upon our side was owned by my master, the one upon the other side was owned by Captain Hatch. I soon learned to manage the boat as well as anyone could and often used to ferry teams across alone. The folks who were acquainted with me used to prefer me to take them across, even when the ferrymen were about. But Captain Hatch did not like me. I used to steal his customers. When I landed my boat upon his side, if anybody was there that wanted to come over to the Bend, before he knew it I would hurry them into my boat and push off from the shore, and leave him swearing. You see, the money I got for fetching back a load was mine, and I stole many a load from old Hatch. I always did, every time I could.

Along with the ferry boat were always one or two skiffs. These we took along to have in readiness in case of accident. When the load was heavy, or when it was windy, two or more ferrymen were required. At such times, I would help them across, but I always came back alone in a skiff. In this way I got so that I could handle the skiff first rate and was very fond of using it. Oftentimes I used to take single passengers over the ferry in a skiff; sometimes two or more at once. This I liked, and they used to pay me well to do it. I had a good name for managing the skiff — they used to say that in using the skiff I could beat any man on the Susquehanna, and I always did beat all that raced with me.

Oftentimes when the ferrymen were at dinner, someone would come to the ferry and holler to let us know that they wanted to cross. Then there would be a race. I'd skip out and down to the wharf so soon that I'd have 'em loaded and pushed off before anyone else could get there and then I'd get the fee. I tell you, if they did not chuck knife and fork and run at once, it was no use — they couldn't run with me — the fee was gone. I've got many a shilling that way, and many a good drink too. My master thought I was smart for doing it. And sometimes, if I had not been in the habit of hurrying things up in this way, people would have waited at the ferry by the hour. They didn't have to wait when I was about and this is why they liked me, and why my master liked me too.

There were plenty of frolics at Great Bend, and I used to go and dance all night. They were some of the best dancers that I ever saw. Folks knew how to dance in those days. Young folks nowadays don't know how to dance. I know they don't. I've seen 'em try and they can't dance a bit. They've got no step. Last winter my neighbors had a party to which they invited me. They had a fiddle and the young folks tried to dance. But they couldn't. Not a damned one of 'em. What was the matter? Why, they had no step. You can't dance unless you have the step, and they were as awkward as the devil and so damned clumsy. Why, if they went to cross their legs, they'd fall down. Nobody can dance much without crossing the legs. But they couldn't do it — they'd get tangled in the rigging and capsize. Why, they cantered over the floor like so many he-goats. I had to show them how to dance. I took a step or two, but I couldn't do it as I used to when I was young. They thought I did well, but they don't know — they've never seen good dancing. When I was young, I could cross my feet ninety-nine times in a minute and never miss the time, strike heel or toe with equal ease and go through the steps as nimble as a witch. But nowadays they're so clumsy that when one takes a foot off the floor, somebody has to hold him up while he shakes it. And then when they reel they push and crowd like a yoke of young steers and bang each other until they are in danger of their lives.

The young think they're great things and very handsome. But they ain't. They're poor scrawny mortals and can't do nothing. Why, the men of the age of my master looked brave. They were tall and commanding and stout of limb and graceful. They had good faces, great high foreheads, large bright eyes and broad mouths with good teeth. They stood up straight and walked with freedom and ease. I tell you, in those old times there were good-looking men — brave looking men. General Washington was, so was Lafayette, and my master, and all the great men that I ever saw, and they were all good dancers and danced whenever they had a chance. They used to say that General Washington was the most beautiful dancer in America, that he was even better than the Marquis de Lafayette.

The big, fine looking yankee men from York State and New England used to come to our house. All tall and dignified, their wives well formed and beautiful and very polite with the best of manners — and they were all good dancers, the best, and they never got tired of dancing. In those days, even the old men and old women danced.

When my master moved into his new house we had a great time. All the grand folks were there and, I tell you, things were lively. We had plenty of brandy, and they drank it too — big time, I tell you.

Anyone can make peach brandy — the best that was ever drunk. You just burn about four pounds of dried peaches until you can rub them to powder in your hands; you must burn 'em in a pot that has a very tight cover on. Then rub 'em fine in your hands, or, if some pieces are too hard for that, pound 'em fine with a hammer. Then put this powder of burnt peaches into a barrel of whiskey, and in four weeks, if you shake the barrel every day, you will have a barrel of peach brandy good enough for anybody.

You make apple brandy in almost the same way. You burn about four pounds of apples dried with the skins on. Make them into powder and put 'em in a barrel of whiskey. Shake the barrel every day for four weeks and you'll have a barrel of apple brandy better than any you ever drank. A little of that will make a fellow talk and won't burn his guts out, neither. Folks used to drink brandy right along — drank it every day — drank plenty of it, and didn't get the delirium, neither. The brandy used to taste good and was pleasant to drink; you can't get none such now, not a bit of it. A drink of brandy nowadays burns like fire all the way down through the guts, worse than a sheet of red-hot sand paper.

I liked to drink, but not 'til towards night; I had too much to do. Whenever there was a keg of brandy that I knew was very well made, for I helped make it, I would leave this keg 'til it was the last thing to be moved. Then, when I and a certain fellow began to move it, we would agree to see if it had kept well. We had no cup, so we would draw it out in an earthen pot, and then we would drink 'til we drank all we could. And if there was still some left in the pot and we couldn't get it back in the keg, for we had no funnel, we would agree that it was too wasteful to throw it away, so we'd drink the rest 'til it was gone. Once, I was so drunk I knew if my master saw me, I'd get a hell of a licking. And some of the rest knew that too. And they didn't want to see me licked, so they got me up and helped me off towards the house to put me to bed.

I used to be subject to the cramps, and sometimes I used to have it so bad that my mistress used to give me medicine for it for fear that I was going to die. Well, I thought now I had better have the cramp, and then maybe I wouldn't get licked. So I began to have pain worse than I'd ever had it before. Anyhow, I made more fuss than I ever had and yelled a good deal louder.

Pretty soon they called missy, and she was awfully frightened; she thought I would die for sure; she said she'd never seen me so weak. She had me carried and placed upon the trundle bed in her own room and attended to me nicely. She gave me some medicine but I was so drunk that I couldn't see, hear, nor feel. For a while I thought I was dead, but by and by the brandy began to wear off and I began to see. There sat missy, fanning me. I cautiously opened my eyes just the least bit, to see how she looked. She looked very pitiful. I was too drunk to laugh, but 'My God,' thought I, 'if you only knew what I am doing, you'd throw that fan away and give me hell.'

That night my master came to bed very late. When he came in to undress, I was making believe that I was asleep. I didn't dare to get well too soon. Mistress began to tell him how sick I was, and how near I came to dying, but I didn't fool him. He looked at me a little and then went to bed. He said, "Paugh! She's only drunk, she's been drinking with the men. Go to sleep, she'll be all right in the morning." And so I was, too, but that cured me of drinking.

I never got drunk after that. Sometimes when others have been drinking, I have taken a dram or two. But I never get drunk. I know my measure and I take no more.

I have laughed about it a great many times. I spoiled my mistress' fun for that night.

My mistress was usually like the very devil himself. Why, she'd beat me with anything she could get hold of — clubs, tongs, a coal shovel, knife, axe, hatchet — anything that was handiest. I tell you, if I intended to sauce her, I made sure to be off always.

Once she beat me 'til I was so stiff that she thought I was dead. Another time, because I was a little saucy, she hit me with the coal shovel and cracked my skull. She thought I was dead then, but I wasn't. I can still feel where the break was, in the side of my head. She smashed it right in — she didn't do things by halves.

One day my master saw her kick me in the stomach so badly that he intervened. I was not grown up then, too young to stand such. He didn't tell her so when I was by, but I have heard him tell her when they thought I was not listening that she was too severe.

This made her worse. It just put the devil in her. And then, just as soon as my master was out of the way, if I was a little saucy, or a little neglectful, I'd catch hell again. But I fixed her. I paid her up for all her spunk. I made up my mind that when I grew up I would do it, and when I had a good chance, when some of her grand company was around, I fixed her. I knocked her down and damned near killed her.

It happened in the barroom. There was some grand folks stopping there and she wanted things to look pretty stylish so she set me to scrubbing up the floor. I felt a little glum and didn't do it to suit her. She scolded me about it and I sauced her. She struck me with her hand. 'It's a good time now to dress you out, and damned if I won't do it,' I thought to myself. I put down the scrubbing brush and squared for a fight. The first whack, I struck her a hell of a blow with my fist. I didn't knock her entirely through the panels of the door, but her fall made a terrible smash. I hurt her so badly that everybody was frightened out of their wits, and I didn't know myself but that I'd killed the old devil. The barroom was full of folks. Some of them were Jersey folks who were going from the Lake Countries home to visit their friends. Some were drovers on their way west. And some were hunters and boatmen staying a while to rest. They were going to take my mistress' part, but I smacked my fists at 'em and told 'em to wade in if they dared and I'd thrash every devil of 'em. There wasn't a damned one that dared to come. Then I got out and pretty quick too.

I knew it wouldn't do to stay there, so I went down to Chenang Point and there went to work. During this time my master was gone to tend court at Wilkes-Barre. He often served as grand jury man and was sometimes gone a week or two. When he came home he sent for me to come back. I had to go. I was a slave, and if I didn't go, he would have brought me, and in a hurry too. In those days the masters made the niggers mind, and when he spoke I knew I must obey. Them old masters, when they got mad, had no mercy on a nigger. They'd cut a nigger all up in a hurry, cut 'em all up into strings, just leave the life, that's all. I've seen 'em do it, many a time.

He didn't scold me much when I came back, but told me that as my mistress and I got along so badly, if I would take my child and go to New Jersey and stay there, he would give me my freedom. I told him I would go. It was late at night; he wrote me a pass, gave it to me, and early the next morning I set out for Flagtown, New Jersey.

My master was a good man and a great man too; all the grand folks liked Minical Dubois. When the great men had their meetings, Minical Dubois was always invited to be with 'em, and he always went, too. He was away from home often; he had a great deal of business and he was known all over the country. I liked my master and so did everybody else.

He never whipped me unless he was sure that I deserved it. He used to let me go to frolics and balls and to have good times away from home with other black folks whenever I wanted to. But when he told me I must come home from a ball at a certain time, when the time came, the jig was out. I knew I must go; it wouldn't do to disappoint Minical Dubois. I was a good negress and always tried to please him. I had good times when he was around, and he always done things right. But you mustn't get him mad.

In the long nights of winter, we often had frolics, almost every week. We'd hardly get over one frolic when we'd begin to fix for another. Then there was the holidays — Christmas, New Year, Easter, the Fourth of July, and General Training. The biggest of 'em all was General Training. That was the biggest day for the nigger, I tell you that was the biggest day. The niggers were all out to General Training — little and big, old and young; and then they'd have some rum — always had rum at general trainings — and then you'd hear 'em laugh a mile. And when they got into a fight, you'd hear 'em yell more than five miles.

There was a great many niggers around the neighborhood of Great Bend. Sometimes we'd meet at one master's house, and sometimes at another's. We was sure to have a fiddle and a frolic and a first rate time, but none of 'em had a better time than myself. I loved frolics. I could dance all night and feel as jolly as a witch all next day. I never tired of frolics — not I — nor at General Training, neither.

I got to Flagtown on foot, to be sure. I came right down through the Beech Woods, all alone, excepting my young one in my arms. Sometimes I didn't see a person for half a day; sometimes I didn't get anything to eat and never had any bed to sleep in. My baby was about a year and a half old, and I had to carry it all the way. The wood was full of panthers, bears, wildcats, and wolves. I often saw 'em in the daytime and always heard 'em howling in the night. Oh that old panther, when he howled it made the hair stand up all over my head.

At Easton, I went on board a raft to go down the Delaware. A man by the name of Brink had his wife and family on board bound for Philadelphia. I went on board to help the wife, for my passage. They were nice folks and I had a good time. I left

the raft not far from Trenton, but I do not know exactly where
— there was no town at the place at which I got off.

Then I proceeded directly to Flagtown to see my mother. I
did not find her there, she had moved to New Brunswick. On
my way, a man called to me, asking me "Whose nigger are
you?" I replied 'I'm no man's nigger. I belong to God. I belong
to no man.'

He then said "Where are you going?" I replied "That's none
of your business. I'm free. I go where I please."

He came toward me. I sat down my young one, showed him
my fist and glared at him. I guess he saw it was no use. He
moseyed off, telling me that he would have me arrested as soon
as he could find a magistrate.

You see, in those days the negroes were all slaves, and they
were sent nowhere, nor allowed to go anywhere without a
pass. And when anyone met a negro who was not with his
master, he had a right to demand of him whose negro he was;
and if the negro did not show his pass, or did not give good
evidence whose he was, he was arrested at once and kept until
his master came for him, paid whatever charges were made,
and took him away. You see, in those days, anybody had
authority to arrest vagrant negroes. They got paid for arresting
them and charges for their keeping 'til their master redeemed
them. But he didn't arrest me, not a bit.

When I got to New Brunswick, I found my mother. Soon
after I went to work, and remained in New Brunswick several
years.

From New Brunswick I went to Princeton to work for Victor
Tulane. I remained in his family a long while. I worked for him
when Paul Tulane was born. Victor Tulane was a great man and
a good man, and he used his servants well. And Paul was a nice
boy and Madam Tulane was a good woman. I liked 'em all, and
so did the other servants.

After a long while, I visited my grandfather, Harry

Compton, who lived at the forks of the road, near this place.

He was then an old man; they say he was more than a hundred years old, and I guess he was. But he was yet quite active; he wanted me to stay with him, so I did. At his death I inherited his property. I lived on the old homestead until a few years ago, when them damned Democrats set fire to my house, and burned up my home and all that I had. Since that time I have lived at this place, with my youngest daughter.

I have suffered a great many hardships, but I ain't tired of living. I'd like to live another hundred years yet — and I don't know but I will, too. My teeth are good, and if I can get enough to eat, I don't know why I should die. There's no use in dying, you ain't good for anything after you are dead, and God knows I ought to have been dead long ago.

I am well and have always been, except sometimes I suffer a cold. I have never had a spell of severe sickness in my life and do not intend to. T'aint no use to be sick. Folks don't feel well when they're sick; they feel best when they're well. Folks wouldn't be sick half so much if they'd behave 'emselves, and stay at home and eat plain vittles. Instead, they want to run all over and be into all kind of nigger shines, and stuff 'emselves with all kinds of things; and their guts won't stand it. Then they get sick and send for a doctor and when he comes, if they're not pretty careful, they'll have a hell of a time for he's sure to go right for the guts, first pass. Never knew one of 'em to miss. A big dose of calomel and jalap to begin business, and then the war is begun. These doctors, they've got no mercy on you, 'specially if you're black. Ah! I've seen 'em, many a time, but, they never come after me, I never gave 'em a chance — not once.

I know every foot of this mountain, every hole and corner of it, every place where anybody lives or ever has lived. And I know the folks, too; and some of 'em are pretty bad ones. In fact, they are all bad, and some of them are worse. What the devil will ever do with them when he has to take 'em, I don't know. Surely he don't want 'em and wouldn't have 'em if he could help it. The only reason that some of these folks up here don't die sooner than they do is, the devil won't have them. He just puts off taking them because he knows what a time he'll have when he gets 'em. Why, some of them are starved to death long enough before they die, but they can't die, there's no place for them to go after they are dead. They ain't fit to go to heaven, and the devil won't have 'em, and so they have to stay here. Why, this mountain is worse than hell itself. If some of these folks don't behave better after they go into the infernal regions than they do while here, the devil will have a time of it. He'll never manage 'em; he'll have to call a congress and have an amendment fixed to the constitution. A brimstone fire won't do; it will never faze 'em; it don't here. I've seen it tried and it don't do at all, only make 'em worse. I tell the truth, and I could tell more of it.

Somebody is killed up here every year. Why, there is more folks killed up here than anybody knows of. And nobody is ever hanged for it. It gets worse and worse. If they kill anybody up here, they just take the murderers off to Flemington and keep them in jail awhile 'til they have a trial, then turn 'em out to come back here, and then they are worse than they were before. They just kill anybody then.

And they steal! Why, you wouldn't believe how much they steal. They don't steal much off one another, because that wouldn't do. If they were caught at that, they'd get killed damned soon, and then they ain't got much to be stolen. But they go off from the mountain, down into the valleys, and there they steal anything they can find — sheep, chickens, grain, meat, clothes — anything that they can eat or wear. And nobody can find anything that has been stolen by the folks up here, for when anything is to be stolen, they all know about it, and they all lie for each other, and they all know where it is to be hid, and they all help to keep folks from finding it, so it does no good to hunt up here for stolen goods. They know so damned well how to hide things, too. They don't hide what they steal in their houses until all the houses have been searched; when they steal anything they hide it in some hole that nobody but mountain folk know of, or else under some rocks, or under some wood, where nobody but the mountain folk would think of looking. That is the way they do business up here, and if you tell 'em of it, they'll kill you. Damned if they won't.

I've lived right here longer than fifty years. I know 'em; I've been to 'em — but they never troubled me much. They know it wouldn't do.

Why, a person is in danger of his life up here and he can't keep nothing. They'd steal the bread out of a blind nigger's mouth, and then murder him if he told of it. That's the way it goes up here, they're worse than the devil himself. No, there ain't no good ones among them, not one. They're all bad and some are worse. You never seen such folks; they're the damnedest that ever lived. A good many of them don't stay long in the same place, neither. They're a set of damned turtles: they carry all they've got on their backs, and that ain't much, neither. They're ready to get up and get out any time, and you catch 'em if you want to. Why, in some of them shanties there are a dozen or more, whites and blacks and all colors, with nothing to eat and nothing to wear and no wood to burn. What can they do? They have to steal. The niggers and whites all live together. The whites are just as good as the niggers, and both are as bad as the devil can make 'em.

When they want to the negroes marry the whites, but they don't do much marrying up here — they don't have to — and then it's no use. It's too much trouble. They have children a plenty and all colors — black and white and yellow and any

other color that you have ever seen, but blue. There ain't no
blue ones yet.

They don't bring up their children. Why, as soon as they are
born, every devil of 'em is for himself, and the devil's for 'em
all. That's how it goes. And, I tell you, they have a hard time of
it, too.

They name 'em after their daddies, to be sure, if they know
who they are. But that don't make any odds, 'cause, before they
are grown up, half of 'em don't know their own young ones
from anybody else's, and the other half of 'em wouldn't own
'em if they did. And the young ones ain't no better. They often
swear they had no daddies. You see, just as soon as they get big
enough, they travel out to get something to eat, and if the feed
is pretty good, maybe they'll stay and never get back. And if
they come back, they find so many more in the nest, they can't
stay if they want to. Why, none of 'em that's good for anything
ever stays here. They go away when they are small and get
work and stay. You'll find folks born on this mountain living in
Princeton, New Brunswick, Trenton, New York, and the devil
knows where, driving for some big bugs or they are waiters in
some great hotel they'll never own. But if one turns out to be a
poor devil and gets into some bad scrape, that fellow is sure to
come back to the mountain. That's the way they keep the ranks
full of the scoundrels that can't stay anywhere else. That's the
way it goes with the folks here.

Why, some of 'em ought to be hanged right up by the neck;
and some of 'em ought to be tied up and licked nearly to death
— tied right up to a post and licked 'til within an inch of their
lives. That's what ought to be done with 'em — that's the way
I'd serve 'em. I'd take 'em up to Flemington, and lick 'em 'til
they'd never want to be licked again.

I've been to Flemington, and it is the damnedest place in the
world. I've got enough against it. You can't get anything there
without money. Nobody is considered anything there unless he

has money. Nobody will tell you anything unless you give 'em money. If you ask a lawyer anything, he won't tell you a bit until he gets your money. You can't get justice there unless you have some money, and you can't get it then, because if another person has more money than you have, they'll all of 'em. Every damned lawyer, the judge and the jury go for him, and a poor body has no show at all. I know 'em — I've been to 'em — they're a bad set.

I've been to the lawyers at Flemington but it didn't do any good. These damned people have been trying to get my property away from me for many years, and I wanted to consult a lawyer to get him to put these devils through, but I couldn't. Not a damned lawyer would take my case, because I had no money. They said they could not talk without money. They couldn't do anything for me unless I paid 'em some money. I couldn't pay 'em, I hadn't a cent to my name.

When they told me that they could do nothing for me without money, I felt like kicking their damned tripes out. They think they are so damned big because they are dressed up a little. If they'd come over on the mountain, we'd show 'em; we'd skin every devil of 'em — I'd do it myself, old as I am. I'd just like to put my fist against their eyes.

I used to go to Flemington often, whenever there was any doings there; whenever the big men had their meetings there. All the niggers used to go to Flemington on those big days; and then they'd get licked — good God, how they'd get licked! Why, they'd tie 'em right up and lick 'em to death — cut 'em into pieces — cut 'em all into string.

Yes, I have seen 'em lick a dozen niggers at a time just for getting so drunk on whiskey and getting into a kinty-koy, and making noise. They'd get into a row or a fight, and then somebody would get hurt, and then the one that got hurt would complain to the authorities, and then the constables would be after the niggers, and when they caught 'em, they'd tie 'em right up without judge or jury and pull off the shirt, and put it right on the bare hide. My God, how they licked 'em — cut the hide all in gashes. That's the way they used to fix the old slaves — give 'em a holiday to have a little sport, and then if they had any fun, lick 'em 'til they'd have a sore back 'til the next holiday come.

The niggers always wanted to go back for the next holiday, back sore or well. Never knew one to miss when his master told him he could go. Then he'd be sure to get licked worse than he was before, because some niggers couldn't have a holiday without getting into a fight.

Tie 'em right up to a post, and give 'em hell, right on the bare back — fetch the blood every time, and they'd holler. "Good God!" they'd howl 'til you could hear 'em a mile; and then, when they'd cut the back all in slits, they'd put salt in the gashes, and then they'd howl some more. Lord God, no panther in the Beech Woods ever made half so much noise. That's the way they fixed the nigger in old times, them damned Flemingtoners — they think they are so damned big.

I was at Flemington when the little nigger was hanged for murdering his mistress. That was the damnedest time I ever saw. The niggers quarreled and fought and pounded each other, and bit each other's ears off, and then pounded each other's noses down, bunged each other's eyes, and some got blamed near killed. Them damned Flemingtoners got after 'em, and they tied 'em up, and licked 'em without mercy cut 'em all in strings — just left the life, no more. I'll never forget that.

Sometimes the niggers deserved to be whipped — most always, I expect. They had to lick 'em; there was no other way; they had to make 'em mind.

The niggers that behaved well never got licked, but some wouldn't behave. They'd always get into a row or steal something, and then they'd be sure to get licked.

ELIZABETH KECKLEY: <u>BEHIND THE SCENES</u>

PREFACE

I have been often been asked to write my life, as those who know me know that it has been an eventful one. At last I have acceded to the importunities of my friends, and have hastily sketched some of the striking incidents that go to make up my history: My life, so full of romance, may sound like a dream to the matter-of-fact reader, nevertheless everything I have written is strictly true; much has been omitted, but nothing has been exaggerated. In writing as I have done I am well aware that I have invited criticism; but before the critic judges harshly, let my explanation be carefully read and weighed. If I have portrayed the dark side of slavery, I also have painted the bright side. The good that I have said of human servitude should be thrown into the scales with the evil that I have said of it. I have kind, true-hearted friends in the South as well as in the North, and I would not wound those southern friends by sweeping condemnation, simply because I was once a slave. They were not so much responsible for the curse under which I was born, as the God of nature and the fathers who framed the Constitution for the United States. The law descended to them, and it was but natural that they should recognise it, since it manifestly was their interest to do so. And yet a wrong was inflicted upon me; a cruel custom deprived me of my liberty, and since I was robbed of my dearest right, I would not have been human had I not rebelled against the robbery. God rules the Universe. I was a feeble instrument in his hands, and through me and the enslaved millions of my race, one of the problems was solved that belongs to the great problem of human destiny; and the solution was developed so gradually that there was no great convulsion of the harmonies of natural laws. A solemn truth was thrown to the surface, and what is better still, it was recognised as a truth by those who give force to moral laws. An act may be wrong, but unless the ruling power recognises the wrong, it is useless to hope for a correction of it. Principles may be right, but they are not established within an hour. The masses are slow to reason, and each principle, to acquire moral force, must come to us from the fire of the crucible; the fire may inflict unjust punishment, but then it purifies and renders stronger the principle, not in itself, but in the eyes of those who arrogate judgment to themselves.

When the war of the Revolution established the independence of the American colonies, an evil was perpetuated, slavery was more firmly established; and since the evil had been planted, it must pass through certain stages before it would be eradicated. In fact, we give but little thought to the plant of evil until it grows to such monstrous proportions that it overshadows important interests; then the efforts to destroy it become earnest. As one of the victims of slavery I drank of the bitter water; but then, since destiny willed it so, and since I aided in bringing a solemn truth to the surface as a truth, perhaps I have no right to complain. Here, as in all things pertaining to life, I can afford to be charitable.

Elizabeth Keckley
14 Carroll Place, New York, March 14, 1868.

My life has been an eventful one. I was born a slave, the child of slave parents. In other words, I came upon the earth free in God-like thought, but fettered in action. My birthplace was Dinwiddie Court House, in Virginia. My recollections of childhood are distinct, perhaps for the reason that many stirring incidents are associated with that period. I am now on the shady side of forty, and as I sit alone in my room the brain is busy, and a rapidly moving panorama brings scene after scene before me, some pleasant and others sad; and when I thus greet old familiar faces, I often find myself wondering if I am not living the past over again. The visions are so terribly distinct that I almost imagine them to be real. Hour after hour I sit while the scenes are being shifted; and as I gaze upon the panorama of the past, I realise how crowded with incidents my life has been. Every day seems like a romance within itself, and the years grow into ponderous volumes. As I cannot condense, I must omit many strange passages in my history. From such a wilderness of events it is difficult to make a selection, but as I am not writing altogether the history of myself, I will confine my story to the most important incidents which I believe influenced the moulding of my character. As I glance over the crowded sea of the past, these incidents stand forth prominently, the guide-posts of memory.

I presume that I must have been four .years old when I first began to remember; at least, I cannot now recall anything occurring previous to this period. My master, Col. A. Burwell, was somewhat unsettled in his business affairs, and while I was yet an infant he made several removals.

While living at Hampton Sidney College, Prince Edward County, Va., Mrs. Burwell gave birth to a daughter, a sweet, black-eyed baby, my earliest and fondest pet. To take care of this baby was my first duty. True, I was but a child of four years old myself but then I had been raised in a hardy school — taught to rely upon myself and to prepare myself to render assistance to others. The lesson was not a bitter one, for I was too young to indulge in philosophy and the precepts that I then treasured and practiced I believe developed those principles of character which have enabled me to triumph over so many difficulties. Notwithstanding all the wrongs that slavery heaped upon me, I can bless it for one thing — youth's important lesson of self-reliance.

The baby was named Elizabeth. It was pleasant to me to be assigned a duty in connection with it, for the discharge of that duty transferred me from the rude cabin to the household of my master. My simple attire was a short dress and a little white apron. My old mistress encouraged me in rocking the cradle, by telling me that if I would watch over the baby well, keep the flies out of its face and not let it cry, I should be its little maid. This was a golden promise and I required no better inducement for the faithful performance of my task. I began to rock the cradle most industriously, when out pitched little pet on the floor.

I instantly cried out, "The baby is on the floor." Not knowing what to do, I seized the coal shovel in my perplexity and was trying to shovel up my tender charge, when my mistress called to me to let the child alone and then ordered that I be taken out and lashed for my carelessness.

The blows were not administered with a light hand, I assure you. Doubtless the severity of the lashing has made me remember the incident so well. This was the first time I was punished in this cruel way, but not the last.

The black-eyed baby that I called my pet grew into a self-willed girl and in after years was the cause of much trouble to me. I grew strong and healthy and, notwithstanding I attended to various kinds of work, I was repeatedly told, when even fourteen years old, that I would never be worth my salt.

When I was eight, Mr. Burwell's family consisted of six sons and four daughters, with a large family of servants. My mother was kind and forbearing; Mrs. Burwell a hard task-master. As mother had so much work to do in making clothes for the family, besides the slaves, I determined to render her all the assistance in my power and in rendering her such assistance my young energies were taxed to the utmost.

I was my mother's only child, which made her love for me all the stronger. I did not know much of my father, for he was the slave of another man and when Mr. Burwell moved from Dinwiddie he was separated from us and only allowed to visit my mother twice a year — during the Easter holidays and Christmas.

Mr. Burwell finally determined to reward my mother by making an arrangement with the owner of my father, by which the separation of my parents could be brought to an end. It was a bright day, indeed, for my mother when it was announced that my father was coming to live with us. The old weary look faded from her face and she worked as if her heart was in every task. But the golden days did not last long. The radiant dream faded all too soon.

In the morning my father called me to him and kissed me, then held me out at arms' length as if he were regarding his child with pride.

"She is growing into a large fine girl," he remarked to my mother. "I dunno which I like best, you or Lizzie, as both are so dear to me."

My mother's name was Agnes and my father delighted to call me his Little Lizzie.

While yet my father and mother were speaking hopefully, joyfully of the future, Mr. Burwell came to the cabin with a letter in his hand. He was a kind master in some things and as gently as possible informed my parents that they must part; for in two hours my father must join his master at Dinwiddie and go with him to the West, where he had determined to make his future home. The announcement fell upon the little circle in that rude-log cabin like a thunderbolt. I can remember the scene as if it were but yesterday; how my father cried out against the cruel separation; his last kiss; his wild straining of my mother to his bosom; the solemn prayer to Heaven; the tears and sobs, the fearful anguish of broken hearts. The last kiss, the last goodbye; and he, my father, was gone, gone forever.

The shadow eclipsed the sunshine and love brought despair. The parting was eternal. The cloud had no silver lining, but I trust that it will be all silver in heaven. We who are crushed to earth with heavy chains, who travel a weary, rugged, thorny road, groping through midnight darkness on earth, earn our right to enjoy the sunshine in the great hereafter. At the grave, at least, we should be permitted to lay our burdens down, that a new world, a world of brightness, may open to us. The light that is denied us here should grow into a flood of effulgence beyond the dark, mysterious shadows of death.

Deep as was the distress of my mother in parting with my father, her sorrow did not screen her from insult. My old mistress said to her: "Stop your nonsense; there is no necessity for you putting on airs. Your husband is not the only slave that has been sold from his family and you are not the only one that has had to part. There are plenty more men about here and if you want a husband so badly, stop your crying and go and find another."

To these unfeeling words my mother made no reply. She turned away in stoical silence with a curl of that loathing scorn upon her lips which swelled in her heart.

My father and mother never met again in this world. They kept up a regular correspondence for years and the most precious mementoes of my existence are the faded old letters that he wrote, full of love and always hoping that the future would bring brighter days. In nearly every letter is a message for me.

Tell my darling little Lizzie, he writes, *to be a good girl and to learn her book. Kiss her for me and tell her that I will come to see her some day.*

Thus he wrote time and again, but he never came. He lived in hope, but died without ever seeing his wife and child.

I note a few extracts from one of my father's letters to my mother, following copy literally:

Shelbyville, Sept. 6, 1833.
MRS. AGNES HOBBS.

Dear Wife. My dear beloved wife I am more than glad to meet with opportunity to write these few lines to you by my Mistress who is now about starting to virginia and several others of my old friends are with her; in company Mrs. Ann Rus the wife of master Thos Rus and Dan Woodiard and his family and I am very sorry that I havn the chance to go with them as I feel determid to see you If life last again. I am now here and out at this place so I am not able to get off at this time. I am write well and hearty and all the rest of masters family. I heard this evening by Mistress that is just from there all sends love to you and all my old frends. I am a living in a town called Shelbyville and I have wrote a great many letters since I've been here and almost been ready to my selfe that its out of the question to write any more at tall, my dear wife. I don't feel no whys like giving out writing to you as yet and I hope when you get this letter that you be incourage to write me a letter. I am well satisfied at my living at this place I am a making money for my own benifit and I hope that it's to yours also. If I live to see Next year I shall have my own time from master by giving, him 100 and twenty dollars a year and I think I shall be doing good bisness at that and have something more than all that. I hope with gods help that I may be able to rejoice with you on the earth and in heave. I am determined to never stop praying, not in this earth and I hope to praise god. In glory there we'll meet to part no more forever. So my dear wife, I hope to meet you in paradise to praise god forever.

I want Elizabeth to be a good girl and not to think that because I am bound so far that God is not able to open the way.

GEORGE PLEASANT,
Hobbs a servant of Grun.

The last letter that my mother received from my father was dated Shelbyville, Tennessee, March 20, 1839. He writes in a cheerful strain and hopes to see her soon. Alas, he looked forward to a meeting in vain. Year after year the one great hope swelled in his heart, but the hope was only realised beyond the dark portals of the grave.

When I was about seven years old I witnessed, for the first time the sale of a human being. We were living at Prince Edward, in Virginia and master had just purchased his hogs for the winter, for which he was unable to pay in full. To escape from his embarrassment it was necessary to sell one of the slaves. Little Joe, the son of the cook, was selected as the victim. His mother was ordered to dress him up in his Sunday clothes and send him to the house. He came in with a bright face, was placed on the scales and was sold, like the hogs, at so much per pound. His mother was kept in ignorance of the transaction, but her suspicions were aroused. When her son started for Petersburgh in the wagon, the truth began to dawn upon her mind and she pleaded piteously that her boy should not be taken from her; but master quieted her by telling her that he was simply going to town with the wagon and would be back in the morning. Morning came, but little Joe did not return to his mother. Morning after morning passed and the mother went down to the grave without ever seeing her child again.

One day she was whipped for grieving for her lost boy. Colonel Burwell never liked to see one of his slaves wear a sorrowful face and those who offended in this particular way were always punished. Alas, the sunny face of the slave is not always an indication of sunshine in the heart.

Colonel Burwell at one time owned about seventy slaves, all of which were sold and in a majority of instances wives were separated from husbands and children from their parents. Slavery in the Border States forty years ago was different from what it was twenty years ago. Time seemed to soften the hearts of master and mistress to insure kinder and more humane treatment to bondsmen and bondswomen.

When I was quite a child, an incident occurred which my mother afterward impressed more strongly on my mind. One of my uncles, a slave of Colonel Burwell, lost a pair of ploughlines. When the loss was made known the master gave him a new pair and told him that if he did not take care of them he would punish him severely. In a few weeks the second pair of lines was stolen. My uncle hung himself rather than meet the displeasure of his master. My mother went to the spring in the morning for a pail of water and, on looking up into the willow tree which shaded the bubbling crystal stream, she discovered the lifeless form of her brother suspended beneath one of the strong branches.

Rather than be punished the way Colonel Burwell punished his servants, he took his own life. Slavery had its dark side as well as its bright side.

When I was about fourteen years old I went to live with my master's eldest son, a Presbyterian minister. His salary was small and he was burdened with a helpless wife, a girl that he had married in the humble walls of life. She was morbidly sensitive and imagined that I regarded her with contemptuous feelings because she was of poor parentage. I was their only servant and a gracious loan at that. They were not able to buy me, so my old master sought to render them assistance by allowing them the benefit of my services.

From the very first, I did the work of three servants and yet I was scolded and regarded with distrust. The years passed slowly. I continued to serve them and at the same time grew into strong, healthy womanhood.

I was nearly eighteen when we removed from Virginia to Hillsboro', North Carolina, where young Mr. Burwell took charge of a church. The salary was small and we still had to practice the closest economy.

Mr. Bingham, a hard, cruel man, the village schoolmaster, was a member of my young master's church and a frequent visitor to the parsonage. She whom I called mistress seemed to be desirous to wreak vengeance on me for something and Bingham became her ready tool. During this time my master was unusually kind to me; he was naturally a goodhearted man, but was influenced by his wife. It was Saturday evening and while I was bending over the bed, watching the baby that I had just hustled into slumber, Mr. Bingham came to the door and asked me to go with him to his study. Wondering what he meant by this strange request, I followed him and when we had entered the study he closed the door and in his blunt way remarked: "Lizzie, I am going to flog you."

I was thunderstruck and tried to think if I had been remiss in anything. I could not recollect of doing anything to deserve punishment and with surprise exclaimed:

"Whip me, Mr. Bingham! What for?"

"No matter," he replied, "I am going to whip you, so take down your dress this instant."

Recollect, I was eighteen years of age, was a woman fully developed and yet this man coolly bade me take down my dress. I drew myself up proudly, firmly and said:

"No, Mr. Bingham, I shall not take down my dress before you. Moreover, you shall not whip me unless you prove the stronger. Nobody has a right to whip me but my own master and nobody shall do so if I can prevent it."

My words seemed to exasperate him. He seized a rope, caught me roughly and tried to tie me. I resisted with all my strength, but he was the stronger of the two and after a hard struggle succeeded in binding my hands and tearing my dress from my back. Then he picked up a rawhide and began to ply it freely over my shoulder. With steady hand and practiced eye he would raise the instrument of torture and with fearful force the rawhide descended upon my quivering flesh. It cut the skin, raised great welts and the warm blood trickled down my back. Oh God, I can feel the torture now — the terrible, excruciating agony of those moments. I did not scream; I was too proud to let my tormentor know what I was suffering. I closed my lips firmly, that not even a groan might escape from them and I stood like a statue while the keen lash cut deep into my flesh. As soon as I was released, stunned with pain, bruised and bleeding, I went home and rushed into the presence of the pastor and his wife, wildly exclaiming:

"Master Robert, why did you let Mr. Bingham flog me? What have I done that I should be so punished?"

"Go away," he gruffly answered, "do not bother me."

I would not be put off thus.

"What have I done? I want to know why I have been flogged."

I saw his cheeks flush with anger, but I did not move. He rose to his feet and, on my refusing to go without an explanation, seized a chair, struck me and felled me to the floor. I rose, bewildered, almost dead with pain, crept to my room, dressed my bruised arms and back as best I could and then lay down, but not to sleep. No, I could not sleep, for I was suffering mental as well as bodily torture. My spirit rebelled against the unjustness that had been inflicted upon me. I tried to smother my anger and to forgive those who had been so cruel to me, it was impossible.

The next morning I was more calm and I believe that I could then have forgiven everything for the sake of one kind word. But the kind word was not proffered and it may be possible that I grew somewhat wayward and sullen.

Though I had faults, I know now, as I felt then, harshness was the poorest inducement for the correction of them. It seems that Mr. Bingham had pledged himself to Mrs. Burwell to subdue what he called my stubborn pride.

On Friday following the Saturday on which I was savagely beaten, Mr. Bingham again directed me to come to his study. I went, but with the determination to offer resistance should he attempt to flog me again. On entering the room I found him prepared with a new rope and a new cowhide. I told him that I was ready to die, but that he could not conquer me. In struggling with him I bit his finger severely, when he seized a heavy stick and beat me with it in a shameful manner. Again I went home sore and bleeding, but with pride as strong and defiant as ever.

The following Thursday Mr. Bingham again tried to conquer me, but in vain. We struggled and he struck me many savage blows.

I stood bleeding before him. Nearly exhausted with his efforts, he burst into tears and declared that it would be a sin to beat me any more. My suffering at last subdued his hard heart; he asked my forgiveness and afterwards was an altered man. He was never known to strike one of his servants from that day forward.

Mr. Burwell, he who preached the love of Heaven, who glorified the precepts and examples of Christ, who expounded the Holy Scriptures Sabbath after Sabbath from the pulpit, when Mr. Bingham refused to whip me any more, was urged by his wife to punish me himself. One morning he went to the wood-pile, took an oak broom, cut the handle off and with this heavy handle attempted to conquer me. I fought him, but he proved the strongest.

At the sight of my bleeding form, his wife fell upon her knees and begged him to desist. My distress even touched her cold, jealous heart. I was so badly bruised that I was unable to leave my bed for five days. I will not dwell upon the bitter anguish of these hours, for even the thought of them now makes me shudder.

The Rev. Mr. Burwell was not yet satisfied. He resolved to make another attempt to subdue my proud, rebellious Spirit — made the attempt and again failed, when he told me, with an air of penitence, that he should never strike me another blow; and faithfully he kept his word.

These revolting scenes created a great sensation at the time, were the talk of the town and neighbourhood and I flatter myself that the actions of those who had conspired against me were not viewed in a light to reflect much credit upon them.

The savage efforts to subdue my pride were not the only things that brought me suffering and deep mortification during my residence at Hillsboro'.

I was regarded as fair-looking for one of my race and for four years a white man (I spare the world his name) had base designs upon me. I do not dare to dwell upon this subject, for it is one that is fraught with pain. Suffice it to say, that he persecuted me for four years and I became a mother. The child of which he was the father was the only child that I ever brought into the world. If my poor boy ever suffered any humiliating pangs on account of birth, he could not blame his mother, for God knows that she did not wish to give him life; he must blame the edicts of that society which deemed it no crime to undermine the virtue of girls in my then position.

Among the old letters preserved by my mother I find the following, written by myself while at Hillsboro':

Hillsboro', April 10, 1838.

My dear mother:—I have been intending to write to you for a long time, but numerous things have prevented and, for that reason, you must excuse me.

I thought very hard of you for not writing to me, but hope that you will answer this letter as soon as you receive it and tell me how you like Marsfield and if you have seen any of my old acquaintances, or if you yet know any of the brick-house people who I think so much of. I want to hear of the family at home very much, indeed. I really believe you and all the family have forgotten me, if not I certainly should have heard from some of you since you left Broyton, if it was only a line. Nevertheless I love you all very dearly and shall, although I may never see you again, nor do I ever expect to.

Miss Anna is going to Petersburg next winter, but she says that she does not intend to take me; what reason she has for leaving me, I cannot tell. I have often wished that I lived where knew I never could see you, for then I would not have my hopes raised and to be disappointed in this manner; however, it is said that a bad beginning makes a good ending, but I hardly expect to see that happy day at this place.

Give my love to all the family, both white and black. I was very much obliged to you for the presents you sent me last summer, though it is quite late in the day to be thanking for them. Tell Aunt Bella that I was very much obliged to her for her present; I have been so particular with it that I have only worn it once.

There have been six weddings since October; the most respectable one was about a fortnight ago. I was asked to be the first attendant, but, as usual with all my expectations, I was disappointed, for on the wedding day I felt more like being locked up in a three cornered box than attending a wedding.

I must now close, although I could fill ten pages with my griefs and misfortunes; no tongue could express them as I feel. Don't forget me though; and answer my letters soon. I will write you again and would write more now, but Miss Anna says it is time I had finished.

Tell Miss Elizabeth that I wish she would make haste and get married, for mistress says that I belong to her when she gets married.

I wish you would send me a pretty frock this summer; if you will send it to Mrs. Robertson's Miss Bet will send it to me.

Farewell, darling mother.

Your affectionate daughter,

ELIZABETH HOBBS.

The years passed and brought many changes to me, but on these I will not dwell, as I wish to hasten to the most interesting part of my story.

My troubles in North Carolina were brought to an end by my unexpected return to Virginia, where I lived with Mr.

Garland, who had married Miss Ann Burwell one of my old master's daughters.

His life was not a prosperous one and after struggling with the world for several years he left his native State, a disappointed man. He moved to St. Louis, hoping to improve his fortune in the West, but ill luck followed him there and he seemed to be unable to escape from the influence of the evil star of his destiny. When his family, myself included, .joined him in his new home on the banks of the Mississippi, we found him so poor that he was unable to pay the dues on a letter waiting in the post-office for him.

The necessities of the family were so great, that it was proposed to place my mother out at service. The idea was shocking to me. Every gray hair in her old head was dear to me and I could not bear the thought of her going to work for strangers. She had been raised in the family, had watched the growth of each child from infancy to maturity; they had been the objects of her kindest care and she was wound round about them as the vine winds itself about the rugged oak. They had been the central figures in her dream of life — a dream beautiful to her, since she had basked in the sunshine of no other. And now they proposed to destroy each tendril of affection, to cloud the sunshine of her existence when the day was drawing to a close, when the shadows of solemn night were rapidly approaching.

My mother, my poor aged mother, go among strangers to toil for a living! No! A thousand times no! I would rather work my fingers to the bone, bend over my sewing 'til the film of blindness gathered in my eyes; nay, even beg from street to street. I told Mr. Garland so and he gave me permission to see what I could do.

I was fortunate in obtaining work and in a short time I had acquired something of a reputation as a seamstress and dress-maker. The best ladies in St. Louis were my patrons and when my reputation was once established I never lacked for orders. With my needle I kept bread in the mouths of seventeen persons for two years and five months.

While I was working so hard that others might live in comparative comfort and move in those circles of society to which their birth gave them entrance, the thought often occurred to me whether I was now worth my salt or not; and then perhaps the lips curled with a bitter sneer. It may seem strange that I should place so much emphasis upon words thoughtlessly, idly spoken, but then we do many strange things in life and cannot always explain the motives that actuate us.

The heavy task was too much for me and my health began to give way. About this time Mr. Keckley, whom I had met in Virginia and learned to regard with more than friendship, came to St. Louis. He sought my hand in marriage and for a long time I refused to consider his proposal; for I could not bear the thought of bringing children into slavery — of adding one single recruit to the millions bound to hopeless servitude, fettered and shackled with chains stronger and heavier than manacles of iron.

I made a proposition to my master to buy myself and my son; the proposition was bluntly declined and I was commanded never to broach the subject again.

I would not be put off thus, for hope pointed to a freer, brighter life in the future. Why should my son be held in slavery, I often asked myself. He came into the world through no will of mine and yet, God only knows how I loved him. The Anglo-Saxon blood as well as the African flowed in his veins; the two currents co-mingled — one singing of freedom, the other silent and sullen with generations of despair. Why should not the Anglo-Saxon triumph? Why should it be weighed down with the rich blood typical of the tropics? Must the life-current of one race bind the other race in chains as strong and enduring as if there had been no Anglo-Saxon taint? By the laws of God and nature, as interpreted by man, one-half of my boy was free and why should not this fair birthright of freedom remove the curse from the other half — raise it into the bright, joyous sunshine of liberty.

I could not answer these questions of my heart that almost maddened me and I learned to regard human philosophy with distrust. Much as I respected the authority of my master, I could not remain silent on a subject that so nearly concerned me. One day, when I insisted on knowing whether he would permit me to purchase myself, and what price I must pay for myself, he turned to me in a petulant manner, thrust his hand into his pocket, drew forth a bright silver quarter of a dollar, and proffering it to me, said:

"Lizzie, I have told you often not to trouble me with such a question. If you really wish to leave me, take this: it will pay the passage of yourself and your boy on the ferry-boat, and when you are on the other side of the river you will be free. It is the cheapest way that I know of to accomplish what you desire."

I looked at him in astonishment and earnestly replied:

"No, master, I do not wish to be free in such a manner. If such had been my wish, I should never have troubled you about obtaining your consent to my purchasing myself. I can cross the river any day, as you well know, and have frequently done so, but will never leave you in such a manner. By the laws of the land I am your slave — you are my master and I will only be free by such means as the laws of the country provide."

He expected this answer and I knew that he was pleased. Some time afterwards he told me that he had reconsidered the question; that I had served his family faithfully; that I deserved my freedom and that he would take $1200 for myself and the boy.

This was joyful intelligence for me and the reflection of hope gave a silver lining to the dark cloud of my life — faint, it is true, but still a silver lining.

Taking a prospective glance at liberty, I consented to marry. The wedding was a great event in the family. The ceremony took place in the parlour, in the presence of the family and a number of guests. Mr. Garland gave me away and the pastor, Bishop Hawks, performed the ceremony, who had solemnised the bridals of Mr. Garland's own children.

The day was a happy one, but it faded all too soon. Mr. Keckley — let me speak kindly of his faults — proved dissipated and a burden instead of a helpmate. More than all, I learned that he was a slave instead of a free man, as he represented himself to be. With the simple explanation that I lived with him eight years, let charity draw around him the mantle of silence.

I went to work in earnest to purchase my freedom, but the years passed and I was still a slave. Mr. Garland's family claimed so much of my attention — in fact, I supported them — that I was not able to accumulate anything. In the mean time Mr. Garland died and Mr. Burwell, a Mississippi planter, came to St. Louis to settle up the estate. He was a kind-hearted man and said I should be free and would afford me every facility to raise the necessary amount to pay the price of my liberty.

Several schemes were urged upon me by my friends. At last I formed a resolution to go to New York, state my case and appeal to the benevolence of the people. The plan seemed feasible and I made preparations to carry it out. When I was almost ready to turn my face northward, Mrs. Garland told me that she would require the names of six gentlemen who would vouch for my return and become responsible for the amount at which I was valued. I had many friends in St. Louis and as I believed that they had confidence in me, I felt that I could readily obtain the names desired. I started out, stated my case and obtained five signatures to the paper and my heart throbbed with pleasure, for I did not believe that the sixth would refuse me. I called, he listened patiently, then remarked:

"Yes, yes, Lizzie; the scheme is a fair one and you shall have my name. But I shall bid you goodbye when you start."

"Goodbye for a short time," I ventured to add.

"No, goodbye for all time," and he looked at me as if he would read my very soul with his eyes.

I was startled.

"What do you mean, Mr. Farrow? Surely you do not think that I do not mean to come back?"

"No."

"No, what then?"

"Simply this: you mean to come back, that is, you mean to now, but you never will. When you reach New York the abolitionists will tell you what savages we are and they will prevail on you to stay there; and we shall never see you again."

"But I assure you, Mr. Farrow, you are mistaken. I not only mean to come back, but will come back and pay every cent of the twelve hundred dollars for myself and my child."

I was beginning to feel sick at heart, for I could not accept the signature of this man when he had no faith in my pledges. No; slavery, eternal slavery rather than be regarded with distrust by those whose respect I esteemed.

"But I am not mistaken," he persisted. "Time will show. When you start for the North, I shall bid you goodbye."

My heart grew heavy. Every ray of sunshine was eclipsed. With humbled pride, weary step, tearful face and a dull, aching pain, I left the house. I walked along the street mechanically. The cloud had no silver lining now. The rosebuds of hope had withered and died without lifting up their heads to receive the kiss of morning. There was no morning, for me. All was night, dark night.

I reached my own home and, weeping, threw myself upon the bed. My trunk was packed, my luncheon was prepared by mother, the carriages were ready to bear me where I would not hear the clank of chains, where I would breathe the free, invigorating breezes of the glorious North. I had dreamed such a happy dream, in imagination had drunk of the water, the pure, sweet crystal water of life, but now the flowers had withered before my eyes; darkness had settled down upon me like a pall and I was left alone with cruel mocking shadows.

The first paroxysm of grief was scarcely over, when a carriage stopped in front of the house. Mrs. Le Bourgois, one of my kind patrons, got out of it and entered the door. She seemed to bring sunshine with her handsome cheery face.

She came to where I was and in her sweet way said:

"Lizzie, I hear that you are going to New York to beg for money to buy your freedom. I have been thinking over the matter and told Ma it would be a shame to allow you to go North to beg for what we should give you. You have many friends in St. Louis and I am going to raise the twelve hundred dollars required among them. I have two hundred dollars put away for a present; am indebted to you one hundred dollars; mother owes you fifty dollars and will add another fifty to it; and as I do not want the present, I will make the money a present to you. Don't start for New York now until I see what I can do among your friends."

Like a ray of sunshine she came and like a ray of sunshine she went away. The flowers no longer were withered, drooping. Again they seemed to bud and grow in fragrance and beauty. Mrs. Le Bourgois, God bless her dear good heart, was more than successful. The twelve hundred dollars were raised and at last my son and myself were free.

Free, free! What a glorious ring to the word. Free. The bitter heart-struggle was over. Free! The soul could go out to heaven and to God with no chains to pull it down. Free. The earth wore a brighter look and the very stars seemed to sing with joy. Yes, free! Free by the laws of man and the smile of God. Heaven bless them who made me so.

The following, copied from the original papers, contain, in brief, the history of my emancipation:

I promise to give Lizzie and her son George their freedom, on the payment of $1200.

ANNE P. GARLAND, *June 27, 1855*

LIZZY—I send you this note to sign for the sum of $75 and when I give you the whole amount you will then sign the other note for $100.

ELLEN M. DOAN

I have received of Lizzy Keckley $95O, which I have deposited with Darby & Barksdale for her—$600 on the 21st July, $300 on the 27th and 28th of July and $5O on 13th August, 1855.

I have and shall make use of said money for Lizzy's benefit and hereby guarantee to her one per cent per month — as much more as can be made she shall have. The one per cent, as it may be checked out, I will be responsible for myself, as well as for the whole amount, when it shall be needed by her.

WILLIS L. WILLIAMS
St. Louis, 13th August, 1855.

Know all men by these presents, that for and in consideration of the love and affection we bear towards our sister, Anne P. Garland, of St. Louis, Missouri, and for the further consideration of $5 in hand paid, we hereby sell and convey unto her, the said Anne P. Garland, a negro woman named Lizzie and a negro boy, her son, named George; said Lizzie now resides at St. Louis and is a seamstress, known there as Lizzie Garland, the wife of a yellow man named James and called James Keckley; said George is a bright mulatto boy and is known in St. Louis as Garland's George. We warrant these two slaves to be slaves for life, but make no representations as to age or health.

Witness our hands and seals, this 10th day of August, 1855.

JAS. R. PUTNAM, E. M. PUTNAM, A. BURWELL

The State of Mississippi, Warren County, City of Vicksburg.

Be it remembered, that on the tenth day of August, in the year of our Lord one thousand eight hundred and fifty-five, before me, Francis N. Steele, a Commissioner, resident in the city of Vicksburg, duly commissioned and qualified by the executive authority and under the Laws of the State of Missouri, to take the acknowledgement of deeds, etc., to be used or recorded therein, personally appeared James R. Putnam and E. M. Putnam, his wife and Armistead Burwell, to me known to be the individuals named in and who executed the foregoing conveyance and acknowledged that they executed the same for the purposes therein mentioned; and the E. M Putnam being by me examined apart from her husband and being fully acquainted with the contents of the foregoing conveyance, acknowledged that she executed the same freely and relinquished her dower and any other claim she might have in and to the property therein mentioned, freely and without fear, compulsion, or undue influence of her said husband.

In witness whereof I have hereunto set my hand and affixed my official seal, this 10th day of August, A.D. 1855.

F. N. STEELE, Commissioner for Missouri

Know all men that I, Anne P. Garland, of the County and City of St. Louis, State of Missouri, for and in consideration of the sum of $1200, to me in hand paid this day in cash, hereby emancipate my negro woman Lizzie and her son George; the said Lizzie is known in St. Louis as the wife of James, who is called James Keckley; is of light complexion, about 37 years of age, by trade a dress-maker and called by those who know her, Garland's Lizzie. The said boy, George, is the only child of Lizzie, is about 16 years of age and is almost white and called by those who know him, Garland's George.

Witness my hand and seal, this 13th day of November, 1855. ANNE P. GARLAND
Witness: JOHN WICKHAM, WILLIS L. WILLLAMS
In St. Louis Circuit Court, October Term., 1855. November 15, 1855.

State of Missouri, County of St. Louis.

Be it remembered, that on this fifteenth day of November, eighteen hundred and fifty-five, in open court came John Wickham and Willis L. Williams, these two subscribing witnesses, examined under oath to that effect, proved the execution and acknowledgment of said deed by Anne P. Garland to Lizzie and her son George, which said proof of acknowledgment is entered on the record of the court of that day.

In testimony whereof I hereto set my hand and affix the seal of said court, at office in the City of St. Louis, the day and year last aforesaid.

Wm J. HAMMOND, Clerk.

State of Missouri, County of St. Louis.

I, Wm. J. Hammond, Clerk of the Circuit Court within and for the county aforesaid, certify the foregoing to be a true copy of a deed of emancipation from Anne P. Garland to Lizzie and her son George, as fully as the same remain in my office.

In testimony whereof I hereto set my hand and affix the seal of said court, at office in the City of St. Louis, this fifteenth day of November, 1855.

Wm. J. HAMMOND, Clerk.

State of Missouri, County of St. Louis.

I, the undersigned Recorder of said county, certify that the foregoing instrument of writing was filed for record in my office on the 14th day of November, 1855; it is truly recorded in Book No. 169, page 288.

Witness my hand and official seal, date last aforesaid.

C. KEEMLE, Recorder.

History of Mary Prince, a West Indian Slave
(RELATED BY HERSELF)

I was born at Brackish Pond, in Bermuda. My mother was a household slave and my father, whose name was Prince, was a sawyer belonging to Mr. Trimmingham, a shipbuilder at Crow Lane. When I was an infant, old Mr. Myners died and there was a division of the slaves and other property among the family. I was bought along with my mother by old Captain Darrel and given to his grandchild, little Miss Betsey Williams. Captain Williams, Mr. Darrel's son-in-law, was master of a vessel which traded to several places in America and the West Indies and he was seldom at home long together.

I had scarcely reached my twelfth year when my mistress became too poor to keep so many of us at home; and she hired me out to Mrs. Pruden, a lady who lived about five miles off, in the adjoining parish, in a large house near the sea.

I cried bitterly at parting with my dear mistress, and when I kissed my mother and brothers and sisters, I thought my young heart would break, it pained me so. But there was no help, I was forced to go. Good Mrs. Williams comforted me by saying that I should still be near the home I was about to quit and might come over and see her and my kindred whenever I could obtain leave of absence from Mrs. Pruden.

I knew that Mrs. Williams could no longer maintain me: that she was fain to part with me for my food and clothing; and I tried to submit myself to the change.

My new mistress was a passionate woman, but yet she did not treat me very unkindly. I do not remember her striking me but once and that was for going to see Mrs. Williams when I heard she was sick and staying longer than she had given me leave to do.

At this time Mrs. Williams died. I was told suddenly of her death and my grief was so great that, forgetting I had the baby in my arms, I ran away directly to my poor mistress's house; but reached it only in time to see the corpse carried out. Oh, that was a day of sorrow — a heavy day! All the slaves cried. My mother cried and lamented her sore; and I (foolish creature!) vainly entreated them to bring my dear mistress back to life. I knew nothing rightly about death then and it seemed a hard thing to bear.

I stayed at Mrs. Pruden's about three months after this. I was then sent back to Mr. Williams to be sold. Oh, that was a sad sad time. I recollect the day well. Mrs. Pruden came to me and said, "Mary, you will have to go home directly; your master is going to be married and he means to sell you and two of your sisters to raise money for the wedding."

Hearing this I burst out crying, though I was then far from being sensible of the full weight of my misfortune, or of the misery that awaited me.

I left Mrs. Pruden's and walked home with a heart full of sorrow. The idea of being sold away from my mother and Miss Betsey was so frightful that I dared not trust myself to think about it.

The black morning at length came, too soon for my poor mother and us. Whilst she was putting on us the new osnaburgs in which we were to be sold, she said in a sorrowful voice, (I shall never forget it) "See, I am shrouding my poor children; what a task for a mother!"

She then called Miss Betsey to take leave of us.

"I am going to carry my little chickens to market," (these were her very words,) "take your last look of them; may be you will see them no more."

"Oh, my poor slaves! My own slaves!" said dear Miss Betsey, "you belong to me; and it grieves my heart to part with you."

Miss Betsey kissed us all and, when she left us, my mother called the rest of the slaves to bid us goodbye. One of them, a woman named Moll, came with her infant in her arms. "Ay!" said my mother, seeing her turn away and look at her child with the tears in her eyes, "your turn will come next."

The slaves could say nothing to comfort us; they could only weep and lament with us. When I left my dear little brothers and the house in which I had been brought up, I thought my heart would burst.

Our mother, weeping as she went, called me away with the children Hannah and Dinah and we took the road that led to Hamble Town which we reached about four o'clock in the afternoon. We followed my mother to the market-place, where she placed us in a row against a large house, with our backs to the wall and our arms folded across our breasts. I, as the eldest, stood first, Hannah next to me then Dinah; and our mother stood beside, crying over us. My heart throbbed with grief and terror so violently, that I pressed my hands quite tightly across my breast, but I could not keep it still and it continued to leap as though it would burst out of my body. But who cared for that? Did one of the many bystanders who were looking at us so carelessly, think of the pain that wrung the hearts of the negro woman and her young ones?

No, no!

They were not all bad, I dare say but slavery hardens white people's hearts towards the blacks; and many of them were not slow to make their remarks upon us aloud without regard to our grief — though their light words fell like pepper on the flesh wounds of our hearts. Oh those white people have small hearts who can only feel for themselves.

At length the venue master, who was to offer us for sale like sheep or cattle, arrived and asked my mother which was the eldest. She said nothing, but pointed to me. He took me by the hand and led me out into the middle of the street and, turning me slowly round, exposed me to the view of those who attended the venue. I was soon surrounded by strange men, who examined and handled me in the same manner that a butcher would a calf or a lamb he was about to purchase and who talked about my shape and size in like words — as if I could no more understand their meaning than the dumb beasts. I was then put up for sale.

The bidding commenced at a few pounds and gradually rose to fifty-seven, when I was knocked down to the highest bidder. The people who stood by said that I had fetched a great sum for so young a slave.

I then saw my sisters led forth and sold to different owners so that we had not the sad satisfaction of being partners in bondage. When the sale was over, my mother hugged and kissed us and mourned over us begging of us to keep up a good heart and do our duty to our new masters.

It was a sad parting; one went one way, one another and our poor mammy went home with nothing.

It was night when I reached my new home. The house was large and built at the bottom of a very high hill; but I could not see much of it that night.

I saw too much of it afterwards, though. The stones and the timber were the best things in it; they were not so hard as the hearts of the owners.

The person I took the most notice of that night was a French Black called Hetty, whom my master took in privateering from another vessel and made his slave. She was the most active woman I ever saw and was tasked to her utmost.

A few minutes after my arrival she came in from milking the cows and put the sweet potatoes on for supper. She then fetched home the sheep and penned them in the fold; drove home the cattle, rubbed down my master's horse and gave the hog and then fed the cows. I liked to look at her and watch all her doings, for hers was the only friendly face I had as yet seen.

She gave me my supper of potatoes and milk and a blanket
to sleep upon, which she spread for me in the passage before
the door of my misstress's chamber.

I got a sad fright that night. I was just going to sleep, when
I heard a noise in my mistress's room; and she presently called
out to inquire if some work was finished that she had ordered
Hetty to do.

"No, Ma'am, not yet," was Hetty's answer from below.

On hearing this, my master started up from his bed and just
as he was, in his shirt, ran down stairs with a long cowskin in
his hand. I heard immediately after, the cracking of the thong
and the house rang to the shrieks of poor Hetty, who kept
crying out, "Oh, Massa, Massa, me dead. Massa! Have mercy
upon me Don't kill me outright."

This was a sad beginning for me. I sat up upon my blanket,
trembling with terror, like a frightened hound and thinking that
my turn would come next. At length the house became still and
I forgot for a little while all my sorrows by falling fast asleep.

The next morning my mistress set about instructing me in
my tasks. She taught me to do all sorts of household work; to
wash and bake, pick cotton and wool and wash floors and
cook. And she taught me (how can I ever forget it!) more things
than these; she caused me to know the exact difference between
the sting of the rope, the cart-whip and the cowskin, when
applied to my naked body by her own cruel hand. And there
was scarcely any punishment more dreadful than the blows I
received on my face and head from her hard heavy fist. She was
a fearful woman and a savage mistress to her slaves.

There were two little slave boys in the house, on whom she
vented her bad temper in a special manner. One of these
children was a mulatto called Cyrus, who had been bought
while an infant in his mother's arms; the other, Jack, was an
African from the coast of Guinea, whom a sailor had given or
sold to my master. Seldom a day passed without these boys

receiving the most severe treatment and often for no fault at all. Both my master and mistress seemed to think that they had a right to ill-use them at their pleasure; and very often accompanied their commands with blows, whether the children were behaving well or ill. I have seen their flesh ragged and raw with licks. They were never secure one moment from a blow and their lives were passed in continual fear. My mistress was not contented with using the whip, but often pinched their cheeks and arms in the most cruel manner.

My pity for these poor boys was soon transferred to myself, for I was licked and flogged and pinched by her pitiless fingers in the neck and arms, exactly as they were. To strip me naked and hang me up by the wrists and lay my flesh open with the cowskin, was an ordinary punishment for even a slight offence.

My mistress often robbed me too of the hours that belong to sleep. She used to sit up very late, frequently even until morning, and I had then to stand at a bench and wash during the greater part of the night, or pick wool and cotton. Often I have dropped down overcome by sleep and fatigue, 'til I roused from a state of stupor by the whip and forced to start up to my tasks.

Poor Hetty was very kind to me and I used to call her my Aunt, but she led a most miserable life and her death was hastened (at least the slaves all believed and said so,) by the dreadful chastisement she received from my master during her pregnancy.

It happened as follows.

One of the cows had dragged the rope away from the stake to which Hetty had fastened it and got loose. My master flew into a terrible rage and ordered the poor woman to be stripped quite naked, notwithstanding her pregnancy and to be tied up to a tree in the yard. He then flogged her as hard as he could lick, both with the whip and cowskin, 'til she was all over streaming with blood. He rested and then beat her again and again.

Her shrieks were terrible. The consequence was that poor
Hetty was brought to bed before her time and was delivered
after severe labour of a dead child. She appeared to recover
after her confinement, so far that she was repeatedly flogged by
both master and mistress afterwards; but her former strength
never returned to her. Before long her body and limbs swelled
to a great size; and she lay on a mat in the kitchen, 'til the water
burst out of her body and she died. All the slaves said that
dying was a good thing for poor Hetty, but I cried very much
for her death. The manner of it filled me with horror. I could not
bear to think about it yet it was always present in my mind for
many a day.

One day a heavy squall of wind and rain came on suddenly
and my mistress sent me round the corner of the house to
empty a large earthen jar. The jar was already damaged with an
old deep crack that divided it in the middle and, in turning it
upside down to empty it, it parted in my hand. I could not help
the accident, but I was dreadfully frightened, looking forward
to a severe punishment.

I ran crying to my mistress, "O mistress, the jar has come in
two."

"You have broken it, have you?" she replied. "Come
directly here to me."

I came trembling.

She stripped and flogged me long and severely with the
cowskin; as long as she had strength to use the lash, for she did
not stop 'til she was quite tired.

When my master came home at night, she told him of my
fault; and he started swearing loudly. After abusing me with
every ill-name he could think of and giving me several heavy
blows with his hand, he said, "I shall come home tomorrow at
none, on purpose to give you a round hundred."

Sadly for me, he kept his word. I cannot easily forget it. He tied me up upon a ladder and gave me a hundred lashes with his own hand and master Benjy stood by to count them for him. When he had licked me for some time, he sat down to take breath. After resting, be beat me again and again until he was quite wearied and so hot (for the weather was very sultry), that he sank back in his chair, as if he was about to faint.

While my mistress went to bring him drink, there was a dreadful earthquake. Part of the roof fell down and every thing in the house went clatter-clatter-clatter.

I thought the end of all things near at hand; and I was so sore with the flogging, that I scarcely cared whether I lived or died. The earth was groaning and shaking, everything tumbling about and my mistress and the slaves were shrieking and crying out, "The earthquake! the earthquake!"

It was an awful day for us all.

During the confusion I crawled away on my hands and knees and laid myself down under the steps of the piazza, in front of the house. I was in a dreadful state. My body covered in blood and bruises, I could not help moaning piteously. The other slaves, when they saw me shook their heads and said, "Poor child! Poor child!"

I lay there 'til the morning, careless of what might happen, for life was very weak in me and I wished more than ever to die. But when we are very young, death always seems a great way off and it would not come that night to me.

The next morning I was forced by my master to rise and go about my usual work, though my body and limbs were so stiff and sore, that I could not move without the greatest pain.

Even after all this severe punishment, I never heard the last of that jar; my mistress was always throwing it in my face.

Some little time after this, one of the cows got loose from the stake and ate one of the sweet-potato slips. I was milking when my master found it out. He came to me and, without any more ado, stooped down and taking off his heavy boot, he struck me such a severe blow in the small of my back, that I shrieked with agony and thought I was killed. I feel a weakness in my back to this day. The cow was frightened at his violence and kicked down the pail and spilt the milk all about. My master knew that this accident was his own fault, but he was so enraged that he seemed glad of an excuse to go on with his ill-usage. I cannot remember how many licks he gave me then, but he beat me 'til I was unable to stand and 'til he himself was weary.

After this I ran away and went to my mother, who was living with Mr. Richard Darrel. My poor mother was both grieved and glad to see me; grieved because I had been so ill-used and glad because she had not seen me for a long, long while. She dared not receive me into the house, but she hid me up in a hole in the rocks nearby and brought me food at night, after everybody was asleep.

My father, who lived at Crow Lane, over the salt-water channel, at last heard of my being hid up in the cavern and he came and took me back to my master.

Oh I was loathe, loathe to go back; but as there was no remedy, I was obliged to submit.

When we got there, my poor father said to my master, "Sir, I am sorry that my child should be forced to run away from her owner; but the treatment she has received is enough to break her heart. The sight of her wounds has nearly broke mine. I entreat you, for the love of God, to forgive her for running away and to be a kind master to her in future."

My master said I was used as well as I deserved and that I ought to be punished for running away.

I then took courage and said that I could stand the floggings no longer, that I was weary of my life and therefore I had run away to my mother; but mothers could only weep and mourn over their children, they could not save them from cruel masters, from the whip, the rope and the cowskin.

My master told me to hold my tongue and go about my

work, or he would find a way to settle me. He did not, however, flog me that day.

For five years after this I remained in his house and almost daily received the same harsh treatment. At length he put me on board a sloop and to my great joy sent me away to Turk's Island. I was not permitted to see my mother or father, or poor sisters and brothers to say goodbye, though going away to a strange land and might never see them again.

Oh the Buckra people who keep slaves think that black people are like cattle, without natural affection. But my heart tells me it is far otherwise.

We were nearly four weeks on the voyage, which was unusually long. Sometimes we had a light breeze, sometimes a great calm and the ship made no way. Our provisions and water ran very low and we were put upon short rations. I should almost have been starved had it not been for the kindness of a black man called Anthony and his wife, who had brought their own victuals and shared them with me.

When we went ashore at the Grand Quay, the captain sent me to the house of my new master, to whom my previous master had sold me.

Grand Quay is a small town upon a sandbank; the houses low and built of wood. Such was my new master's.

The first person I saw on my arrival was my new master, a stout sulky looking man who carried me through the hall to show me to his wife and children. Next day I was put up for valuation to know how much I was worth. I was valued at one hundred pounds currency.

My new master was one of the owners or holders of the salt ponds, and he received a certain sum for every slave that worked upon his premises, whether they were young or old. This sum was allowed him out of the profits arising from the salt works.

I was immediately sent to work in the salt water with the

rest of the slaves. This work was perfectly new to me. I was given a half barrel and a shovel and had to stand up to my knees in the water, from four o'clock in the morning 'til nine, when we were given some Indian corn boiled in water, which we were obliged to swallow as fast as we could for fear the rain should fall and melt the salt. We were then called again to our tasks and worked through the heat of the day; the sun flaming upon our heads like fire and raising salt blisters in those parts which were not completely covered.

Our feet and legs, from standing in the salt water for so many hours, soon became full of dreadful boils, which eat down in some cases to the very bone, afflicting the sufferers with great torment.

We came home at twelve, ate our corn soup as fast as we could and went back to our employment 'til dark at night We then shovelled up the salt in large heaps and went down to the sea where we washed the pickle from our limbs and cleaned the barrows and shovels from the salt. When we returned to the house, our master gave us each our allowance of raw Indian corn, which we pounded in a mortar and boiled in water for our suppers.

We slept in a long shed, divided into narrow slips, like the stalls used for cattle. Boards fixed upon stakes driven into the ground, without mat or covering, were our only beds.

On Sundays, after we had washed the salt bags and done other work required of us, we went into the bush and cut the long soft grass, of which we made trusses for our legs and feet to rest upon, for they were so full of the salt boils that we could get no rest lying upon the bare boards.

Though we worked from morning 'til night, there was no satisfying our master. I hoped when I left my previous master that I should have been better off, but I found it was but going from one butcher to another. There was this difference between them: my former master used to beat me while raging and foaming with passion while my new master was usually quite calm. He would stand by and give orders for a slave to be cruelly whipped and assist in the punishment without moving a muscle of his face; walking about and taking snuff with the greatest composure. Nothing could touch his hard heart — neither sighs, nor tears, nor prayers, nor streaming blood; he was deaf to our cries and careless of our sufferings. He has often stripped me naked, hung me up by the wrists and beat me with the cowskin, with his own hand, 'til my body was raw with gashes. Yet there was nothing very remarkable in this; for it might serve as a sample of the common usage of the slaves on that horrible island.

When we were ill, let our complaint be what it might, the only medicine given to us was a great bowl of hot salt water which made us very sick. If we could not keep up with the rest of the gang of slaves, we were put in the stocks and severely flogged the next morning. Yet, not the less, our master expected, after we had thus been kept from our rest and our limbs rendered stiff and sore with ill-usage, that we should still go through the ordinary tasks of the day all the same.

Sometimes we had to work all night, measuring salt to load a vessel, or turning a machine to draw water out of the sea for the salt-making. Then we had no sleep — nor rest — but were forced to work as fast as we could and go on again all next day the same as usual.

I I had worked in the salt ponds at Turk's Island about ten years when my master retired to a house he had in Bermuda, leaving his son to succeed him on the island. He took me with him to wait upon his daughters and I was joyful, for I was sick, sick of Turk's Island and my heart yearned to see my native place again, my mother and my kindred.

After I left Turk's Island, I was told by some negroes that came over from it, that the poor slaves had built up a place with boughs and leaves, where they might meet for prayers, but the white people pulled it down twice and would not allow them even a shed for prayers. A flood came down soon after and washed away many houses, filled the place with sand and overflowed the ponds. I do think that this was for their wickedness; for the Backra men there were very wicked. I sat and heard much that was very very bad at that place.

Back in my native place I worked for several years in the grounds of my master's home, planting and hoeing sweet-potatoes, Indian corn, plantains, bananas, cabbages, pumpkins, onions and so on. I did all the household work, carried out all the errands and attended upon a horse and cow besides. I had more than enough to do, but still it was not so very bad as Turk's Island.

After that I was hired to work at Cedar Hills and, every Saturday night, I handed my earnings to my master. I had plenty of work to do there, plenty of washing; but yet I made myself pretty comfortable. I earned two dollars and a quarter a week, which is twenty pence a day.

Mr. Wood took me with him to Antigua, to the town of St. John's, where he lived. This was about fifteen years ago. He did not then know whether I was to be sold, but Mrs. Wood found that I could work and she wanted to buy me. Her husband then wrote to my master to inquire whether I was to be sold? My master wrote in reply that I should not be sold to anyone that would treat me ill.

It was strange he should say this, when he had treated me so ill himself. So I was purchased by Mr. Wood for 300 dollars (£100 Bermuda currency.)

My work there was to attend the chambers and nurse the child and to go down to the pond and wash clothes. But I soon fell ill of the rheumatism and grew so very lame that I was forced to walk with a stick. I got the Saint Anthony's fire, also, in my left leg and became quite a cripple. No one cared much to come near me and I was ill a long long time, for several months I could not lift the limb. I had to lie in a little old out-house, that was swarming with bugs and other vermin, which tormented me greatly; but I had no other place to lie in. I got the rheumatism by catching cold at the pond, from washing in the fresh water; in the salt water I never got cold.

The person who lived in the next yard (a Mrs. Greene), could not bear to hear my cries and groans. She was kind and used to send an old slave woman to help me, who sometimes brought me a little soup.

When the doctor found I was so ill, he said I must be put into a bath of hot water. The old slave got the bark of some bush that was good for the pains, which she boiled in the hot water and every night she came and put me into the bath and did what she could for me. I don't know what I should have done, or what would have become of me, had it not been for her.

Though I was still very ill with the rheumatism, my mistress was always abusing and fretting after me. It is not possible to tell all her ill-language. I bore in silence a great deal of ill-words until my heart was quite full and I finally told her that she ought not to use me so; that when I was ill I might have lain and died for what she cared; and no one would then come near me to nurse me, because they were afraid of my mistress.

This was a great affront. She called her husband and told him what I had said. He flew into a passion, but did not beat me then. He only abused and swore at me, and then gave me a note and bade me go and look for a new owner. Not that he meant to sell me; but he did this to please his wife and to frighten me.

I went to Adam White, a cooper, a free black who had money, and asked him to buy me. He went directly to Mr. Wood, but was informed that I was not to be sold.

The next day my master whipped me.

Some time after I began to attend the Moravian Church, I met with Daniel James, afterwards my dear husband. He was a carpenter and cooper to his trade, an honest, hard-working, decent black man and a widower. He had purchased his freedom off his mistress, old Mrs. Baker, with money he had earned whilst a slave. When he asked me to marry him, I took time to consider the matter over with myself and would not say yes 'til he went to church with me.

He was very industrious after he bought his freedom and he had hired a comfortable house and had convenient things about him. We were joined in marriage Christmas 1826, in the Moravian Chapel at Spring Gardens, by the Rev. Mr. Olufsen. We could not be married in the English Church. English marriage is not allowed to slaves and no free man can marry a slave woman.

When Mr.Wood heard of my marriage, he flew into a great rage and sent for Daniel, who was helping to build a house for his old mistress.

Mr. Wood asked him who gave him a right to marry a slave of his?

My husband said, "Sir, I am a free man and thought I had a right to choose a wife. If I had known Molly was not allowed to have a husband, I should not have asked her to marry me."

Mrs. Wood was more vexed than her husband. She could not forgive me for getting married and stirred up Mr. Wood to flog me dreadfully with the horsewhip.

I thought it very hard to be whipped at my time of life for getting a husband. I told her so. She said that she would not have nigger men about the yards and premises, or allow a nigger man's clothes to be washed in the same tub where hers were washed.

She was fearful, I think, that I should lose her time, in order to wash and do things for my husband, but I had then no time to wash for myself. I was obliged to find someone to wash my own clothes, though I was always at the wash-tub.

I had not much happiness in my marriage, owing to my being a slave. It made my husband sad to see me so ill-treated. Mrs. Wood was always abusing me about him. She did not lick me herself, but she got her husband to do it for her, whilst she fretted the flesh off my bones. Yet for all this, she would not sell me. She sold five slaves whilst I was with her; but though she was always finding fault with me, she would not part with me.

Mr. Wood eventually allowed Daniel to have a place to live in our yard, which we were very thankful for.

About this time my master and mistress were going to England to put their son to school and bring their daughters home and they took me with them to take care of the child. I was willing to come to England: I thought that by going there I should probably get cured of my rheumatism and should return quite well, to my husband.

My husband was willing for me to come away, for he had heard that my master would free me, and I also hoped this might prove true; but it was all a false report.

When we drew near to England, the rheumatism seized all my limbs worse than ever and my body was dreadfully swelled. When we landed at the Tower, I showed my flesh to my mistress, but she took no great notice of it.

We were obliged to stop at the tavern 'til my master got a house, and a day or two after, my mistress sent me down into the washhouse to learn to wash in the English way. In the West Indies we wash with cold water, in England with hot.

I told my mistress I was afraid that putting my hands first into the hot water and then into the cold, would increase the pain in my limbs. The doctor had told my mistress long before I came from the West Indies that I was a sickly body and that washing did not agree with me. But Mrs. Wood would not release me from the tub, so l was forced to do as I could.

I grew worse and could not stand to wash and through pain and weakness was reduced to kneel or sit down on the floor to finish my task.

When I complained to my mistress of this, she only got into a passion as usual and said washing in hot water could not hurt any one; that I was lazy and insolent and wanted to be free of my work, but that she would make me do it.

I thought her very hard on me and my heart rose up within me. However I kept still at that time and went down again to wash the child's things. The English washerwomen who were there with me, when they saw that I was so ill, had pity upon me and washed them for me.

I am often much vexed and I feel great sorrow when I hear some people say that the slaves do not need better usage and do not want to be free. They believe the foreign people who deceive them and say slaves are happy. I say, not so. How can slaves be happy when they have the halter round their neck and the whip upon their back, and are disgraced and thought no more of than beasts, are separated from their mothers and husbands and children and sisters, just as cattle are sold and separated? Is it happiness for a driver in the field to take down his wife or sister or child and strip them and whip them in such a disgraceful manner? Women have had their children exposed in the open field to shame! There is no modesty or decency shown by the owner to his slaves. Men, women and children are exposed alike.

Since I have been in England, I have often wondered how English people can go out into the West Indies and act in such a beastly manner. When they go there they forget God and all feeling of shame, I think, since; they can see and do such things. They tie up slaves like hogs and beat them like hogs never were flogged. And yet they come home and say and make some good people believe, that slaves don't want to get out of slavery.

It is not so. I never heard a slave say so. All slaves want to be free — to be free is very sweet. I have been a slave myself, I know what slaves feel. I know what they have told me. The man that says slaves are quite happy in slavery is either ignorant or a liar. Such people ought to be ashamed of themselves. They can't do without slaves, they say. What's the reason they can't do without slaves as well as in England? No slaves here, no whips, no stocks, no punishment, except for wicked people. They hire servants in England; and if they don't like them, they send them away. They can't lick them. Let them work ever so hard in England, they are far better off than slaves in the West Indies. Here, if they get a bad master, they give warning and go hire to another. They have their liberty. That's just what we want. We don't mind hard work, if we had proper treatment and proper wages like English servants and proper time given in the week to keep us from breaking the Sabbath. But they won't give it. They will have work, work, work, night and day, sick or well, 'til we are quite done up; and we must not speak up nor look amiss, however much we be abused. And then when we are quite done up, who cares for us, more than for a lame horse? This is slavery. I tell it, to let English people know the truth; and I hope they will never leave off to pray God and call loud to the great King of England, 'til all the poor blacks be given free and slavery done up for evermore.

Lucy A. Delaney's Story

In the year 18— , Mr. and Mrs. John Woods and Mr. and Mrs. Andrew Posey lived as one family in the State of Illinois. Living with Mrs. Posey was a little negro girl named Polly Crocket, who had made it her home there, in peace and happiness for five years. On a dismal night in the month of September, Polly, with four other colored persons, were kidnapped and, after being securely bound and gagged were put into a boat which carried them across the Mississippi River to the city of St. Louis. Shortly after, these unfortunate negroes were taken up the Missouri River and sold into slavery. Polly was purchased by a farmer. Thomas Botts, with whom she resided for a year, when, overtaken by business reverses, he was obliged to sell all he possessed, including his negroes.

Among those present on the day set apart for the sale was Major Taylor Berry, a wealthy gentleman who had travelled a long distance for the purpose of purchasing a servant girl for his wife. As was the custom, all the negroes were brought out and placed in a line so that the buyers could examine their good points at leisure. Major Berry was immediately attracted by the bright and alert appearance of Polly and at once negotiated with the trader, paid the price agreed upon and started for home to present his wife with this flesh and blood commodity, which money could so easily procure in our vaunted land of freedom.

Mrs. Fanny Berry highly pleased with Polly's manner and appearance decided to make a seamstress of her.

Major Berry had a mulatto servant who was as handsome as an Apollo and when he and Polly met each other, day after day, the natural result followed and, in a short time, with the full consent of Major Berry and his wife, were married. Two children were the fruit of this marriage, my sister Nancy and myself, Lucy A. Delaney.

While living in Franklin county, Major Berry became involved in a quarrel with some gentleman and a duel was resorted to, to settle the difficulty and avenge some fancied insult. The Major arranged his affairs and made his will, leaving his negroes to his wife during. her lifetime and at her death they were to be free. This was his expressed wish.

My father accompanied Major Berry to New Madrid, where the fatal duel was fought, and slayed by him until the end came, received his last sign, his last words and closed his dying eyes and afterwards conveyed the remains of his best friend to the bereaved family with a sad heart.

Major Berry was consigned with loving hands to his last resting place. Though sympathizing deeply with them in their affliction, my father was much disturbed as to what disposition would be made of him and his family.

A few years after, Major Berry's widow married Robert Wash, an eminent lawyer, who afterwards became Judge of the Supreme Court. One child was born to them, who, when she grew to womanhood, became Mrs. Francis W. Goode, whom I shall always hold in grateful remembrance as long as life lasts and God bless her in her old age, is my fervent prayer for her kindness to me, a poor little slave girl.

We lived in the old Wash mansion some time until Mrs. Wash lost her health and, on the advice of a physician, went to Pensacola, Florida, accompanied by my mother. There she died and her body was brought back to St. Louis and there interred.

After Mrs. Wash's death, the troubles of my parents and their children may be said to have really commenced.

Though in direct opposition to the will of Major Berry, Judge Wash tore my father from his wife and children and sold him "way down South."

Slavery, cursed slavery!

What crimes has it invoked and, oh, what retribution has a righteous God visited upon these traders in human flesh. The rivers of tears shed by us helpless ones in captivity, were turned to lakes of our blood!

How often have we cried in our anguish, *Oh Lord, how long, how long?*

But the handwriting was on the wall, and tardy justice came at last and avenged the woes of an oppressed race. Atlanta and Gettysburgh spoke in thunder tones that John Brown's body had indeed marched on and we, the ransomed ones, glorify God and dedicate ourselves to His service and acknowledge His greatness and goodness in rescuing us from such bondage as parts husband from wife, the mother from her children, yes, even the babe from her breast.

Major Berry's daughter, Mary, shortly after, married H. S. Cox of Philadelphia and they went to that city to pass their honeymoon, taking my sister Nancy with them as waiting-maid.

When my father was sold South, my mother registered a solemn vow that her children should not continue in slavery all their lives and she never spared an opportunity to impress it upon us, that we must get our freedom whenever the chance offered. So here was an unlooked-for avenue of escape which presented much that was favorable in carrying out her desire to see Nancy a free woman.

Having been brought up in a free State, mother had learned much to her advantage which would have been impossible in a slave State and which she now proposed to turn to account for the benefit of her daughter. So mother instructed my sister not to return with Mr. and Mrs. Cox but to run away, as soon as chance offered, to Canada where a friend of our mother's lived who was also a runaway slave living in freedom and happiness in Toronto.

As the happy couple wandered from city to city in search of

pleasure, my sister was constantly turning over in her mind various plans of escape.

Fortune finally favored her and she took her opportunity. As she told me later:

"Though the air was chill and gloomy, I felt the warmth of freedom as I neared the Canada shore. I landed, without question and found my mother's friend with but little difficulty, who assisted me to get work and support myself.

"Not long afterwards, I married a prosperous farmer who provided me with a happy home where I brought my children into the world without the sin of slavery to strive against."

On the return of Mrs. Cox to St. Louis she sent for my mother and told her that Nancy had run away. Mother was very thankful and in her heart arose a prayer of thanksgiving, but outwardly she pretended to be vexed and angry.

Oh, the impenetrable mask of these poor black creatures! How much of joy, sorrow, misery and anguish have they hidden from their tormentors?

I was a small girl at that time, but remember how wildly mother showed her joy at Nancy's escape when we were alone together. She would dance, clap her hands and, waving them above her head, would indulge in one of those weird negro melodies, which so charm and fascinate the listener.

Mrs. Cox commenced housekeeping on a grand and extended scale, having a large acquaintance, she entertained lavishly. My mother cared for the laundry and I, who was living with a Mrs. Underhill from New York and was having rather good times, was compelled to go live with Mrs. Cox to mind the baby.

My pathway was thorny enough and, though there may be no roses without thorns, I had thorns in plenty with no roses.

I was beginning to plan for freedom and was forever on the alert for a chance to escape and join my sister. I was then twelve years old and often talked the matter over with mother and canvassed the probabilities of both of us getting away.

Mrs. Cox was always very severe and exacting with my mother and, on one occasion when something did not suit her, turned on mother like a fury and declared, "I am tired out with the 'white airs' you put on. If you don't behave differently, I will make Mr. Cox sell you down the river at once."

Although mother turned grey with fear, she presented a bold front and retorted that she didn't care, she was tired of that place and didn't like to live there, nohow.

This so infuriated Mr. Cox that he cried, "How dare a negro" say what she liked or what she did not 1ike; and he would show her what he should do.

So, on the day following, he took my mother to an auction room on Main Street and sold her, to the highest bidder, for five hundred and fifty dollars.

Oh, God, the pity of it! In the home of the brave and the land of the free, in the sight of the stars and stripes — that symbol of freedom — sold away from her child, to satisfy the anger of a peevish mistress.

My mother returned to the house to get her few belongings and, straining me to her breast, begged me to be a good girl, that she was going to run away and would buy me as soon as she could.

With all the inborn faith of a child, I believed it most fondly and, when I heard that she had actually made her escape three weeks after, my heart gave an exultant throb and cried, "God is good!"

A large reward was offered, the bloodhounds (curse them and curse their masters) were set loose on her trail. In the daytime she hid in caves and the surrounding woods and in the night time, guided by the wondrous North Star, that blessed lodestone of a slave people, my mother finally reached Chicago, where she was arrested by the negro-catchers.

At this time the Fugitive Slave Law was in full operation

and it was against the law of the whole country to aid and protect an escaped slave; not even a drink of water, for the love of the Master, might be given. Those who dared to do it (and there were many such brave hearts, thank God!) placed their lives in danger.

The presence of bloodhounds and 'nigger-catchers' in their midst, created great excitement and scandalized the community. Feeling ran high and hundreds of people gathered together and declared that mother should not be returned to slavery, but fearing that Mr. Cox would wreak his vengeance upon me, my mother finally gave herself up to her captors and returned to St. Louis.

And so the mothers of Israel have been ever slain through their deepest affections.

After my mother's return, she decided to sue for her freedom and, for that purpose, employed a good lawyer. She had ample testimony to prove that she was kidnapped and it was so fully verified that the jury decided that she was a free woman and papers were made out accordingly.

In the meanwhile, Miss Martha Berry had married Mr. Mitchell and taken me to live with her.

Mrs. Mitchell commanded me to do the weekly washing. I had no more idea how it was to be done than Mrs. Mitchell herself. That I made the effort to do what she required and my failure would have been amusing had it not been so appalling. In those days filtering was unknown and the many ways of cleansing water were to me an unsolved riddle. I never had to do it, so it never concerned me how the clothes were ever washed clean, as the Mississippi water was muddy.

On the morning of the 8th of September 1842, my mother sued Mr. D. D. Mitchell for the possession of her child, Lucy Ann Berry. My mother, accompanied by the sheriff, took me from my hiding place and conveyed me to the jail which was located on Sixth Street, between Chestnut and Market where the Laclede Hotel now stands, and there met Mr. Mitchell with Mr. H. S. Cox, his brother-in-law.

Judge Bryant Murphy read the Law to Mr. Mitchell, which stated that if Mr. Mitchell took me back to his house he must give bond and security to the amount of two thousand dollars and, furthermore, I should not be taken out of the State of Missouri until I had a chance to prove my freedom.

Mr. H S. Cox became his security and Mr. Mitchell gave bond accordingly, and then demanded that I should be put in jail.

"Why do you want to put that poor young girl in jail?" demanded my lawyer.

"Because," he retorted, "her mother or some of her crew might run off with her, just to make me pay the two thousand dollars. I would like to see her lawyer, or any other man, in jail who would take up a nigger case like that."

"You need not think, Mr. Mitchell," Mr. Murdock calmly replied, "because my client is colored that she has no rights and can be cheated out of her freedom. She is just as free as you are and the court will so decide it, as you will see."

However, I was put in a cell, under lock and key and there remained for seventeen long and dreary months listening to the foreign echoes from the streets. Faint sounds of revelling, traffic, conflict.

My only crime was seeking for that freedom which was my birthright. I heard Mr. Mitchell tell his wife that he did not believe in slavery yet, through his instrumentality, I was shut away from the sunlight because he was determined to prove me a slave and thus keep me in bondage.

At the time my mother entered suit for her freedom she was not instructed to mention her two children Nancy and Lucy, so the white people took advantage of this flaw and showed a determination to the every means in their power to prove that

I was not her child.

This gave my mother an immense amount of trouble, but she had girded up her loins for the fight and knowing that she was right was resolved, by the help of God and a good lawyer, to win my case against all opposition.

After advice by competent persons, mother went to Judge Edward Bates and begged him to plead the case. After fully considering the proofs and learning that my mother was a poor woman, he consented to undertake the case and make his charges only sufficient to cover his expenses.

It would be well here to give a brief sketch of Judge Bates, as many people wondered that such a distinguished statesman would take up the case of an obscure negro girl.

Edward Bates was born in Belmont, Virginia in September 1795. He was of Quaker descent and inherited all the ways of that peace-loving people. In 1813, he received a midshipman's warrant and was only prevented from following the sea by the influence of his mother to whom he was greatly attached. Edward emigrated to Missouri in 1814 and entered upon the practice of Law. In 1816, he was appointed prosecuting lawyer for the St. Louis Circuit.

Back in the courthouse, after the evidence from both sides was all in, Mr. Mitchell's lawyer, Thomas Hutchinson, commenced to plead.

For one hour he talked so bitterly against me and against my being in possession of my liberty that I was trembling, for I certainly thought everybody must believe him. Indeed, I almost believed the dreadful things he said myself. As I listened I closed my eyes with sickening dread, for I could just see myself floating down the river and my heart throbs seemed to be the throbs of the mighty engine which propelled me from my mother and freedom forever.

Oh, what a relief it was to me when he finally finished his harangue and resumed his seat. As I had never heard anyone plead before, I was very much alarmed, although I knew in my heart that every word he uttered was a lie. Yet how was I to make people believe? It seemed a puzzling question.

Judge Bates arose and his soulful eloquence and earnest pleading made such an impression on my sore heart, I listened with renewed hope. I felt the black stormy clouds of doubt and despair were fading away and that I was drifting into the safe harbor of the realms of truth. I felt as if everybody must believe him, for he clung to the truth and I wondered how Mr. Hutchinson could so lie about a poor defenseless girl like me.

Judge Bates gripped his hearers with the graphic history of my mother's life, from that time she played on Illinois river banks, through her trials in slavery, her separation from her husband, her efforts to become free, her voluntary return to slavery for the sake of her child and her subsequent efforts in securing her own freedom. All these incidents he lingered over step by step and, concluding, he said:

"Gentlemen of the jury, I am a slaveholder myself, but, thanks to the Almighty God I am above the base principle of holding anybody a slave that has as good right to her freedom as this girl has been proven to have. She was free before she was born; her mother was free but kidnapped in her youth and sacrificed to the greed of negro traders. No free woman can give birth to a slave child, as it is in direct violation of the laws of God and man."

At this juncture he read the affidavit of Mr. A. Posey with whom my mother lived at the time of her abduction. Also affidavits of Mr. and Mrs. Woods in corroboration of the previous facts duly set forth. Judge Bates then said:

"Gentleman of the jury, here I rest this case, as I would not want any better evidence for one of my own children. The testimony of Judge Wash is alone sufficient to substantiate the claim of Polly Crockett Berry to the defendant as being her own child."

The case was then submitted to the jury about 8 o clock in the evening. I was returned to the jail and locked in the cell which I had occupied for seventeen months, filled with the most intense anguish.

Blessed mother, how she fought for me. No work was too hard for her to undertake. Others would have crumpled before the obstacles which confronted her, but undauntedly she pursued her way until my freedom was established by every right and without a questioning doubt.

On the morning of my return to court I was so overcome with fright and emotion and the alternating feelings of despair and hope that I could not stand still long enough to dress myself. I trembled like an aspen leaf; so I sent a message to Mrs Lacy to request permission for me to go to her room, that she might assist me in dressing. I had done a great deal of sewing for Mrs. Lacy, for she had showed me much kindness and was a good Christian. She gladly assisted me and under her willing hands I was soon made ready. Promptly at nine o'clock the sheriff called and escorted me to the courthouse.

At last the courthouse was reached and I had taken my seat in such a condition of helpless terror that I could not tell one person from another. Friends and foes were as one and vainly did I try to distinguish them. My long confinement, burdened with harrowing anxiety, the sleepless night I had just spent, and the unaccountable absence of my mother had brought me to an indescribable condition. I felt dazed as if I were no longer myself. I seemed to be another person — an onlooker — and in my heart dwelt a pity for the poor, lonely girl with downcast face sitting on the bench apart from anyone else in that noisy room. I found myself wondering where Lucy's mother was and how she would feel if the trial went against her. I seemed to have lost all feeling about it, but was speculating what Lucy would do and what her mother would do, if the hand of Fate was raised against poor Lucy. Oh, how sorry I did feel for myself.

At the sound of a gentle voice, I gathered courage to look upward and caught the kindly gleam of Judge Bates' eyes as he turned his gaze upon me and smiling said, "I will have you discharged in a few minutes, Miss Lucy."

Some other business occupied the attention of the court and, when I had begun to think they had forgotten all about me, Judge Bates arose and said calmly:

"Your Honor, I desire to have this girl, Lucy A. Berry, discharged before going into any other business."

Judge Murphy answered, "Certainly."

Then the verdict was called for and rendered and the jurymen resumed their places. Mr. Mitchell's lawyer jumped up and exclaimed:

"Your Honor, my client demands that this girl be remanded in jail. He does not consider that the case has had a fair trial. I am not informed as to what course he intends to pursue but I am now expressing this present wishes."

Judge Bates was on his feet in a second and cried:

"For shame! Is it not enough that this girl has been deprived of her liberty for a year and a half that you must still pursue her after a fair and impartial trial before a jury, in which it was clearly proven and decided that she had every right to freedom? I demand that she be set at liberty at once!"

"I agree with Judge Bates," responded Judge Murphy "The girl may go."

Oh, the overflowing thankfulness of my grateful heart at that moment, who could picture it? None but the good God above us. I could have kissed the feet of my deliverers to express my thanks. With a voice trembling with tears I tried to thank Judge Bates for all his kindness.

I returned to the jail to bid them all goodbye and thank them for their good treatment of me while under their care. They rejoiced with me and wished me much success and happiness in years to come.

I was much concerned at my mother's prolonged absence and was deeply anxious to meet her and pour out my joy on her faithful bosom. Surely it was the hands of God which prevented mother's presence at the trial, for broken down with anxiety and lack of sleep on my account, the emotion would have been greater than her over-wrought heart could have sustained.

As soon as she heard of the result she hurried to meet me and, hand in hand we gazed into each others eyes and saw the light of freedom there and felt in our hearts that we could with one accord cry out: "Glory to God in the highest and peace and good will towards men."

Dear, dear mother, how solemnly I invoke your spirit as I review these trying scenes of my girlhood so long gone. Your patient face and neatly-dressed figure stands ever in the foreground of that checkered time.

After the trial was over and my mother had at last been awarded the right to own her own child, her next thought reverted to sister Nancy who had been gone so long and from whom we had never heard. The greatest ambition mother now had was to see her child Nancy.

We earnestly set ourselves to work to reach the desired end, which was to visit Canada and seek the long-lost girl. With my mother, a first-class laundress and myself, an expert seamstress, it was easy to find all the work we could do and command our own prices.

We found, as well as the whites, a great difference between slave and free labor. While the first was compulsory and, therefore, at the best perfunctory, the latter must be superior in order to create a demand. Realizing this fully mother and I expelled the utmost care in our respective callings and were well rewarded for our efforts.

By exercising rigid economy and much self-denial, we at last accumulated sufficient to enable mother to start for Canada. Oh, how rejoiced I was when that dear overworked woman approached the time when her hard-earned and long-deferred holiday was about to begin.

The uses of adversity is a worn theme, but when it is considered how much of sacrifice the poverty-stricken must bear in order to procure the slightest gratification, should it not impress the thinking mind with amazement, how much of fortitude and patience the honest poor display in the exercise of self-denial.

Mother arrived in Toronto two weeks after she left St. Louis and surprised my sister Nancy, in a pleasant home. She had married a prosperous farmer who owned the farm on which they lived as well as some property in the city nearby. Mother was indescribably happy in finding her child so pleasantly situated and took much pleasure with her bright little grandchildren; and after a long visit, returned home, although strongly urged to remain the rest of her life with Nancy. But old people are like old trees, uproot them and transplant to other scenes they droop and die, no matter how bright the sunshine, or how balmy the breezes.

On her return, mother found me with Mrs. Elsie Thomas, where I had lived during her absence; still sewing for a livelihood. Those were the days in which sewing machines were unknown and no stitching or sewing of any description was allowed to pass inspection unless each stitch looked as if it were a part of th cloth. The art of fine sewing was lost when sewing machines were invented and, though doubtless they have given women more leisure, they have destroyed that extreme neatness in the craft, which was obtained in the days of long ago.

Time passed happily on with us, with no event to ruffle life's peaceful stream. Until 1845, when I met Frederick Turner and, in a few short months, we were made man and wife.

After our marriage, we removed to Quincy, Ill., but our happiness was of short duration as my husband was killed in the explosion of the steamboat *Edward Bates,* on which he was employed. To my mind it seemed a singular coincidence that the boat which bore the name of the great and good man who had given me the first joy of my meagre life — the precious boon of freedom — should be the means of weighing me with my first great sorrow. This thought seemed to reconcile me to my grief, for that name was ever sacred and I could not speak it without reverence.

The number of killed and wounded were many and they were distributed among friends and hospitals. My husband was carried to a friend's, where he breathed his last.

Telegraphs were wanting in those times, so days passed before this wretched piece of news reached me and, there being no railroads and many delays, I reached the home of my friend only to be told that my husband was dead and buried. Intense grief was mine and my grieving worried mother greatly. She never believed in fretting about anything that could not be helped. My only consolation from her was, "Cast your burden on the Lord. My husband is down South and I don't know where he is; he may be dead, he may be alive, he may be happy and comfortable, he may be kicked, abused and half-starved. Your husband, honey, is in heaven; and mine — God only knows where he is."

In those few words, I knew her burden was heavier than mine, for I had been taught that there was hope beyond the grave, but hope was left behind when sold "down Souf".

I resolved to conceal my grief and devote myself to my mother who had done so much and suffered so much for me.

We then returned to St. Louis and took up the old life, minus the contentment which had always buoyed us up in our daily trials, and with an added sorrow which cast a sadness over us.

But Time, the great healer, taught us patience and resignation and once more we were waiting when fortune sheds brightly her smile. There always is something to wait for the while.

Four years afterwards, I became the wife of Zachariah Delaney of Cincinatti, with whom I have had a happy married life, continuing forty two years. Four children were born to us and many were the plans we mapped out for their future, but two of our little girls were called from us while still in their childhood. My remaining daughter attained the age of twenty-two years, and left life behind while the brightest of prospects was hers, and my son the fullness of a promising youth, at the age of twenty-four, "turned his face to the wall."

So my cup of bitterness was full to the brim and overflowing; yet one consolation was always mine. Our children were born free and died free! Their childhood and my maternity were never shadowed with a thought of separation. The grim reaper did not spare them, but they were as treasures laid up in heaven. Such a separation one could accept from the hand of God with humble submission, *for He calleth His own.*

Mother always made her home with me until the day of her death. She had lived to see the joyful time when her race was made free, their chains struck off and their right to their own flesh and blood lawfully acknowledged. Her life, so full of sorrow, was ended. Full of years and surrounded by many friends, both black and white, who recognized and appreciated her sufferings and sacrifices and rejoiced that her old age was spent in freedom and plenty. The azure vault of heaven bends over us all and the gleaming moonlight brightens the marble tablet which marks her last resting place, *to fame and fortune unknown,* but in the eyes of Him who judgeth us, hers was a heroism which outvied the most famous.

I frequently thought of father and wondered if he were alive or dead; and at the time of the great exodus of negroes from the

South a few years ago, a large number arrived in St. Louis and were cared for by the colored people of that city. They were sheltered in churches, huts and private houses, until such time as they could pursue their journey. I hoped I might find him in this motley crowd of all ages, from the crowing babe in its mother's arms, to the aged and decrepit, on whom the marks of slavery were still visible.

I made inquiry upon inquiry until after long and persistent search, I learned that my father had always lived on the same plantation, fifteen miles from Vicksburg.

I wrote to my father and begged him to come and see me and make his home with me

When he finally reached St. Louis, it was with great joy that I received him. Old, grizzled and gray, time had dealt harshly with him and he looked very little like the dapper master's valet, whose dark beauty won my mother's heart.

Forty-five years of separation, hard work, rough times and heart-longings had perseveringly performed its work and instead of a man bearing his years with upright vigor, he was made prematurely old by the accumulation of troubles.

My sister Nancy came from Canada and we had a most joyful reunion and only the absence of our mother left a vacuum, which we deeply and sorrowfully felt.

Father could not be persuaded to stay with us when he found his wife dead. He longed to get back to his old associations of forty-five years standing, he felt like a stranger in a strange land and,m taking pity on him, I urged him no more, but let him go, though with great reluctance.

There are abounding in public and private libraries of all sorts, lives of people which fill our minds with amazement admiration, sympathy and, indeed, with as many feelings as there are people, so I scarcely expect that the reader of these episodes of my life will meet with more than a passing interest, but as such I will commend it to your thoughts for a brief hour.

To be sure, I am deeply aware that this story, as written, is not a very striking performance, but I have brought you with me face to face with but only a few of the painfull facts engendered by slavery and the rest can be drawn from history.

Just have patience a little longer and I have done.

I became a member of the Methodist Episcopal Church in 1855; was elected President of the first colored society called the Female Union, which was the first ever organized exclusively for women; was elected President of a society known as the Daughters of Zion three years in succession, and was Most Ancient Matron of the Grand Court of Missouri.

A SLAVE GIRL'S STORY

Once a slave girl, I have endeavored to fill these pages with some of the most interesting thoughts that my mind is so full of and not with something that is dry.

This sketch is written for the good of those that have written and prayed that the slaves might be a freed people and have schools and books and learn to read and write for themselves. The Lord, in His love for us and to us as a race, has ever found favor in His sight, for when we were in the land of bondage He heard the prayers of the faithful ones and came to deliver them out of the Land of Egypt.

For God loves those that are oppressed and will save them when they cry unto him and when they put their trust in Him.

Some of the dear ones have gone to the better land, but this is one of the answers to their prayers.

We, as the Negro Race, are a free people and God be praised for it. We as the Negro Race, need to feel proud of the race and I for one do with all my heart and soul and mind, knowing as I do, for I have labored for the good of the race, that their children might be the bright and shining lights. And we can see the progress that we are making in an educational way in a short time and I think that we should feel very grateful to God and those who are trying to help us forward. God bless such with their health and heart full of that same love, that this world can not give nor taketh away.

There are many doors that are shut to keep us back as a race, but some are opened to us and God be praised for them. There are many that have lost their lives in the far South in trying to get an education, but there are many that have done well and we feel like giving God all the praise.

I was born in Old Virginia, in or near the Valley, the other side of Petersburg, of slave parents. I can just call to mind the time when the war began, for I was not troubled then about wars, as I was feeling as free as any one could feel, for I was sought by all of the rich whites of the neighborhood, as they all loved me, as noble whites will love a child, like I was in those days, and they would send for me if I should be at my play and have me to talk for them. All of their friends learned to love me and send me presents and I would stand and talk and preach for some time to them.

My dear mother was sold, at the beginning of the war, from all of her little ones, after the death of the lady that she belonged to and who was so kind to my dear mother and all of the rest of the negroes of the place. She never liked the idea of holding us as slaves and she always said that we were all that she had on the earth to love; and she did love me to the last.

The money that my mother was sold for was to keep the rich man from going to the field of battle, as he sent a poor white man in his stead and should the war end in his favor, the poor white man should have given to him one negro and that would fully pay for all of his service in the army. But my God moves in a way unknown to men and they can never understand His ways, for He can plant His footsteps on the North, the South, the East, the West and outride any man's ideas. How wonderful are all of His ways. And if we, as a race, will only put our trust in Him, we shall gain the glorious victory and be a people whose God is the God of all this broad earth and may we humble ourselves before Him and call Him, Blessed.

I told you that my white mother did not like the idea of calling us her slaves and she always prayed God that I should never know what slavery was, for she said I was never born to serve as did the slaves of some of the people that owned them.

And God, in His love for me and to me, never let me know of it, as did some of my own dear sisters, for some of them were hired out after the old home was broken up.

My mother was sold at Richmond, Virginia. A gentleman bought her who lived in Georgia and we did not know that she was sold until she was gone. The saddest thing was that I never knew which way she had gone. I used to go outside and look up to see if there was anything that would direct me. I saw a clear place in the sky and it seemed to me the way she had gone. I watched it three and a half years, not knowing what that meant and it was there the whole time that mother was gone from her little ones.

On one bright Sunday I asked my older sister to go with me for a nice walk and she did so, for she was the one that was so kind to the rest of us. We saw some sweet flowers on the wayside and began to have delight in picking them, when all at once I was led to leave her alone with the flowers and to go where I could look up at that nice, clear spot. I wanted to get as near to it as I could. I got on the fence and as I looked that way I saw a form coming to me that looked like my dear mother's and called my sister Frances to come at once and see if that did not look like my dear mother. She came to us, so glad to see us and to ask after her baby that she was sold from that was only six weeks old when she was taken from it.

I would that the whole world could have seen the joy of a mother and her two girls on that heaven-made day — a mother returning back to her own once more, a mother that we did not know that we should ever see her face on this earth more. And mother, not feeling good over the past events, had made up her mind that she would take her children to a part of this land where she thought that they would never be in bondage any more on this earth.

So she sought out the head man that was placed there by the North to look after the welfare of lately emancipated negroes of the South, to see that they should have their rights as a freed people.

This gentleman's name was Major Bailey, who was a gentleman of the highest type and it was this loving man that sent my dear mother and her ten little girls on to this lovely city. He even informed the people of Brooklyn that we were on the way and what time we should reach there; and it seemed as though the whole city were out to meet us. As God would have it, six of us had homes on that same day and the people had their carriages there to take us to our new homes.

This God-sent blessing was of a great help to mother, as she could get the money to pay her rent, which was ten dollars per month, and God bless those of my sisters who could help mother to care for her little ones, for they had not been called home then and God be praised for all that we have ever done for her love and comfort while she kept house.

But after all the hard trials we reached this lovely city, where there are those that love and fear God and who love the souls of the negro as well as those of the white, the red, the yellow or brown races of the earth, for we have ever found some of the people who do not forget us day or night in their prayers, that God will send a blessing to us as a race.

To my story of a life of slavery:

My dear mother had a dear husband that she was sold from also and he, not knowing that he should ever see his wife any more, as the times were then, he waited for a while and then he found him another wife. When mother came and found that he was married to another she tried to get him, but she could do nothing about it; so she had to leave him behind to look after her family, although it seemed hard for her to do so.

My mother had a large family to take care of, but the Lord was good to her and helped her, for she had laid some of them away and then there were ten little girls to care for. My brother was lost to us and to mother also, as he was sent to the war to do service for his owner and we did not know if he was alive or not and he was my mother's only boy, as this is a girl family that you do not see or hear of every day, for that made seventeen girls to have battle through life had they all have lived to this time.

My mother did not know where my brother was before she was sold, for we heard that he had tried to get over to the Northern side and had been taken to Richmond, Va. and put into Castle Thunder. That was the last that we heard of him during the war.

We were on our way North when, to our surprise, we learned that he was going to school; that the Northern people had teachers there in the South to teach them to read and to write; and he, learning that we had gone North made himself ready and came on. But he did not know where to find us, so getting a place to work and at the same time telling those that he worked for that his people were here somewhere, they found mother and got her to go to the place where he was and, sure enough, there was her dead and lost boy.

The joy and love that came to that dear, loving mother and her only son on that day will never be known on this side of the grave, as they have both gone to the land of the blessed, for my brother never used any bad language in his life and when he took the Lord for his own, it was his meat and his drink to live for Him and to follow where He led and died a true child of the King.

A few years later and mother's name was enrolled in the Lambs' *Book of Life,* for she gladly answered to the roll call and fell asleep in the arms of Jesus.

Well, my first place was in Adelphi Street, with a family by the name of Hammond. I was there to help do the work and, when they found that I liked to work so well, they wanted me to do so much that I left that place and got me another. I did not get out to church or to Sunday School and that was not the way that I had been trained, for when I was three years old my white mother had taken me to church with her on horseback.

Well, I said that I saw these children going to school on every weekday but Saturdays and on Sundays to Sunday School and I there at work as if it were not the Lord's day. I never shall like to work on that day as I was born on Sunday morning.

I was two and a half years, as near as I can remember, when my own slave mother's house was burned to the ground. I shall never forget that Saturday night. My mother's husband had gone to a dance and mother was there alone with her little ones and we all came near getting burned up.

We were all asleep when I awoke and found the house in a blaze. I was so scared that I did not call to my mother, but I think that she heard me when I rolled out of the bed. She was out of the bed quick as could be and, getting the feather beds, she threw them out of the door and got the children and threw them out as well. Finding that she did not have them all, she ran in the house to look and found me under the bed.

God be praised that I was saved from that fire and I have not had the time to run after any fires since, for that fire was all the fire I want.

I had not to stay there then, for the time is near at hand when I shall go to my white mother's to live, for she is in Tennessee and will come home soon to be with her darling child; and when she shall start again I shall go. Now the times are all well for me as then, but the time has come that the Lord has called her away from her child to be with Him and how could I live without her? And she was to leave her sick child there for her own mother to care for and God will raise up friends in this lonely world to look after those that cry unto heaven, believing that He is a hearer of the true prayer. I shall always remember that Saturday afternoon when for me and all of humanity and I love to think of her love and to know how wonderful it would be to see her sweet face on this green earth and it does seem to me as if I could almost see her by thinking of her so much.

I have said that we came to this lovely city in the year of our Lord 1865 and, in that year, I went to live with a good family that were members of the church, where the Lord spoke peace to my soul, under the preaching of the Rev. David Moore, then the beloved leader of the noblest band of God's children on this earth and a more beloved people never lived. They were always on the lookout for any strangers that might come in the church. They soon found me, as I was a stranger, in the Monday night meeting. The dear pastor came to me, for he did not stop to think whether I was an African or what nation I had come from, but he saw in me a soul and he wanted to find out if there was any room for Jesus to live or what I should do with Jesus, or what should I do for Him, who had done so much for me. My poor heart was ready and waiting for someone to come to its rescue. It was then and there that I yielded my life and my all to the one that can save to the uttermost all that come unto Him by the Lord Jesus Christ.

I followed my Lord and Master in the Jordan in the year of our Lord 1866 and those sweet moments have never left me once. As the years go by they seem to be the more sweet to my sinful soul and I am trying to wing my way to these bright mansions above, where I shall meet those dear ones who have gone before.

I have had some of the darkest days of my life while on this voyage of life, but when it is dark Jesus says, "Peace, be still and fear not, for I will pilot thee."

And then my heart can sing. I have no joy like the joy there is in the Lord.

My dear mother found peace in Jesus before she went to that land of song. When the Lord sent the death angel to call her name she was ready to answer, "Here am I ready to go in, to come out no more."

My mother left us on the 28th day of February, 1894, in the

triumph of faith in the Lord Jesus Christ. What a blessed thought that I shall soon be with her on the other side of the river to help her *crown Him Lord of all.*

To my story:

The subject of this sketch, as I said, was born again under the preaching of Rev. David Moore, of the Washington Avenue Baptist Church, which is one of the noblest churches of this city and it has some of the best people in it of any church in the world, for there is more done for those in need in other lands. When I became a member of that church I could not read. There was a gentleman in the church by the name of Mr. Lansberry, who, finding that I was one of those that was going to learn, went to a store and bought me a *First Reader* and gave it to me and I did not lose any of my time at nights. I went to the meetings every night and came back and got a lady, who was a sister of Mr. Bailey, to be my teacher. Sometimes she used to be so very sleepy that she could not keep her eyes open and I would shake her and say that my lesson was to be learned and it was always well learned. Then I went to the Sunday school to let my Sunday school teacher hear it on Sundays and he, Mr. Ward, always said that he was sure that I would learn so fast I would soon catch up with his Bible Class. It was not long before I could lay my *Reader* down and take my lessons in the Bible. I can bless God for all of this, for the love and the kindness that I received of all that knew me was a token of His great love for me. I know that He was near me all the time to bring me nearer to the Light.

My mind was then fixed that I should some day go to school and I could not rest night or day. I was so anxious to go to school, but my dear mother could not send me. She had poor health and no one to help her to take care of the younger children. I had to work and do the best I could with my books, hoping that the time would come that I should see myself sitting in some school studying, the same time asking mother to let two of the other children go to school every day. She did let them go for awhile, but someone came and wanted her to let them go to work again and she let them go out to work:

Well, I said that I would go to school some day and they had a fine time laughing at my high ideas. I let them laugh all that they wanted to, but I worked hard and long to get the means that I might be able to go, as I said, to some pay school, where I could not be stopped at any time. When I was almost ready to leave for some school the smallpox took me and I was laid aside for three or four years; that is, I was not well and thought that my plans were all broken. I still trusted in God, for I knew that He would do all things for me as long as I put my trust in Him.

Well, as time rolled on I found myself improving slowly and I was then living with a dear, good lady by the name of Miss L. A. Pousland, who is one of the loveliest ladies that ever lived. She loves me today as a mother, though she is in eightieth odd year and is doing well for an old lady.

We were living in South Oxford Street when I took sick of the smallpox and she did not want me taken away from there, as she wanted to take care of me herself. I felt that I would gladly follow Him to be buried to the world. I have found it to be one of those times when the Father was pleased with His own dear beloved Son and I know that He will be pleased whenever we do please Him, for God so loved the world of sinful men that He gave His only begotten Son that whosoever believeth in Him should have everlasting life, for God sent not His Son into the world to condemn it, but that through Him all might believe in Him and have everlasting life.

I wish that I could know that the whole world was receiving this life and that we all could help to crown Him, as the angels are crowning Him, the King of Kings and Lord of Heaven and of this earth.

It is a blessed hope to know that God is love and they that

worship Him must worship Him in spirit and in truth.

I joined the church in 1866 and began to try and follow in this good old way that leads from earth to glory and it has not always been a path of the sweetest flowers, but I have never failed to find my all in the Lord Jesus Christ.

He led me on, day by day, and after awhile I found that He had led me to go away from home that I might get ready for the work that my heart was so full of, for every time that I saw the newspaper there was someone of our race in the far South getting killed for trying to teach and I made up my mind that I would die to see my people taught. I was willing to go to prepare to die for my people, for I could not rest until my people were educated. Now they are in a fair way to be the people that God speaks of in the Holy Word, as He says that Ethiopia shall yet stretch forth her hand and all nations shall bow unto her. I long to see the day that the Ethiopians shall all bow unto God as the One that we should all bow unto, for it is to Him that we all owe our homage and to be very grateful to Him for our deliverance as a race. If we should fail to give him the honor due there would a curse come to us as a race, for we remember those of olden times were of the same descent of our people and some of those that God honored most were of the Ethiopians, such as the Unica and even Moses, the law-giver, was of the same seed.

Not so long ago darkness hung over the face of this race and God moved upon the face of this dark earth and the light came forth.

How wonderfully solemn and yet grand are these inspired thoughts and words of a race whose God is so loving and forgiving and we, contemplating the grand mystery of the world beyond this vale of tears, for God does preserve all that He has planted on this earth.

No subject can surely be a more delightful study than the history of a slave girl and the many things that are linked to this life that man may search and research in the ages to come. I do not think there ever can be found any that should fill the mind as this book.

This is a perfect representation of things as I can remember them and to think how wonderful are these most beneficent streams of God's providence to all those of our race that have prayed that their loving children might feel the warm streams of an education flowing through every child. Tens of thousands of miles, North, South, West and East, God has thrown His mantle of love all around us and it is that which should make us love and fear Him, who is able to destroy both soul and body, for His searching eye rests on all of the negro race, to see what use they are going to make of their time and talent.

Some slaves were hung and, later, the skeleton of one of these men was found in the office of a doctor in Clayton.

After the men were hung, the bones were put in an old deserted house. Somebody that cared for the bones used to put them in the sun in bright weather and back in the house when it rained. Finally the bones disappeared, although the boxes that had contained them still remained.

At one time, when they were building barns on the plantation, one of the big boys got a little brandy and gave us children all a drink, enough to make us drunk. Four doctors were sent for, but nobody could tell what was the matter with us, except they thought we had eaten something poisonous. They wanted to give us some castor oil, but we refused to take it, because we thought that the oil was made from the bones of the dead men we had seen. Finally, we told about the big white boy giving us the brandy and the mystery was cleared up.

The times changed from slavery days to freedom days. As young as I was, my thoughts were mystified to see such wonderful changes; yet I did not know their meaning. But days glided by and, in my mystified way, I could see and hear many strange things. I would see my master and mistress in close conversation and they seemed anxious about something that I, a child, could not know the meaning of.

But as weeks went by, I began to understand.

Young as I was then, I remember this conversation between master and mistress, when he had received the latest war news:

"William, what is the news from the seat of war?"

"A great battle was fought at Bull Run and the Confederates won," he replied.

"Oh, good, good," said mistress, "and what did Jeff Davis say?"

" 'Look out for the blockade. I do not know what the end may be soon'," he answered.

"What does Jeff Davis mean by that?" she asked.

"Sarah Anne, I don't know, unless he means that the niggers will be free."

"O, my God, what shall we do?"

"I presume," he said, "we shall have to put our boys to work and hire help."

"But," she said, "what will the niggers do if they are free. Why, they will starve if we don't keep them."

"Oh, well," he said, "let them wander, if they will not stay with their owners. I don't doubt that many owners have been good to their slaves and they would rather remain with their owners than wander about without home or country."

My mistress often told me that my father was a planter who owned a plantation about two miles from ours. He was a white man, born in Liverpool, England. He died in Lewisville, Alabama, in the year 1875.

I will venture to say that I only saw my father a dozen times, when I was about four years old; and those times I saw him only from a distance, as he was driving by the great house of our plantation. Whenever my mistress saw him going by, she would take me by the hand and run out upon the piazza and exclaim, "Stop there, I say. Don't you want to see and speak to and caress your darling child? She often speaks of you and wants to embrace her dear father. See what a bright and beautiful daughter she is, a perfect picture of yourself. Well, I declare, you are an affectionate father."

I well remember that whenever my mistress would speak thus and upbraid him, he would whip up his horse and get out of sight and hearing as quickly as possible. My mistress's action was, of course, intended to humble and shame my father. I never spoke to him and cannot remember that he ever noticed me, or in any way acknowledged me to be his child.

My mother and my mistress were children together and grew up to be mothers together. My mother was the cook in my mistress's household. One morning when master was away, my mother and my mistress got into an argument, the consequence of which was that my mother was whipped for the first time in her life. Whereupon, my mother refused to do any more work and ran away from the plantation. For three years we did not see her again.

Our plantation was one of several thousand acres, comprising large level fields, upland and considerable forests of Southern pine. Cotton, corn, sweet potatoes, sugar cane, wheat and rye were the principal crops raised on the plantation. It was situated near the river and about twenty-three miles from Clayton, Ala.

One day my master heard that the Yankees were coming our way and he immediately made preparations to get his goods and valuables out of their reach. The big six-mule team was brought to the smoke-house door and loaded with hams and provisions. After being loaded, the team was put in the care of two of the most trustworthy and valuable slaves that my master owned, and driven away. It was master's intention to have these things taken to a swamp and there concealed in a pit that had recently been made for the purpose. But just before the team left the main road for the by-road that led to the swamp, the two slaves were surprised by the Yankees, who at once took possession of the provisions and started the team toward Clayton, where the Yankees had headquarters. The road to Clayton ran past our plantation. One of the slave children happened to look up the road and saw the Yankees coming and gave warning. Whereupon, my master left unceremoniously for the woods and remained concealed there for five days. The niggers had run away whenever they got a chance, but now it was master's and the other white folks' turn to run.

All around the plantation was left barren. Day after day I could run down to the gate and see down the road troops and troops of Garrison's Brigade and in the midst of them gangs and gangs of negro slaves who joined with the soldiers, shouting, dancing and clapping their hands. The war was nearly ended and from Mobile Bay to Clayton, Ala., all along the road, on all the plantations, the slaves thought that if they joined the Yankee soldiers they would be perfectly safe.

As I looked on these I did not know what it meant, for I had never seen such a circus. The Yankee soldiers found that they had such an army of men and women and children, that they had to build tents and feed them to keep them from starving. But from what I, a little child, saw and heard the older ones say, that must have been a terrible time of trouble.

The Yankees rode up to the piazza of the great house and inquired who owned the plantation. They gave orders that nothing must be touched or taken away, as they intended to return shortly and take possession. My mistress and the slaves watched for their return day and night for more than a week, but the Yankees did not come back.

One morning in April, 1865, my master got the news that the Yankees had left Mobile Bay and crossed the Confederate lines and that the Emancipation Proclamation had been signed by President Lincoln. Mistress suggested that the slaves should not be told of their freedom; but master said he would tell them, because they would soon find it out. Mistress, however, said she could keep my mother's three children, for my mother had now been gone so long.

All the slaves left the plantation upon the news of their freedom, one by one disappearing (for night and day they kept going) until there was not one to be seen, except those who were feeble or sickly. With the help of these, the crops were gathered. My mistress and her daughters had to go to the kitchen and to the washtub. My little half-brother, Henry and myself had to gather chips and help all we could. My sister, Caroline, who was twelve years old, could help in the kitchen.

After the war, the Yankees took all the good mules and horses from the plantation and left their old army stock. We children chanced to come across one of the Yankees' old horses, that had *U.S.* branded on him. We called him 'Old Yank' and got him fattened up. One day in August, six of us children took Old Yank and went away back on the plantation for watermelons. Coming home, we thought we would make the old horse trot. When Old Yank commenced to trot, our big melons dropped off, but we couldn't stop the horse for some time. Finally, one of the big boys went back and got some more melons and left us eating what we could find of the ones that had been dropped. Then all six of us, with our melons, got on Old Yank and went home. We also used to hitch Old Yank into a wagon and get wood. But one sad day in the fall, the Yankees came back again and gathered up their old stock and took Old Yank away.

They never came back to our plantation and I could only speak of my own home, but I thought to myself, what would become of my good times all over the old plantation. Oh, the harvesting times, the great hog-killing times when several hundred hogs were killed and we children watched and got our share of the slaughter in pig's liver roasted on a bed of coals, eaten ashes and all. Then came the great sugar-cane grinding time, when they were making the molasses and we children would be hanging round, drinking the sugar-cane juice and awaiting the moment to help ourselves to everything good. We did, too, making ourselves sticky and dirty with the sweet stuff being made. Not only were the slave children there, but the little white children from Massa's house would join us and have a jolly time. The negro child and the white child knew not the great chasm between their lives, only that they had dainties and we had crusts. They would be put to bed in their luxurious bedrooms, while we little slaves would find what homes we could on some lumber under the house.

But it was a sad, sad change on the old plantation and the beautiful, proud sunny South, with its masters and mistresses, was bowed beneath the sin brought about by slavery. It was a terrible blow to the owners of plantations and slaves and their children would feel it more than they, for they had been reared to be waited upon by willing or unwilling slaves.

One day mistress sent me out to do some churning under a tree. I went to sleep and jerked the churn over on top of me and consequently got a whipping.

My mother came for us at the end of the year 1865 and demanded that her children be given up to her. This, mistress refused to do and threatened to set the dogs on my mother if she did not at once leave the place. My mother went away and remained with some of the neighbors until supper time. Then she got a boy to tell Caroline to come down to the fence. When she came, my mother told her to go back and get Henry and myself and bring us down to the gap in the fence as quick as she could.

My mother took Henry in her arms and my sister carried me on her back. We climbed fences and crossed fields and after several hours came to a little hut which my mother had secured on a plantation. We had no more than reached the place and made a little fire, when master's two sons rode up and demanded that the children be returned. My mother refused to give us up. Upon her offering to go with them to the Yankee headquarters to find out if it were really true that all negroes had been made free, the young men left and troubled us no more.

The cabin that was now our home was made of logs. It had one door. An opening in a wall with an inside shutter was the only window. The door was fastened with a latch. Our beds were some straw.

We were six in our little family; my mother, Caroline, Henry, two other children that my mother had brought with her upon her return, and myself.

We had little to eat and little to sleep on save some old pieces of horse-blankets and hay that the soldiers gave us. The first day in the hut was a rainy day; and as night drew near it grew more fierce and we children had gathered some little fagots to make a fire by the time mother came home with something for us to eat, such as she had gathered through the day. It was only corn meal and peas and ham-bone and skins which she had for our supper. She had started a little fire and said, "One of you close that door," for it was cold. She swung the pot over the fire and filled it with the peas and ham-bone and skins. Then she seated her little brood around the fire on the pieces of blanket, where we watched with all our eyes, our hearts filled with desire, looking to see what she would do next. She took down an old broken earthen bowl and tossed into it the little meal she had brought, stirring it up with water, making a hoe cake.

"I will put a tin plate over this and put it away for your breakfast," she said.

We five children were eagerly watching the pot boiling,

with the peas and ham-bone. The rain was pattering on the roof of the hut. All at once there came a knock at the door. My mother answered the knock. When she opened the door, there stood a white woman and three little children, all dripping with rain.

My mother said, "In the name of the Lord, where are you going on such a night with these children?"

The woman said, "Auntie, I am travelling. Will you please let me stop here tonight, out of the rain, with my children?"

My mother said, "Yes, honey. I ain't got much, but what I have got I will share with you."

"God bless you."

They all came in.

We children looked in wonder at what had come. But my mother scattered her own little brood and made a place for the forlorn wanderers.

She said, "Wait, honey, let me turn over that hoe cake."

Then the two women fell to talking, each telling a tale of woe.

After a time, my mother called out, "Here, you, Louise, or some one of you, put some fagots under the pot so these peas can get done."

We couldn't put them under fast enough, first one and then another of us children, the mothers still talking.

Soon my mother said, "Draw that hoe cake one side, I guess it is done."

We hoped the talk was most ended, for we were anxiously watching that pot. Pretty soon my mother seemed to realize our existence. She exclaimed, "My Lord! I suppose the little children are nearly starved. Are those peas done, young ones?"

She turned and said to the white woman, "Have you-all had anything to eat?"

"We stopped at a house about dinner time, but the woman didn't have anything but some bread and buttermilk."

My mother said, "Well, honey, I ain't got but a little, but I will divide with you."

The woman said, "Thank you, Auntie. You just give my children a little; I can do without it."

Then came the dividing. We all watched to see what the shares would be. My mother broke a mouthful of bread and put it on each of the tin plates. Then she took the old spoon and equally divided the pea soup.

We children were seated around the fire, with some little wooden spoons. But the wooden spoons didn't quite go round and some of us had to eat with our fingers. Our share of the meal, however, was so small that we were as hungry when we finished as when we began.

"Take that rag and wipe your face and hands and give it to the others and let them use it, too," my mother said. "Put those plates upon the table."

We immediately obeyed orders and took our seats again around the fire.

"One of you go and pull that straw out of the corner and get ready to go to bed."

We all lay down on the straw, the white children with us and my mother covered us over with the blanket. We were soon in the Land of Nod, forgetting our empty stomachs. The two mothers still continued to talk, sitting down on the only seats, a couple of blocks. A little back against the wall my mother and the white woman slept.

Bright and early in the morning we were called up and the rest of the hoe cake was eaten for breakfast, with a little meat, some coffee sweetened with molasses. The little wanderers and their mother shared our meal and then they started again on their journey towards their home among their kinsfolk. We never saw them again.

My mother said, "God bless you. I wish you all good luck. I hope you will reach your home safely." Then mother said to us,

"You young ones put away that straw and sweep up the place, because I have to go to my work."

But she came at noon and brought us a nice dinner, more satisfactory than the supper and breakfast we had had. We children were delighted that there were no little white children to share our meal this time.

The man on whose plantation this cabin stood, hired my mother as cook and gave us this little home. We children used to sell blueberries and plums that we picked. One day the man on whom we depended for our home and support, left. Then my mother did washing by the day, for whatever she could get. Caroline was hired out to take care of a baby. We were sent to get cold victuals from hotels and such places. A man wanting hands to pick cotton, my brother Henry and I were set to help in this work. We had to go to the cotton field very early every morning. For this work, we received forty cents for every hundred pounds of cotton we picked.

In time, my older sister, Caroline and myself got work among good people, where we soon forgot all the hard times in the little log cabin by the roadside in Clayton, Alabama.

In 1866, another man hired the plantation on which our hut stood and we moved into Clayton, to a little house my mother secured there. A rich lady came to our house one day, looking for someone to take care of her little daughter. I was taken and adopted into this family. This rich lady was Mrs. E. M. Williams, a music teacher, the wife of a lawyer. We called her Mis' Mary.

Some rich people in Clayton who had owned slaves, opened the Methodist church on Sundays and began the work of teaching the negroes. My new mistress sent me to Sunday school every Sunday morning and I soon got so that I could read. Mis' Mary taught me every day at her knee. I soon could read nicely and went through Sterling's *Second Reader* and then into Mcauthrie's *Third Reader*. The first piece of poetry I recited in Sunday school was taught to me by Mis' Mary during the week. Mis' Mary's father-in-law, an ex-judge, of Clayton, Alabama, heard me recite it and thought it was wonderful. It was this:

> *I am glad to see you, little bird*
> *It was your sweet song I heard.*
> *What was it I heard you say:*
> *'Give me crumbs to eat today.'*
> *Here are crumbs I brought for you*
> *Eat your dinner, eat away*
> *Come and see us every day.*

After this Mis' Mary kept on with my studies and taught me to write. As I grew older, she taught me to cook and how to do housework. During this time Mis' Mary had given my mother one dollar a month in return for my services; now as I grew up to young womanhood, I thought I would like a little money of my own. Accordingly, Mis' Mary began to pay me four dollars a month, besides giving me my board and clothes. For two summers she hired me out while she was away and I got five dollars a month.

While I was with Mis' Mary, I had my first sweetheart, one of the young fellows who attended Sunday school with me. Mis' Mary, however, objected to the young man's coming to the house to call, because she did not think I was old enough to have a sweetheart.

I owe a great deal to Mis' Mary for her good training of me, in honesty, uprightness and truthfulness. She told me that when I went out into the world all white folks would not treat me as she had, but that I must not feel bad about it, but just do what I was employed to do and if I wasn't satisfied, to go elsewhere; but always to carry an honest name.

One Sunday, when my sweetheart walked to the gate with

me, Mis' Mary met him and told him she thought I was too young for him and that she was sending me to Sunday school to learn, not to catch a beau. It was a long while before he could see me again — not until later in the season, in watermelon time, when Mis' Mary and my mother gave me permission to go to a watermelon party one Sunday afternoon. Mis' Mary did not know, however, that my sweetheart had planned to escort me.

We met around the corner of the house. After the party he escorted me back to the same place. After that I saw him occasionally at barbecues and parties. I was permitted to go with him some evenings to church, but my mother always walked ahead or behind us.

We went together for four years. During that time, although I still called Mis' Mary's my home, I had been out to service in one or two families.

Finally, my mother and Mis' Mary consented to our marriage and the wedding day was to be in May. The winter before that May, I went to service in the family of Dr. Drury in Eufaula.

Just a week before I left Clayton I dreamed that my sweetheart died suddenly. The night before I was to leave, we were invited out to tea. He told me he had bought a nice piece of poplar wood, with which to make a table for our new home. When I told him my dream, he said:

"Don't let that trouble you, there is nothing in dreams."

But one month from that day he died, and his coffin was made from the piece of poplar wood he had bought for the table.

After his death, I remained in Clayton for two or three weeks with my people and then went back to Eufaula, where I stayed two years.

My sweetheart's death made a profound impression on me and I began to pray as best I could. Often I remained all night on my knees.

Going on an excursion to Macon, Georgia one time, I liked the place so well that I did not go back to Eufaula. I got a place as cook in the family of an Episcopal clergyman and remained with them eight years, leaving when the family moved to New Orleans.

During these eight years, my mother died in Clayton and I had to take the three smallest children into my care. My oldest sister was now married and had a son.

I now went to live with a Mrs. Maria Campbell, a colored woman who adopted me and gave me her name. Mrs. Campbell did washing and ironing for her living. While living with her, I went six months to Lewis' High School in Macon. Then I went to Atlanta and obtained a place as first-class cook with Mr. E. N. Inman. But I always considered Mrs. Campbell's my home. I remained about a year with Mr. Inman and received as wages ten dollars a month.

One day, when the family were visiting in Memphis, I chanced to pick up a newspaper and read the advertisement of a Northern family for a cook to go to Boston. I went at once to the address given and made agreement to take the place, but told the people that I could not leave my present position until Mr. Inman returned home.

Mr. and Mrs. Inman did not want to let me go, but I made up my mind to go North. The Northern family whose service I was to enter had returned to Boston before I left and had made arrangements with a friend, Mr. Bullock, to see me safely started North.

After deciding to go North, I went to Macon to make arrangements with Mrs. Campbell for the care of my two sisters who lived with her. One sister was now about thirteen and the other fifteen, both old enough to do a little for themselves. My brother was dead. He went to Brunswick in 1875 and died there of the yellow fever in 1876. One sister I brought in later years to

Boston. I stayed in Macon two weeks and was in Atlanta three or four days before leaving for the North.

About the 15th of June, 1879, I arrived at the Old Colony Station in Boston and had my first glimpse of the country I had heard so much about. From Boston I went to Newtonville, where I was to work. The gentleman whose service I was to enter, Mr. E. N. Kimball, was waiting at the station for me and drove me to his home on Warner Street. For a few days, until I got somewhat adjusted to my new circumstances, I had no work to do. On June 17th the family took me with them to Auburndale. But in spite of the kindness of Mrs. Kimball and the colored nurse, I grew very homesick for the South and would often look in the direction of my old home and cry.

The washing, a kind of work I knew nothing about, was given to me; but I could not do it and it was finally given over to a hired woman, though I had to do the ironing of the fancy clothing for Mrs. Kimball and the children.

About five or six weeks after my arrival, Mrs. Kimball and the children went to the White Mountains for the summer and I had more leisure. Mr. Kimball went up to the mountains every Saturday night to stay with his family over Sunday; but he and his father-in-law were at home other nights and I had to have dinner for them.

To keep away the homesickness and loneliness as much as possible, I made acquaintance with the hired girl across the street.

One morning I climbed up into the cherry tree that grew between Mr. Kimball's yard and the yard of his next-door neighbor, Mr. Roberts. I was thinking of the South and as I picked the cherries, I sang a Southern song. Mr. Roberts heard me and gave me a dollar for the song.

By agreement, Mrs. Kimball was to give me three dollars and a half a week, instead of four, until the difference amounted to my fare from the South; after that, I was to have four dollars. I had, however, received but little money. In the fall, after the family came home, we had a little difficulty about my wages and I had to leave and find work elsewhere.

Having obtained a situation, I sent to Mr. Kimball's for my trunk. I remained in my new place a year and a half. At the end of that time the family moved to Dorchester and, because I did not care to go out there, I left their service.

From this place, I went to Narragansett Pier to work as a chambermaid for the summer. In the fall, I came back to Boston and obtained a situation with a family in Berwick Park. This family afterward moved to Jamaica Plain and I went with them. With this family I remained seven years. They were very kind to me, gave me two or three weeks' vacation without loss of pay.

In June 1884, I went with them to their summer home in the Isles of Shoals, as housekeeper for some guests who were coming from Paris. On the 6th of July I received word that my sister Caroline had died in June. This was a great blow to me. I remained with the Reeds until they closed their summer home, but I was not able to do much work after the news of my sister's death.

I wrote home to Georgia, to the white people who owned the house in which Caroline had lived, asking them to take care of her boy Lawrence until I should come in October.

When we came back to Jamaica Plain in the fall, I was asked to decide what I should do in regard to this boy. Mrs. Reed wanted me to stay with her and promised to help pay for the care of the boy in Georgia. Of course, she said, I could not expect to find positions if I had a child with me. As an inducement to remain in my present place and leave the boy in Georgia, I was promised provision for my future days, as long as I should live.

It did not take me long to decide what I should do. The last time I had seen my sister, a little over a year before she died, she had said, when I was leaving, "I don't expect ever to see you again, but if I die I shall rest peacefully in my grave because I know you will take care of my child."

I left Jamaica Plain and took a room on Village Street for the two or three weeks until my departure for the South.

Back South, I fetched Lawrence and we went at once to a neighbor's house for the night. The next day I got a room in the yard of a house belonging to some white people. Here we stayed two weeks. The only return I was asked to make for the room was to weed the garden. Lawrence and I dug out some weeds and burned them, but came so near setting fire to the place that we were told we need not dig any more weeds, but that we might have the use of the room so long as we cared to stay.

In about a week and a half more we got together such things as we wanted to keep and take away with us.

The last time I saw my sister, I had persuaded her to open a bank account and she had done so and had made small deposits from time to time. When I came to look for the bankbook, I discovered that her lodger, one Mayfield, had taken it at her death and nobody knew where it might be now. I found out that Mayfield had drawn thirty dollars from the account for my sister's burial and also an unknown amount for himself. He had done nothing for the boy. I went down to the bank and was told that Mayfield claimed to look after my sister's burial and her affairs. He had made one Reuben Bennett, who was no relation and had no interest in the matter, administrator for Lawrence, until his coming of age. But Bennett had as yet done nothing for him. The book was in the bank, with some of the account still undrawn, how much I did not know. I next went to see a lawyer, to find out how much it would cost me to get this book. The lawyer said fifteen dollars. I said I would call again. In the meantime, I went to the courthouse and when the case on trial was adjourned I went to the judge and stated my case. The judge, who was slightly acquainted with my sister and me, told me to have Reuben Bennett in court next morning at nine o'clock and to bring Lawrence with me. When we had all assembled before the judge, he told Bennett to take Lawrence and go to the bank and get the money belonging to my sister. Bennett went and collected the money, some thirty-five dollars. The boy was then given into my care by the judge. For his kindness, the judge would accept no return.

Happy at having obtained the money so easily, we went back to our room and rested until our departure the next night for Jacksonville, Florida. I had decided to go to this place for the winter, on account of Lawrence, thinking the Northern winter would be too severe for him.

My youngest sister, who had come to Macon from Atlanta a few days before my arrival, did not hear of Caroline's death until within a few days of our departure. This youngest sister decided to go to Florida with us for the winter.

Our trunks and baggage were taken to the station in a team. We had a goodly supply of food, given us by our friends and by the people whose hospitality we had shared during the latter part of our stay.

The next morning we got into Jacksonville. My idea was to get a place as chambermaid at Green Cove Springs, Florida, through the influence of the head waiter at a hotel there, whom I knew. After I got into Jacksonville I changed my plans. I did not see how I could move my things any farther and we went to a hotel for colored people, hired a room for two dollars and boarded ourselves on the food which had been given us in Macon. This food lasted about two weeks. Then I had to buy.

My money was going every day and none coming in, I did not know what to do. One night the idea of keeping a restaurant came to me and I decided to get a little home for the three of us and then see what I could do in this line of business.

After a long and hard search, I found a little house of two rooms where we could live, and the next day I found a place to start my restaurant. For house furnishings, we used at first, to the best advantage we could, the things we had brought from Macon. Caroline's cookstove had been left with my foster-mother in Macon. After hiring the room for the restaurant, I sent for this stove and it arrived in a few days. Then I went to a dealer in second-hand furniture and got such things as were actually needed for the house and the restaurant, on the condition that he would take them back at a discount when I got through with them.

Trade at the restaurant was very good and we got along nicely. My sister got a position as nurse for fifteen dollars a month.

One day the cook from a shipwrecked vessel came to my restaurant and in return for his board and a bed in the place, agreed to do my cooking. After trade became good, I changed my residence to a house of four rooms and put three cheap cots in each of two of the rooms and let the cots at a dollar a week apiece to colored men who worked nearby in hotels. Lawrence and I did the chamber work at night, after the day's work in the restaurant.

I introduced 'Boston baked beans' into my restaurant, much to the amusement of the people at first; but after they had once eaten them it was hard to meet the demand.

It is now six years since the inspiration to write this book came to me in the Franklin evening school. I have struggled on, helped by friends. God said, "Write the book and I will help you." And He has.

Linda Brent: <u>Incidents In The Life Of A Slave Girl</u>

Reader, be assured this narrative is no fiction. I am aware that some of my adventures may seem incredible, but they are, nevertheless, strictly true. I have not exaggerated the wrongs inflicted by slavery, on the contrary, my descriptions fall far short of the facts. I have concealed the names of places, and given persons fictitious names. I had no motive for secrecy on my own account, but I deemed it kind and considerate towards others to pursue this course.

I wish I were more competent to the task I have undertaken. But I trust my readers will excuse deficiencies in consideration of circumstances. I was born and reared in slavery, and I remained in a slave State twenty-seven years. Since I have been in the North, it has been necessary for me to work diligently for my own support and the education of my children. This has not left me much leisure to make up for the loss of early opportunities to improve myself, and it has compelled me to write these pages at irregular intervals, whenever I could snatch an hour from household duties.

When I first arrived in Philadelphia, Bishop Paine advised me to publish a sketch of my life, but I told him I was altogether incompetent to such an undertaking. Though I have improved my mind somewhat since that time, I still remain of the same opinion, but I trust my motives will excuse what might otherwise seem presumptuous. I have not written my experiences in order to attract attention to myself, on the contrary, it would have been more pleasant to me to have been silent about my own history. Neither do I care to excite sympathy for my own sufferings. But I do earnestly desire to arouse the women of the North to a realizing sense of the condition of two millions of women in the South, still in bondage, suffering what I suffered, and most of them far worse. I want to add my testimony to that of abler pens to convince the people of the Free States what slavery really is. Only by experience can anyone realize how deep, and dark, and foul is that pit of abominations. May the blessing of God rest on this imperfect effort in behalf of my persecuted people.

I was born a slave, but I never knew it till six years of happy childhood had passed away. My father was a carpenter, and considered so intelligent and skillful in his trade, that when buildings were to be erected, he was sent for from long distances, to be head workman. On condition of paying his mistress two hundred dollars a year, and supporting himself, he was allowed to work at his trade and manage his own affairs. His strongest wish was to purchase his children, but though he several times offered his hard earnings for that purpose, he never succeeded.

In complexion my parents were a light shade of brownish-yellow, and were termed mulattos. They lived together in a comfortable home and, though we were all slaves, I was so fondly shielded that I never dreamed I was a piece of merchandise, trusted to them for safe keeping, and liable to be demanded of them at any moment.

I had one brother, William, who was two years younger than myself — a bright, affectionate child. I had also a great treasure in my maternal grandmother, who was a remarkable woman in many respects. She was the daughter of a planter in South Carolina, who, at his death, left her mother and his three children free, with money to go to St. Augustine, where they had relatives. It was during the Revolutionary War, and they were captured on their passage, carried back, and sold to different purchasers.

Such was the story my grandmother used to tell me, but I do not remember all the particulars. She was a little girl when she was captured and sold to the keeper of a large hotel. I have often heard her tell how hard she fared during childhood. But as she grew older she evinced so much intelligence, and was so faithful, that her master and mistress could not help seeing it was in their interest to take care of such a valuable piece of property. She became an indispensable personage in the household, officiating in all capacities, from cook and wet nurse to seamstress. She was much praised for her cooking, and her nice crackers became so famous in the neighborhood that many people were desirous of obtaining them. In consequence of numerous requests of this kind, she asked permission of her mistress to bake crackers at night, after all the household work was done, and she obtained leave to do it, provided she would clothe herself and her children from the profits. Upon these terms, after working hard all day for her mistress, she began her midnight bakings, assisted by her two oldest children.

The business proved profitable, and each year she laid by a little, which was saved for a fund to purchase her children.

Her master died, and the property was divided among his heirs. The widow had the hotel, which she continued to keep open. My grandmother remained in her service as a slave, but her children were divided among her master's children. As she had five, Benjamin, the youngest, was sold, in order that each heir might have an equal portion of dollars and cents. There was so little difference in our ages that he seemed more like my brother than my uncle. He was a bright, handsome lad, nearly white, for he inherited the complexion my grandmother had derived from Anglo-Saxon ancestors. Though only ten years old, seven hundred and twenty dollars were paid for him.

His sale was a terrible blow to my grandmother, but she was naturally hopeful, and she went to work with renewed energy, trusting in time to be able to purchase some of her children.

She had saved three hundred dollars, which her mistress one day begged as a loan, promising to pay her soon. The reader probably knows that no promise or writing given to a slave is legally binding. According to Southern laws, a slave, being property, can hold no property. When my grandmother lent her hard earnings to her mistress, she trusted solely to her honor. The honor of a slaveholder to a slave.

To this good grandmother I was indebted for many comforts. My brother Willie and I often received portions of the crackers, cakes and preserves she made to sell, and after we ceased to be children we were indebted to her for many more important services.

Such were the unusually fortunate circumstances of my early childhood. When I was six years old, my mother died, and then, for the first time, I learned, by the talk around me, that I was a slave. My mother's mistress was the daughter of my grandmother's mistress. She was the foster sister of my mother, they were both nourished at my grandmother's breast. In fact, my mother had been weaned at three months old, so that the babe of the mistress might obtain sufficient food. They played together as children and, when they became women, my mother was a most faithful servant to her whiter foster sister.

On my mother's death-bed her mistress promised that her children should never suffer for anything, and during her lifetime she kept her word. They all spoke kindly of my dead mother, who had been a slave merely in name, but in nature was noble and womanly. I grieved for her, and my young mind was troubled with the thought of who would now take care of me and my little brother.

I was told that my home was now to be with my mother's mistress, and I found it a happy one. No toilsome or disagreeable duties were imposed upon me. She was so kind to me that I was always glad to do her bidding, and proud to labor for her as much as my young years would permit. I would sit by her side for hours, sewing diligently, with a heart as free from care as that of any freeborn white child. When she thought I was tired, she would send me out to run and jump, and away I bounded, to gather berries or flowers to decorate her room.

Those were happy days — too happy to last. The slave child had no thought for the morrow, but there came that blight, which too surely waits on every human being born to be a chattel.

When I was nearly twelve years old, my kind mistress sickened and died. As I saw the cheek grow paler, and the eye more glassy, how earnestly I prayed in my heart that she might live. I loved her, for she had been almost like a mother to me. My prayers were not answered. She died, and they buried her in the little churchyard, where, day after day, my tears fell upon her grave.

I was sent to spend a week with my grandmother. I was now old enough to begin to think of the future, and again and again I asked myself what they would do with me. I felt sure I should never find another mistress so kind as the one who was gone. She had promised my dying mother that her children should never suffer for anything, and when I remembered that, and recalled her many proofs of attachment to me, I could not help having some hopes that she had left me free. My friends were almost certain it would be so. They thought she would be sure to do it, on account of my mother's love and faithful service. But, alas, we all know that the memory of a faithful slave does not avail much to save her children from the auction block.

After a brief period of suspense, the will of my mistress was read, and we learned that she had bequeathed me to her sister's daughter, a child of five years old.

So vanished our hopes. My mistress had taught me the precepts of God's Word:

Thou shalt love thy neighbor as thyself.

Whatsoever ye would that men should do unto you, do

ye even so unto them.

But I was her slave, and I suppose she did not recognize me as her neighbor. I would give much to blot out from my memory that one great wrong. As a child, I loved my mistress and, looking back on the happy days I spent with her, I try to think with less bitterness of this act of injustice. While I was with her, she taught me to read and spell, and for this privilege, which so rarely falls to the lot of a slave, I bless her memory.

She possessed but few slaves, and at her death they were all distributed among her relatives. Five of them were my grandmother's children, and had shared the same milk that nourished her mother's children. Notwithstanding my grandmother's long and faithful service to her owners, not one of her children escaped the auction block. These God-breathing machines are no more, in the sight of their masters, than the cotton they plant, or the horses they tend.

Dr. Flint, a physician in the neighborhood, had married the sister of my mistress, and I was now the property of their little daughter. It was not without murmuring that I prepared for my new home. What added to my unhappiness was the fact that my brother William was purchased by the same family. My father, by his nature, as well as by the habit of transacting business as a skillful mechanic, had more of the feelings of a freeman than is common among slaves. My brother was a spirited boy, and being brought up under such influences, he early detested the name of master and mistress. One day, when his father and his mistress both happened to call him at the same time, he hesitated between the two, being perplexed to know which had the strongest claim upon his obedience. He finally concluded to go to his mistress.

When my father reproved him for it, he said, "You both called me, and I didn't know which I ought to go to first."

"You are my child," replied our father, "and when I call you, you should come immediately, if you have to pass through fire and water."

Poor Willie. He was now to learn his first lesson of obedience to a master.

Grandmother tried to cheer us with hopeful words, and they found an echo in the credulous hearts of youth.

When we entered our new home we encountered cold looks, cold words and cold treatment. We were glad when the night came. On my narrow bed I moaned and wept, I felt so desolate and alone.

I had been there nearly a year, when a dear little friend of mine was buried. I heard her mother sob as the clods fell on the coffin of her only child. I turned away from the grave, feeling thankful that I still had something left to love. I met my grandmother, who said, "Come with me, Linda." From her tone I knew that something sad had happened. She led me apart from the people and then said, "My child, your father is dead."

Dead!

How could I believe it? He had died so suddenly I had not even heard that he was sick. I went home with my grandmother. My heart rebelled against God who had taken from me mother, father, mistress and friend.

The good grandmother tried to comfort me.

"Who knows the ways of God?" said she. "Perhaps they have been kindly taken from the evil days to come."

Years afterwards I often thought of this. She promised to be a mother to her grandchildren, so far as she might be permitted to do so and, strengthened by her love, I returned to my master's.

I thought I should be allowed to go to my father's house the next morning, but I was ordered to go for flowers, that my mistress's house might be decorated for an evening party. I spent the day gathering flowers and weaving them into festoons, while the dead body of my father was lying within a mile away. What cared my owners for that? He was merely a piece of property. Moreover, they thought he had spoiled his children, by teaching them to feel that they were human beings. This was blasphemous doctrine for a slave to teach, presumptuous in him, and dangerous to the masters.

The next day I followed his remains to a humble grave beside that of my dear mother. There were those who knew my father's worth, and respected his memory.

My home now seemed more dreary than ever. The laugh of the little slave children sounded harsh and cruel. It was selfish to feel so about the joy of others. My brother moved about with a very grave face. I tried to comfort him, by saying, "Take courage, Willie, brighter days will come by and by."

"You don't know anything about it, Linda," he replied. "we shall have to stay here all our days, we shall never be free."

I argued that we were growing older and stronger and that perhaps we might, before long, be allowed to hire our own time, and then we could earn money to buy our freedom. William declared this was much easier to say than to do, moreover, he did not intend to buy his freedom. We held daily controversies upon this subject.

Little attention was paid to the slaves' meals in Dr. Flint's house. If they could catch a bit of food while it was going, well and good. I gave myself no trouble on that score, for on my various errands I passed my grandmother's house, where there was always something to spare for me. I was frequently threatened with punishment if I stopped there, and my grandmother, to avoid detaining me, often stood at the gate with something for my breakfast or dinner. I was indebted to her for all my comforts, spiritual or temporal. It was her labor that supplied my scanty wardrobe. I have a vivid recollection of the linsey-woolsey dress given me every winter by Mrs. Flint. How I hated it. It was one of the badges of slavery.

While my grandmother was thus helping to support me from her hard earnings, the three hundred dollars she had lent her mistress were never repaid. When her mistress died, her son-in-law, Dr. Flint, was appointed executor. When grandmother applied to him for payment, he said the estate was insolvent, and the law prohibited payment. It did not, however, prohibit him from retaining the silver candelabra, which had been purchased with that money. I presume they will be handed down in the family, from generation to generation.

My grandmother's mistress had always promised her that, at her death, she should be free, and it was said that in her will she made good the promise. But when the estate was settled, Dr. Flint told the faithful old servant that, under existing circumstances, it was necessary she should be sold.

On the appointed day, the customary advertisement was posted up, proclaiming that there would be a *Public sale of negroes and horses*. Dr. Flint called to tell my grandmother that he was unwilling to wound her feelings by putting her up at auction, and that he would prefer to dispose of her in a private sale. My grandmother saw through his hypocrisy, she understood very well that he was ashamed of the job. She was a very spirited woman, and if he was base enough to sell her, when her mistress intended she should be free, she was determined the public should know it. She had for a long time supplied many families with crackers and preserves, consequently, 'Aunt Marthy', as she was called, was generally known, and everybody who knew her respected her intelligence and good character. Her long and faithful service in the family was also well known, and the intention of her mistress to leave her free.

When the day of sale came, she took her place among the chattels, and at the first call she sprang upon the auction block. Many voices called out, "Shame! Shame! Who is going to sell you, Aunt Marthy? Don't stand there. That is no place for you."

Without saying a word, she quietly awaited her fate. No one

bid for her.

At last, a feeble voice said, "Fifty dollars."

It came from a maiden lady, seventy years old, the sister of my grandmother's deceased mistress. She had lived forty years under the same roof with my grandmother, she knew how faithfully she had served her owners, and how cruelly she had been defrauded of her rights, and she resolved to protect her. The auctioneer waited for a higher bid, but her wishes were respected, no one bid above her. She could neither read nor write, and when the bill of sale was made out, she signed it with a cross. But what consequence was that, when she had a big heart overflowing with human kindness? She gave the old servant her freedom.

At that time, my grandmother was just fifty years old. Laborious years had passed since then, and now my brother and I were slaves to the man who had defrauded her of her money, and tried to defraud her of her freedom. One of my mother's sisters, called Aunt Nancy, was also a slave in his family. She was a kind, good aunt to me, and supplied the place of both housekeeper and waiting maid to her mistress. She was, in fact, at the beginning and end of everything.

Mrs. Flint, like many Southern women, was totally deficient in energy. She had not strength to superintend her household affairs, but her nerves were so strong that she could sit in her easy chair and see a woman whipped till the blood trickled from every stroke of the lash. She was a member of the church, but partaking of the Lord's supper did not seem to put her in a Christian frame of mind. If dinner was not served at the exact time on that particular Sunday, she would station herself in the kitchen, and wait till it was dished, and then spit in all the kettles and pans that had been used for cooking. She did this to prevent the cook and her children from eking out their meager fare with the remains of the gravy and other scrapings. The slaves could get nothing to eat except what she chose to give them. Provisions were weighed out by the pound and ounce, three times a day. I can assure you she gave them no chance to eat wheat bread from her flour barrel. She knew how many biscuits a quart of flour would make, and exactly what size they ought to be.

Dr. Flint was an epicure. The cook never sent a dinner to his table without fear and trembling, for if there happened to be a dish not to his liking, he would either order her to be whipped, or compel her to eat every mouthful of it in his presence. The poor, hungry creature might not have objected to eating it, but she did object to having her master ram it down her throat till she choked.

They had a pet dog that was a nuisance in the house. The cook was ordered to make some Indian mush for him. The dog refused to eat, and when his head was held over it, the froth flowed from his mouth into the basin. He died a few minutes after. When Dr. Flint came in, he said the mush had not been well cooked, and that was the reason the animal would not eat it. He sent for the cook, and compelled her to eat it. He thought that the woman's stomach was stronger than the dog's, but her sufferings afterwards proved that he was mistaken. This poor woman endured many cruelties from her master and mistress. Sometimes she was locked up, away from her nursing baby, for a whole day and night.

When I had been in the family a few weeks, one of the plantation slaves was brought to town, by order of his master. It was near night when he arrived, and Dr. Flint ordered him to be taken to the work house and tied up to the joist, so that his feet would just escape the ground. In that situation he was to wait till the doctor had taken his tea. I shall never forget that night. Never before, in my life, had I heard hundreds of blows fall, in succession, on a human being. His piteous groans, and his "Pray don't, massa," rang in my ear for months afterwards.

There were many conjectures as to the cause of this terrible punishment. Some said master accused him of stealing corn, others said the slave had quarreled with his wife in presence of the overseer, and had accused his master of being the father of her child. They were both black, and the child was very fair.

I went into the work house next morning, and saw the cowhide still wet with blood, and the boards all covered with gore. The poor man lived, and continued to quarrel with his wife. A few months afterwards Dr. Flint handed them both over to a slave-trader. The guilty man put their value into his pocket, and had the satisfaction of knowing that they were out of sight and hearing. When the mother was delivered into the trader's hands, she said, "You promised to treat me well." To which Dr. Flint replied, "You have let your tongue run too far, damn you."

She had forgotten that it was a crime for a slave to tell who was the father of her child.

From others than the master, persecution also comes in such cases. I once saw a young slave girl dying soon after the birth of a child nearly white. In her agony she cried out, "Lord, come and take me."

Her mistress stood by, and mocked at her like an incarnate fiend.

"You suffer, do you?" she exclaimed. "I am glad of it. You deserve it all, and more too."

The girl's mother said, "The baby is dead, thank God, and I hope my poor child will soon be in heaven, too."

"Heaven!" retorted the mistress. "There *is* no such place for the like of her and her bastard."

The poor mother turned away, sobbing. Her dying daughter called her, feebly, and as she bent over her, I heard her say, "Don't grieve so, mother. God knows all about it, and He will have mercy upon me."

Her sufferings afterwards became so intense, that her mistress felt unable to stay. When she left the room, the scornful smile was still on her lips.

Though seven children called her mother, the poor black woman had but the one child, whose eyes she saw closing in death, while she thanked God for taking her away from the greater bitterness of life.

Dr. Flint owned a fine residence in town, several farms, and about fifty slaves, besides hiring a number by the year. Hiring day in the South takes place on the first of January.

On the second, the slaves are expected to go to their new masters. On a farm, they work until the corn and cotton are laid. They then have two days off. Some masters give them a good dinner under the trees. This over, they work until Christmas Eve. If no heavy charges are meantime brought against them, they are given four or five days off, whichever the master or overseer may think proper. Then comes New Year's Eve, and they gather together their little alls, or more properly speaking, their little nothings, and wait anxiously for the dawning of day. At the appointed hour the grounds are thronged with men, women, and children, waiting, like criminals, to hear their doom pronounced. The slave is sure to know who is the most humane, or cruel master, within forty miles of him.

It is easy to find out, on that day, who clothes and feeds his slaves well, for he is surrounded by a crowd, begging, "Please, massa, hire me this year. I will work very hard, massa."

If a slave is unwilling to go with his new master, he is whipped, or locked up in jail, until he consents to go, and promises not to run away during the year. Should he chance to change his mind, thinking it justifiable to violate an extorted promise, woe unto him if he is caught. The whip is used till the blood flows at his feet, and his stiffened limbs are put in chains, to be dragged in the field for days and days.

If he lives until the next year, perhaps the same man will hire him again, without even giving him an opportunity of going to the hiring ground. After those for hire are disposed of, those for sale are called up.

Oh, you happy free women, contrast your New Year's Day with that of the poor bondwoman. With you it is a pleasant season, and the light of the day is blessed. Friendly wishes meet you everywhere, and gifts are showered upon you. Even hearts that have been estranged from you soften at this season, and lips that have been silent echo back, "I wish you a happy New Year." Children bring their little offerings and raise their rosy lips for a caress. They are your own, and no hand but that of death can take them from you.

But to the slave mother, New Year's Day comes laden with peculiar sorrows. She sits on her cold cabin floor, watching the children who may all be torn from her the next morning, and often does she wish that she and they might die before the day dawns. She may be an ignorant creature, degraded by the system that has brutalized her from childhood, but she has a mother's instincts, and is capable of feeling a mother's agonies.

On one of these sale days, I saw a mother lead seven children to the auction block. She knew that some of them would be taken from her, but they took all. The children were sold to a slave-trader, and their mother was bought by a man in her own town. Before night her children were all far away. She begged the trader to tell her where he intended to take them, this he refused to do. How could he, when he knew he would sell them, one by one, wherever he could command the highest price? I met that mother in the street, and her wild, haggard face lies today in my mind. She wrung her hands in anguish, and exclaimed, "Gone. All gone. Why don't God kill me?" I had no words wherewith to comfort her. Instances of this kind are of daily, yea, of hourly occurrence.

Slaveholders have a method, peculiar to their institution, of getting rid of old slaves whose lives have been worn out in their service. I knew an old woman, who for seventy years faithfully served her master. She had become almost helpless from hard labor and disease. Her owners moved to Alabama, and the old black woman was left to be sold to anybody who would give twenty dollars for her.

Two years had passed since I entered Dr. Flint's family, and those years had brought much of the knowledge that comes from experience, though they had afforded little opportunity for any other kinds of knowledge.

My grandmother had, as much as possible, been a mother to her orphan grandchildren. By perseverance and unwearied industry, she was now mistress of a snug little home, surrounded with the necessaries of life. She would have been happy could her children have shared them with her. There remained but three children and two grandchildren, all slaves. Most earnestly did she strive to make us feel that it was the will of God: that He had seen fit to place us under such circumstances and, though it seemed hard, we ought to pray for contentment.

It was a beautiful faith, coming from a mother who could not call her children her own. But I, and Benjamin, her youngest boy, condemned it. We reasoned that it was much more the will of God that we should be situated as she was. We longed for a home like hers. There we always found sweet balsam for our troubles. She was so loving, so sympathizing. She always met us with a smile, and listened with patience to all our sorrows. She spoke so hopefully that unconsciously the clouds gave place to sunshine. There was a grand big oven there, too, that baked bread and nice things for the town, and we knew there was always a choice bit in store for us.

But, alas, even the charms of the old oven failed to reconcile us to our hard lot. Benjamin was now a tall, handsome lad, strongly and gracefully made, and with a spirit too bold and daring for a slave. My brother William, now twelve years old, had the same aversion to the word 'master' that he had when he was an urchin of seven years. I was his confidant. He came to me with all his troubles. I remember one instance in particular. It was on a lovely spring morning. When I marked the sunlight dancing here and there, its beauty seemed to mock my sadness. For my master, whose restless, craving, vicious nature roved about day and night, seeking whom to devour, had just left me, with stinging, scorching words that scathed ear and brain like fire. How I despised him. I thought how glad I should be if some day when he walked the earth, it would open and swallow him up, and disencumber the world of a plague.

When he told me that I was made for his use, made to obey his command in everything, that I was nothing but a slave, whose will must and should surrender to his, never before had my puny arm felt half so strong.

So deeply was I absorbed in painful reflections afterwards, that I neither saw nor heard the entrance of anyone, till the voice of William sounded close beside me.

"Linda," said he, "what makes you look so sad? Linda, isn't this a bad world? Everybody seems so cross and unhappy. I wish I had died when poor father did."

I told him that everybody was not cross, or unhappy, that those who had pleasant homes and kind friends, and who were not afraid to love them, were happy. But we, who were slave children, without father or mother, could not expect to be happy. We must be good, perhaps that would bring us contentment.

"Yes," he said, "I try to be good, but what's the use? They are all the time troubling me."

Then he proceeded to relate his afternoon's difficulty with young master Nicholas. It seemed that the brother of master Nicholas had pleased himself with making up stories about William. Master Nicholas said he should be flogged, and he would do it. Whereupon he went to work, but William fought bravely, and the young master, finding his slave was getting the better of him, undertook to tie his hands behind him. He failed in that likewise. By dint of kicking and punching, William came out of the skirmish none the worse for a few scratches.

He continued to discourse on his young master's meanness, how Nicholas whipped the little boys, but was a perfect coward when a tussle ensued between him and white boys of his own size. On such occasions Nicholas always took to his legs. William had other charges to make against him. One was his rubbing up pennies with quicksilver, and passing them off for quarters of a dollar on an old man who kept a fruit stall. William was often sent to buy fruit, and he earnestly inquired of me what he ought to do under such circumstances. I told him it was certainly wrong to deceive the old man, and that it was his duty to tell him of the impositions practiced by his young master. I assured him the old man would not be slow to comprehend the whole, and there the matter would end. William thought it might with the old man, but not with Nicholas. He said he did not like the idea of being whipped.

While I advised him to be good and forgiving I was not unconscious of the beam in my own eye. It was the very knowledge of my own shortcomings that urged me to retain, if possible, some sparks of my brother's God-given nature. I had not lived fourteen years in slavery for nothing. I had felt, seen, and heard enough to read the characters and question the motives, of those around me. The war of my life had begun, and though one of God's most powerless creatures, I resolved never to be conquered. Alas for me!

If there was one pure, sunny spot for me, I believed it to be in Benjamin's heart, and in another's, whom I loved with all the ardor of a girl's first love. My owner knew of it, and sought in every way to render me miserable. He did not resort to corporal punishment, but to all the petty, tyrannical ways that human ingenuity could devise.

I remember the first time I was punished. It was in the month of February. My grandmother had taken my old shoes, and replaced them with a new pair. I needed them, for several inches of snow had fallen, and it still continued to fall. When I walked through Mrs. Flint's room, the creaking of the shoes grated harshly on her refined nerves. She called me to her, and asked what I had about me that made such a horrid noise. I told her it was my new shoes. "Take them off," said she, "and if you put them on again, I'll throw them into the fire."

I took them off, and my stockings also. She then sent me a long distance, on an errand. As I went through the snow, my bare feet tingled. That night I was very hoarse, and I went to bed thinking the next day would find me sick, perhaps dead. What was my grief on waking to find myself quite well!

I had imagined if I died, or was laid up for some time, that my mistress would feel a twinge of remorse that she had so hated 'the little imp', as she styled me. It was my ignorance of that mistress that gave rise to such extravagant imaginings.

Dr. Flint occasionally had high prices offered for me, but he always said, "She don't belong to me. She is my daughter's property and I have no right to sell her." Good, honest man. My young mistress was still a child, and I could look for no protection from her. I loved her. She returned my affection. I once heard her father allude to her attachment to me. His wife promptly replied that it proceeded from fear. This put unpleasant doubts into my mind. Did the child feign what she did not feel, or was her mother jealous of the mite of love she bestowed on me? I concluded it must be the latter. I said to myself, "Surely, little children are true."

One afternoon I sat at my sewing, feeling unusual depression of spirits. My mistress had been accusing me of an offense, of which I assured her I was perfectly innocent, but I saw, by the contemptuous curl of her lip, that she believed I was telling a lie.

I wondered for what wise purpose God was leading me through such thorny paths, and whether still darker days were in store for me. As I sat musing thus, the door opened softly, and William came in.

"Well, brother," said I, "what is the matter this time?"

"Linda, Ben and his master have had a dreadful time," said he.

My first thought was that Benjamin was killed.

"Don't be frightened, Linda," said William, "I will tell you all about it."

It appeared that Benjamin's master had sent for him, and he did not immediately obey the summons. When he did, his master was angry and began to whip him. He resisted. Master and slave fought, and finally the master was thrown. Benjamin had cause to tremble, for he had thrown to the ground his master — one of the richest men in town. I anxiously awaited the result.

That night I stole to my grandmother's house, and Benjamin also stole thither from his master's. My grandmother had gone to spend a day or two with an old friend living in the country.

"I have come," said Benjamin, "to tell you goodbye. I am going away."

I inquired where.

"To the North," he replied.

I looked at him to see whether he was in earnest. I saw it all in his firm, set mouth. I implored him not to go, but he paid no heed to my words. He said he was no longer a boy, and every day made his yoke more galling. He had raised his hand against his master, and was to be publicly whipped for the offense. I reminded him of the poverty and hardships he must encounter among strangers. I told him he might be caught and brought back, and that was terrible to think of.

He grew vexed, and asked if poverty and hardships with freedom, were not preferable to our treatment in slavery.

"Linda," he continued, "we are dogs here, cattle. No, I will not stay. Let them bring me back. We don't die but once."

He was right, but it was hard to give him up.

"Go," said I, "and break your mother's heart."

I repented my words ere they were out.

"Linda," said he, speaking as I had not heard him speak that evening, "how could you say that? Poor mother! Be kind to her, Linda."

Farewells were exchanged, and the bright, kind boy, endeared to us by so many acts of love, vanished from my sight.

It is not necessary to state how he made his escape. Suffice it to say, he was on his way to New York when a violent storm overtook the vessel. The captain said he must put into the nearest port. This alarmed Benjamin, who was aware that he would be advertised in every port near his own town. His embarrassment was noticed by the captain. To port they went. There the advertisement met the captain's eye. Benjamin so exactly answered its description, that the captain laid hold on him, and bound him in chains. The storm passed, and they proceeded to New York. Before reaching that port Benjamin managed to get off his chains and throw them overboard. He escaped from the vessel, but was pursued, captured, and carried back to his master.

When my grandmother returned home and found her youngest child had fled, great was her sorrow, but, with characteristic piety, she said, "God's will be done." Each morning, she inquired if any news had been heard from her boy. Yes, news was heard. The master was rejoicing over a letter, announcing the capture of his human chattel.

That day seems but as yesterday, so well do I remember it. I saw him led through the streets in chains, to jail. His face was ghastly pale, yet full of determination. He had begged one of the sailors to go to his mother's house and ask her not to meet him. He said the sight of her distress would take from him all self-control. She yearned to see him, and she went, but she screened herself in the crowd, that it might be as her child had said.

We were not allowed to visit him, but we had known the jailer for years, and he was a kind-hearted man. At midnight he opened the jail door for my grandmother and myself to enter, in disguise. When we entered the cell not a sound broke the stillness.

"Benjamin, Benjamin," whispered my grandmother.

No answer.

"Benjamin!" she again faltered. There was a jingle of chains. The moon had just risen, and cast an uncertain light through the bars of the window. We knelt down and took Benjamin's cold hands in ours. We did not speak. Sobs were heard, and Benjamin's lips were unsealed, for his mother was weeping on his neck. How vividly does memory bring back that sad night. Mother and son talked together. He asked her pardon for the suffering he had caused her. She said she had nothing to forgive, she could not blame his desire for freedom. He told her that when he was captured, he broke away, and was about casting himself into the river, when thoughts of her came over him, and he desisted. She asked if he did not also think of God. I fancied I saw his face grow fierce in the moonlight. He answered, "No, I did not think of him. When a man is hunted like a wild beast he forgets there is a God, a heaven. He forgets everything in his struggle to get beyond the reach of the bloodhounds."

"Don't talk so, Benjamin," said she. "Put your trust in God. Be humble, my child, and your master will forgive you."

"Forgive me for what, mother? For not letting him treat me like a dog? No! I will never humble myself to him. I have worked for him for nothing all my life, and I am repaid with stripes and imprisonment. Here I will stay till I die, or till he sells me."

The poor mother shuddered at his words. I think he felt it, for when he next spoke, his voice was calmer.

"Don't fret about me, mother. I ain't worth it," said he. "I wish I had some of your goodness. You bear everything patiently, just as though you thought it was all right. I wish I could."

She told him she had not always been so. Once, she was like him, but when sore troubles came upon her and she had no arm to lean upon, she learned to call on God, and He lightened her burdens. She besought him to do likewise.

We overstayed our time, and were obliged to hurry from the jail.

Benjamin had been imprisoned three weeks when my grandmother went to intercede for him with his master. He was immovable. He said Benjamin should serve as an example to the rest of his slaves, he would be kept in jail till he was subdued, or be sold if he got but one dollar for him. However, he afterwards relented in some degree. The chains were taken off, and we were allowed to visit him.

As his food was of the coarsest kind, we carried him as often as possible a warm supper, accompanied with some little luxury for the jailer.

Three months elapsed, and there was no prospect of release or of a purchaser. One day he was heard to sing and laugh. This piece of indecorum was told to his master, and the overseer was ordered to re-chain him. He was now confined in a cell with other prisoners, who were covered with filthy rags. Benjamin was chained near them, and was soon covered with vermin. He worked at his chains till he succeeded in getting out of them. He passed them through the bars of the window, with a request that they should be taken to his master, and he should be informed that he was covered with vermin.

This audacity was punished with heavier chains, and prohibition of our visits.

My grandmother continued to send him fresh changes of clothes. The old ones were burned up. The last night we saw him in jail his mother still begged him to send for his master, and beg his pardon. Neither persuasion nor argument could turn him from his purpose. He calmly answered, "I am waiting his time."

Those chains were mournful to hear.

Another three months passed, and Benjamin left his prison walls. We that loved him waited to bid him a long and last farewell. A slave-trader had bought him. You remember, I told you what price he brought when ten years of age. Now he was more than twenty years old, and sold for three hundred dollars. The master had been blind to his own interest. Long confinement had made his face too pale, his form too thin, moreover, the trader had heard something of his character, and it did not strike him as suitable for a slave. He said he would give any price if the handsome lad was a girl. We thanked God that he was not.

Could you have seen that mother clinging to her child when they fastened the irons upon his wrists, could you have heard her heart-rending groans and seen her bloodshot eyes wander wildly from face to face, vainly pleading for mercy? Could you have witnessed that scene as I saw it, you would exclaim, slavery is damnable!

Benjamin, her youngest, her pet, was forever gone. She could not come to terms with it. She had had an interview with the trader for the purpose of ascertaining if Benjamin could be purchased. She was told it was impossible, as he had given bonds not to sell him till he was out of the State. He promised that he would not sell him till he reached New Orleans.

With a strong arm and unvaried trust, my grandmother

began her work of love. Benjamin must be free. If she succeeded, she knew they would still be separated, but the sacrifice was not too great. Day and night she labored. The trader's price would treble that he gave, but she was not discouraged.

She employed a lawyer to write to a gentleman, whom she knew, in New Orleans. She begged him to interest himself for Benjamin, and he willingly favored her request. When he saw Benjamin, and stated his business, he thanked him, but said he preferred to wait a while before making the trader an offer. He knew he had tried to obtain a high price for him, and had invariably failed. This encouraged him to make another effort for freedom. So one morning, long before day, Benjamin was missing. He was riding over the blue billows, bound for Baltimore.

For once his white face did him a kindly service. They had no suspicion that it belonged to a slave, otherwise the law would have been followed out to the letter and the thing rendered back to slavery.

The brightest skies are often overshadowed by the darkest clouds. Benjamin was taken sick and compelled to remain in Baltimore three weeks. His strength was slow in returning and his desire to continue his journey seemed to retard his recovery. How could he get strength without air and exercise? He resolved to venture on a short walk. A side street was selected, where he thought himself secure of not being met by anyone who knew him, but a voice called out, "Hello, Ben, my boy. What are you doing here?"

His first impulse was to run, but his legs trembled so that he could not stir. He turned to confront his antagonist, and behold, there stood his old master's next door neighbor. He thought it was all over with him now but it proved otherwise. That man was a miracle. He possessed a goodly number of slaves, and yet was not quite deaf to that mystic clock, whose ticking is rarely heard in the slaveholder's breast.

"Ben, you are sick," said he. "Why, you look like a ghost. I guess I gave you something of a start. Never mind, Ben, I am not going to touch you. You had a pretty tough time of it, and you may go on your way rejoicing for all me. But I would advise you to get out of this place pretty quick, for there are several gentlemen here from our town." He described the nearest and safest route to New York, and added, "I shall be glad to tell your mother I have seen you. Goodbye, Ben."

Benjamin turned away, filled with gratitude, and surprised that the town he hated contained such a gem — a gem worthy of a purer setting.

This gentleman was a northerner by birth, and had married a Southern lady. On his return, he told my grandmother that he had seen her son, and of the service he had rendered him.

Benjamin reached New York safely and concluded to stop there until he had gained strength enough to proceed further. It happened that my grandmother's only remaining son had sailed for the same city on business for his mistress. Through God's providence, the brothers met. You may be sure it was a happy meeting.

"Oh Phil," exclaimed Benjamin, "I am here at last." Then he told him how near he came to dying, almost in sight of free land, and how he prayed that he might live to get one breath of free air. He said life was worth something now, and it would be hard to die. In the old jail he had not valued it. Once, he was tempted to destroy it, but something, he did not know what, had prevented him, perhaps it was fear. He had heard those who profess to be religious declare there was no heaven for self-murderers, and as his life had been pretty hot here, he did not desire a continuation of the same in another world. "If I die now," he exclaimed, "thank God, I shall die a free man."

He begged my uncle Phillip not to return south, but stay and work with him till they earned enough to buy those at home. His brother told him it would kill their mother if he deserted her in her trouble. She had pledged her house, and with difficulty had raised money to buy him. Would he be bought?

"No, never," he replied. "Do you suppose, Phil, when I have got so far out of their clutches, I will give them one red cent? No! And do you suppose I would turn mother out of her home in her old age? That I would let her pay all those hard-earned dollars for me, and never to see me? For you know she will stay south as long as her other children are slaves. What a good mother. Tell her to buy you, Phil. You have been a comfort to her, I have been a trouble. And Linda, poor Linda, what'll become of her? Phil, you don't know what a life they lead her. She has told me something about it, and I wish old Flint was dead, or a better man. When I was in jail, he asked her if she didn't want him to ask my master to forgive me, and take me home again. She told him no, that I didn't want to go back. He got mad, and said we were all alike. I never despised my own master half as much as I do that man. There is many a worse slaveholder than my master, but for all that I would not be his slave."

While Benjamin was sick, he had parted with nearly all his clothes to pay necessary expenses. But he did not part with a little pin I fastened in his bosom when we parted. It was the most valuable thing I owned, and I thought none more worthy to wear it. He had it still.

His brother furnished him with clothes and gave him what money he had.

They parted with moistened eyes, and as Benjamin turned away, he said, "Phil, I part with all my kindred."

And so it proved. We never heard from him again.

Uncle Phillip came home, and the first words he uttered when he entered the house were, "Mother, Ben is free. I have seen him in New York."

She stood looking at him with a bewildered air.

"Mother, don't you believe it?" he said, laying his hand softly upon her shoulder.

She raised her hands, and exclaimed, "God be praised. Let us thank him."

She dropped on her knees and poured forth her heart in prayer. Then Phillip must sit down and repeat to her every word Benjamin had said. He told her all, except how sick and pale her darling looked. Why should he distress her when she could do Benjamin no good?

The brave old woman still toiled on, hoping to rescue some of her other children. After a while she succeeded in buying Phillip. She paid eight hundred dollars, and came home with the precious document that secured his freedom. The happy mother and son sat together by the old hearthstone that night, telling how proud they were of each other, and how they would prove to the world that they could take care of themselves, as they had long taken care of others. We all concluded by saying, "He that is willing to be a slave, let him be a slave."

During the first years of my service in Dr. Flint's family, I was accustomed to sharing some indulgences with the children of my mistress. Though this seemed to me no more than right, I was grateful for it, and tried to merit the kindness by the faithful discharge of my duties. But I now entered on my fifteenth year — a sad epoch in the life of a slave girl. My master began to whisper foul words in my ear. Young as I was, I could not remain ignorant of their import. I tried to treat them with indifference or contempt. The master's age, my extreme youth, and the fear that his conduct would be reported to my grandmother, made him bear this treatment for many months. He was a crafty man, and resorted to many means to accomplish his purposes. Sometimes he had stormy ways that made his victims tremble, sometimes he assumed a gentleness that he thought must surely subdue. Of the two, I preferred his stormy moods, although they left me trembling. He tried his utmost to corrupt the pure principles my grandmother had instilled. He peopled my young mind with unclean images, such as only a vile monster could think of. I turned from him with disgust and hatred. But he was my master. I was compelled to live under the same roof with him, where I saw a man forty years my senior daily violating the most sacred commandments of nature. He told me I was his property, that I must be subject to his will in all things. My soul revolted against the mean tyranny. But where could I turn for protection? No matter whether the slave girl be as black as ebony or as fair as her mistress, in either case there is no shadow of law to protect her from insult, violence, or even from death. All these are inflicted by fiends who bear the shape of men. The mistress, who ought to protect the helpless victim, has no other feelings towards her but those of jealousy and rage. The degradation, the wrongs, the vices that grow out of slavery are more than I can describe. They are greater than you would willingly believe. Surely, if you credited one half the truths that are told you concerning the helpless millions suffering in this cruel bondage, you in the North would not help to tighten the yoke. You surely would refuse to do for the masters on your own soil, the mean and cruel work which trained bloodhounds and the lowest class of whites do for him in the South.

Everywhere the years bring to all enough of sin and sorrow, but in slavery the very dawn of life is darkened by these shadows. Even the little child, who is accustomed to wait on her mistress and her children, will learn, before she is twelve years old, why it is that her mistress hates such and such a one among the slaves. Perhaps the child's own mother is among those hated ones. She listens to violent outbreaks of jealous passion, and cannot help understanding what is the cause. She will become prematurely knowing in evil things. Soon she will learn to tremble when she hears her master's footsteps. She will be compelled to realize that she is no longer a child. If God has bestowed beauty upon her, it will prove her greatest curse. That which commands admiration in the white woman only hastens the degradation of the female slave. I know that some are too much brutalized by slavery to feel the humiliation of their position, but many slaves feel it most acutely, and shrink from the memory of it. I cannot tell how much I suffered in the presence of these wrongs, nor how I am still pained by the retrospect. My master met me at every turn, reminding me that I belonged to him, and swearing by heaven and earth that he would compel me to submit to him. If I went out for a breath of fresh air, after a day of unwearied toil, his footsteps dogged me. If I knelt by my mother's grave, his dark shadow fell on me even there. The light heart which nature had given me became heavy with sad forebodings. The other slaves in my master's house noticed the change. Many of them pitied me, but none dared to ask the cause. They had no need to inquire. They knew too well the guilty practices under that roof, and they were aware that to speak of them was an offense that never went unpunished.

I longed for someone to confide in. I would have given the world to have laid my head on my grandmother's faithful bosom, and told her all my troubles. But Dr. Flint swore he would kill me if I was not as silent as the grave. Then, although my grandmother was all in all to me, I feared her as well as loved her. I had been accustomed to look up to her with a respect bordering upon awe. I was very young, and felt shamefaced about telling her such impure things, especially as I knew her to be very strict on such subjects. Moreover, she was a woman of a high spirit. She was usually very quiet in her demeanor, but if her indignation was once roused, it was not very easily quelled. I had been told that she once chased a white gentleman with a loaded pistol, because he insulted one of her daughters. I dreaded the consequences of a violent outbreak, and both pride and fear kept me silent. But though I did not confide in my grandmother, and even evaded her vigilant watchfulness and inquiry, her presence in the neighborhood was some protection to me. Though she had been a slave, Dr. Flint was afraid of her. He dreaded her scorching rebukes. Moreover, she was known and patronized by many people, and he did not wish to have his villainy made public. It was lucky for me that I did not live on a distant plantation, but in a town not so large that the inhabitants were ignorant of each other's affairs. Bad as are the laws and customs in a slaveholding community, the doctor, as a professional man, deemed it prudent to keep up some outward show of decency.

What days and nights of fear and sorrow that man caused me. Reader, it is not to awaken sympathy for myself that I am telling you truthfully what I suffered in slavery. I do it to kindle a flame of compassion in your hearts for my sisters who are still in bondage, suffering as I once suffered.

I once saw two beautiful children playing together. One was a fair white child, the other was her slave, and also her sister. When I saw them embracing each other, and heard their joyous laughter, I turned sadly away from the lovely sight. I foresaw the inevitable blight that would fall on the little slave's heart. I knew how soon her laughter would be changed to sighs. The fair child grew up to be a still fairer woman. From childhood to womanhood her pathway was blooming with flowers, and arched by a sunny sky. Scarcely one day of her life had been clouded when the sun rose on her happy bridal morning.

How had those years dealt with her slave sister, the little playmate of her childhood? She, also, was very beautiful, but the flowers and sunshine of love were not for her. She drank the cup of sin, shame and misery, whereof her persecuted race are compelled to drink.

In view of these things, why are ye silent, ye free men and women of the North? Why do your tongues falter in maintenance of the right? Would that I had more ability. But my heart is so full, my pen so weak. There are noble men and women who plead for us, striving to help those who cannot help themselves. God bless them. God give them strength and courage to go on. God bless those, everywhere, who are laboring to advance the cause of humanity.

I would ten thousand times rather that my children should be the half-starved paupers of Ireland than to be the most pampered among the slaves of America. I would rather drudge out my life on a cotton plantation, till the grave opened to give me rest, than to live with an unprincipled master and a jealous mistress. The felon's home in a penitentiary is preferable. He may repent and turn from the error of his ways, and so find peace, but it is not so with a favorite slave. She is not allowed to have any pride of character. It is deemed a crime in her to wish to be virtuous.

Mrs. Flint possessed the key to her husband's character before I was born. She might have used this knowledge to counsel and to screen the young and the innocent among her slaves, but for them she had no sympathy. They were the objects of her constant suspicion and malevolence. She watched her husband with unceasing vigilance, but he was well practiced in means to evade it. What he could not find opportunity to say in words he manifested in signs. He invented more than were ever thought of in a deaf and dumb asylum. I let them pass, as if I did not understand what he meant, and many were the curses and threats bestowed on me for my stupidity.

One day, he caught me teaching myself to write. He frowned, as if he was not well pleased, but I suppose he came to the conclusion that such an accomplishment might help to advance his favorite scheme.

Before long, notes were often slipped into my hand. I would return them, saying, "I can't read them, sir."

"Can't you?" he replied, "then I must read them to you." He always finished the reading by asking, "Do you understand?" Sometimes he would complain of the heat of the tea room, and order his supper to be placed on a small table in the piazza. He would seat himself there with a well-satisfied smile, and tell me to stand by and brush away the flies. He would eat very slowly, pausing between the mouthfuls. These intervals were employed in describing the happiness I was so foolishly throwing away, and in threatening me with the penalty that finally awaited my stubborn disobedience. He boasted much of the forbearance he had exercised towards me, and reminded me that there was a limit to his patience. When I succeeded in avoiding opportunities for him to talk to me at home, I was ordered to come to his office, to do some errand. When there, I was obliged to stand and listen to such language as he saw fit to address me. Sometimes I so openly expressed my contempt for him that he would become violently enraged, and I wondered why he did not strike me. Circumstanced as he was, he probably thought it was better policy to be forbearing. But the state of things grew worse and worse daily. In desperation I told him that I must and would apply to my grandmother for protection. He threatened me with death, and worse than death, if I made any complaint to her. Strange to say, I did not despair. I was naturally of a buoyant disposition, and always I had a hope of somehow getting out of his clutches. Like many a poor, simple slave before me, I trusted that some threads of joy would yet be woven into my dark destiny.

I had entered my sixteenth year, and every day it became more apparent that my presence was intolerable to Mrs. Flint. Angry words frequently passed between her and her husband. He had never punished me himself, and he would not allow anybody else to punish me. In that respect, she was never satisfied, but, in her angry moods no terms were too vile for her to bestow upon me. Yet I, whom she detested so bitterly, had far more pity for her than he had, whose duty it was to make her life happy. I never wronged her, or wished to wrong her, and one word of kindness from her would have brought me to her feet.

After repeated quarrels between the doctor and his wife, he announced his intention to take his youngest daughter, then four years old, to sleep in his apartment. It was necessary that a servant should sleep in the same room, to be on hand if the child stirred. I was selected for that office, and informed for what purpose that arrangement had been made. By managing to keep within sight of people as much as possible during the day time, I had hitherto succeeded in eluding my master, though a razor was often held to my throat to force me to change this line of policy. At night I slept by the side of my great aunt, where I felt safe. He was too prudent to come into her room. She was an old woman, and had been in the family many years. Moreover, as a married man, and a professional man, he deemed it necessary to save appearances in some degree. But he resolved to remove the obstacle in the way of his scheme, and he thought he had planned it so that he should evade suspicion. He was well aware how much I prized my refuge by the side of my old aunt, and he determined to dispossess me of it. The first night the doctor had the little child in his room alone. The next morning I was ordered to take my station as nurse the following night. A kind Providence interposed in my favor. During the day Mrs. Flint heard of this new arrangement, and a storm followed. I rejoiced to hear it rage.

After a while my mistress sent for me to come to her room. Her first question was, "Did you know you were to sleep in the doctor's room?"

"Yes, ma'am."

"Who told you?"

"My master."

"Will you answer truly all the questions I ask?"

"Yes, ma'am."

"Tell me, then, as you hope to be forgiven, are you innocent of what I have accused you?"

"I am."

She handed me a Bible, and said, "Lay your hand on your heart, kiss this holy book, and swear before God that you tell me the truth."

I took the oath she required, and I did it with a clear conscience.

"You have taken God's holy word to testify your innocence," said she. "If you have deceived me, beware! Now take this stool, sit down, look me directly in the face, and tell me all that has passed between your master and you."

I did as she ordered. As I went on with my account her color changed frequently, she wept, and sometimes groaned. She spoke in tones so sad that I was touched by her grief. The tears came to my eyes, but I was soon convinced that her emotions arose from anger and wounded pride. She felt that her marriage vows were desecrated, her dignity insulted, but she had no compassion for the poor victim of her husband's perfidy. She pitied herself as a martyr, but she was incapable of feeling for the condition of shame and misery in which her unfortunate, helpless slave was placed.

Yet perhaps she had some touch of feeling for me, for when the conference was ended, she spoke kindly, and promised to protect me. I should have been much comforted by this assurance if I could have had confidence in it, but my experiences in slavery had filled me with distrust. She was not a very refined woman, and had not much control over her passions. I was an object of her jealousy and, consequently, of her hatred. I knew I could not expect kindness or confidence from her under the circumstances in which I was placed. I could not blame her. Slaveholders' wives feel as other women would under similar circumstances. The fire of her temper kindled from small sparks, and now the flame became so intense that the doctor was obliged to give up his intended arrangement.

I knew I had ignited the torch, and I expected to suffer for it afterwards, but I felt too thankful to my mistress for the timely aid she rendered me to care much about that. She now took me to sleep in a room adjoining her own. There I was an object of her especial care, though not of her especial comfort, for she spent many a sleepless night watching over me. Sometimes I woke up, and found her bending over me. At other times she whispered in my ear, as though it was her husband who was speaking to me, and listened to hear what I would answer. If she startled me, on such occasions, she would glide stealthily away, and the next morning she would tell me I had been talking in my sleep, and ask who I was talking to. At last, I began to be fearful for my life. It had been often threatened, and you can imagine, better than I can describe, what an unpleasant sensation it must produce to wake up in the dead of night and find a jealous woman bending over you. Terrible as this experience was, I had fears that it would give place to one more terrible.

My mistress grew weary of her vigils, they did not prove satisfactory. She changed her tactics. She now tried the trick of accusing my master of crime, in my presence, and gave my name as the author of the accusation. To my utter astonishment, he replied, "I don't believe it, but if she did acknowledge it, you tortured her into exposing me."

Tortured into exposing him! Truly, Satan had no difficulty in distinguishing the color of his soul.

I understood his object in making this false representation.

It was to show me that I gained nothing by seeking the protection of my mistress, that the power was still all in his own hands. I pitied Mrs. Flint. She was a second wife, many years the junior of her husband, and the hoary-headed miscreant was enough to try the patience of a wiser and better woman. She was completely foiled, and knew not how to proceed. She would gladly have had me flogged for my supposed false oath but, as I have already stated, the doctor never allowed anyone to whip me. The old sinner was politic. The application of the lash might have led to remarks that would have exposed him in the eyes of his children and grandchildren. How often did I rejoice that I lived in a town where all the inhabitants knew each other. If I had been on a remote plantation, or lost among the multitude of a crowded city, I should not be a living woman at this day.

The secrets of slavery are concealed like those of the Inquisition. My master was, to my knowledge, the father of eleven slaves. But did the mothers dare to tell who was the father of their children? Did the other slaves dare to allude to it, except in whispers among themselves? No, indeed. They knew too well the terrible consequences.

My grandmother could not avoid seeing things which excited her suspicions. She was uneasy about me, and tried various ways to buy me, but the never-changing answer was always repeated: "Linda does not belong to me. She is my daughter's property, and I have no legal right to sell her."

The conscientious man! He was too scrupulous to sell me, but he had no scruples whatever about committing a much greater wrong against the helpless young girl placed under his guardianship, as his daughter's property. Sometimes my persecutor would ask me whether I would like to be sold. I told him I would rather be sold to anybody than to lead such a life as I did.

On such occasions he would assume the air of a very injured

individual, and reproach me for my ingratitude.

"Did I not take you into the house and make you the companion of my own children?" he would say. "Have I ever treated you like a negro? I have never allowed you to be punished, not even to please your mistress. And this is the recompense I get, you ungrateful girl."

I answered that he had reasons of his own for screening me from punishment, and that the course he pursued made my mistress hate me and persecute me.

If I wept, he would say, "Poor child. Don't cry. Don't cry. I will make peace for you with your mistress. Only let me arrange matters in my own way. Poor, foolish girl, you don't know what is for your own good. I would cherish you. I would make a lady of you. Now go, and think of all I have promised you."

I did think of it.

Reader, I draw no imaginary pictures of Southern homes. I am telling you the plain truth. Yet when victims make their escape from this wild beast of slavery, northerners consent to act the part of bloodhounds and hunt the poor fugitive back into his den, 'full of dead men's bones, and all uncleanness'. Nay, more, they are not only willing, but proud, to give their daughters in marriage to slaveholders. The poor girls have romantic notions of a sunny clime and of the flowering vines that all the year round shade a happy home.

To what disappointments are they destined. The young wife soon learns that the husband in whose hands she has placed her happiness pays no regard to his marriage vows. Children of every shade of complexion play with her own fair babies, and too well she knows that they are born unto him of his own household. Jealousy and hatred enter the flowery home, and it is ravaged of its loveliness.

Southern women often marry a man knowing that he is the father of many little slaves. They do not trouble themselves about it. They regard such children as property, as marketable as the pigs on the plantation, and it is seldom that they do not make them aware of this by passing them into the slave-trader's hands as soon as possible, and thus getting them out of their sight. I am glad to say there are some honorable exceptions.

I have myself known two Southern wives who exhorted their husbands to free those slaves towards whom they stood in a 'parental relation', and their request was granted. These husbands blushed before the superior nobleness of their wives' natures. Though they had only counseled them to do that which it was their duty to do, it commanded their respect, and rendered their conduct more exemplary. Concealment was at an end and confidence took the place of distrust.

Though this bad institution deadens the moral sense, even in white women, to a fearful extent, it is not altogether extinct. I have heard Southern ladies say of such a one, "He not only thinks it no disgrace to be the father of those little niggers, but he is not ashamed to call himself their master. I declare, such things ought not to be tolerated in any decent society."

Why does the slave ever love? Why allow the tendrils of the heart to twine around objects which may at any moment be wrenched away by the hand of violence? When separations come by the hand of death, the pious soul can bow in resignation, and say, "Not my will, but thine be done, O Lord!" But when the ruthless hand of man strikes the blow, regardless of the misery he causes, it is hard to be submissive. I did not reason thus when I was a young girl. Youth will be youth. I loved, and I indulged the hope that the dark clouds around me would turn out a bright lining. I forgot that in the land of my birth the shadows are too dense for light to penetrate. A land

Where laughter is not mirth, nor thought the mind,
Nor words a language, nor e'en men mankind.
Where cries reply to curses, shrieks to blows,

And each is tortured in his separate hell.

There was in the neighborhood a young colored carpenter, a free-born man. We had been well acquainted in childhood, and frequently met together afterwards. We became mutually attached, and he proposed to marry me. I loved him with all the ardor of a young girl's first love. But when I reflected that I was a slave and that the laws gave no sanction to the marriage of such, my heart sank within me. My lover wanted to buy me, but I knew that Dr. Flint was too willful and arbitrary a man to consent to that arrangement. From him, I was sure of experiencing all sorts of opposition, and I had nothing to hope from my mistress. She would have been delighted to have got rid of me, but not in that way. It would have relieved her mind of a burden if she could have seen me sold to some distant State, but if I was married near home I should be just as much in her husband's power as I had previously been, for the husband of a slave has no power to protect her. Moreover, my mistress, like many others, seemed to think that slaves had no right to any family ties of their own, that they were created merely to wait upon the family of the mistress. I once heard her abuse a young slave girl, who told her that a colored man wanted to make her his wife.

"I will have you peeled and pickled, my lady," said she, "if I ever hear you mention that subject again. Do you suppose that I will have you tending my children with the children of that nigger?"

The girl to whom she said this had a mulatto child, of course not acknowledged by its father. The poor black man who loved her would have been proud to acknowledge his helpless offspring.

Many and anxious were the thoughts I revolved in my mind. I was at a loss what to do. Above all things, I was desirous to spare my lover the insults that had cut so deeply into my own soul. I talked with my grandmother about it, and partly told her my fears. I did not dare to tell her the worst. She had long suspected all was not right, and if I confirmed her suspicions I knew a storm would rise that would prove the overthrow of all my hopes.

This love-dream had been my support through many trials, and I could not bear to run the risk of having it suddenly dissipated. There was a lady in the neighborhood, a particular friend of Dr. Flint's, who often visited the house. I had a great respect for her and she had always manifested a friendly interest in me.

Grandmother thought she would have great influence with the doctor. I went to this lady, and told her my story. I told her I was aware that my lover's being a free-born man would prove a great objection, but he wanted to buy me, and if Dr. Flint would consent to that arrangement, I felt sure he would be willing to pay any reasonable price. She knew that Mrs. Flint disliked me, therefore, I ventured to suggest that perhaps my mistress would approve of my being sold, as that would rid her of me. The lady listened with kindly sympathy, and promised to do her utmost to promote my wishes. She had an interview with the doctor, and I believe she pleaded my cause earnestly, but it was all to no purpose.

How I dreaded my master now. Every minute I expected to be summoned to his presence, but the day passed, and I heard nothing from him. The next morning, a message was brought to me: "Master wants you in his study."

I found the door ajar, and I stood a moment gazing at the hateful man who claimed a right to rule me, body and soul. I entered. Tried to appear calm. I did not want him to know how my heart was bleeding. He looked at me with an expression which seemed to say, "I have half a mind to kill you on the spot."

He eventually broke the silence. A relief to both of us.

"So you want to be married, do you?" said he. "And to a

free nigger."

"Yes, sir."

"Well, I'll soon convince you whether I am your master, or the nigger fellow you honor so highly. If you must have a husband, you may take up with one of my slaves."

What a situation I should be in, as the wife of one of his slaves even if my heart had been interested.

I replied, "Don't you suppose, sir, that a slave can have some preference about marrying? Do you suppose that all men are alike to her?"

"Do you love this nigger?" said he, abruptly.

"Yes, sir."

"How dare you tell me so," he exclaimed, in great wrath. After a slight pause, he added, "I supposed you thought more of yourself, that you felt above the insults of such puppies."

I replied, "If he is a puppy I am a puppy, for we are both of the negro race. It is right and honorable for us to love each other. The man you call a puppy never insulted me, sir, and he would not love me if he did not believe me to be a virtuous woman."

He sprang upon me like a tiger and gave me a stunning blow. It was the first time he had ever struck me, and fear did not enable me to control my anger. When I had recovered a little from the effects, I exclaimed, "You have struck me for answering you honestly. How I despise you!"

There was silence for some minutes. Perhaps he was deciding what should be my punishment, or perhaps he wanted to give me time to reflect on what I had said, and to whom I had said it. Finally, he asked, "Do you know what you just said?"

"Yes, sir, but your treatment drove me to it."

"Do you know that I have a right to do as I like with you, that I can kill you, if I please?"

"You have tried to kill me, and I wish you had, but you have no right to do as you like with me."

"Silence!" he exclaimed, in a thundering voice. "By heavens, girl, you forget yourself too far. Are you mad? If you are, I will soon bring you to your senses. Do you think any other master would bear what I have borne from you this morning? Many masters would have killed you on the spot. How would you like to be sent to jail for your insolence?"

"I know I have been disrespectful, sir," I replied, "but you drove me to it, I couldn't help it. As for the jail, there would be more peace for me there than there is here."

"You deserve to go there," said he, "and to be under such treatment that you would forget the meaning of the word peace. It would do you good. It would take some of your high notions out of you. But I am not ready to send you there yet, notwithstanding your ingratitude for all my kindness and forbearance. You have been the plague of my life. I have wanted to make you happy, and I have been repaid with the basest ingratitude, but though you have proved yourself incapable of appreciating my kindness, I will be lenient towards you, Linda. I will give you one more chance to redeem your character. If you behave yourself and do as I require, I will forgive you and treat you as I always have done, but if you disobey me, I will punish you as I would the meanest slave on my plantation. Never let me hear that fellow's name mentioned again. If I ever know of your speaking to him, I will cowhide you both. If I catch him lurking about my premises, I will shoot him as soon as I would a dog. Do you hear what I say? I'll teach you a lesson about marriage and free niggers. Now go, and let this be the last time I have occasion to speak to you on this subject."

Reader, did you ever hate? I hope not. I never did but once, and I trust I never shall again. Somebody has called it 'the atmosphere of hell', and I believe it is so.

For a fortnight the doctor did not speak to me. He thought

to mortify me, to make me feel that I had disgraced myself by receiving the honorable addresses of a respectable colored man, in preference to the base proposals of a white man. But though his lips disdained to address me, his eyes were very loquacious No animal ever watched its prey more narrowly than he watched me. He knew that I could write, though he had failed to make me read his letters, and he was now troubled lest I should exchange letters with another man. After a while he became weary of silence, and I was sorry for it. One morning, as he passed through the hall to leave the house, he contrived to thrust a note into my hand. I thought I had better read it and spare myself the vexation of having him read it to me. It expressed regret for the blow he had given me, and reminded me that I myself was wholly to blame for it. He hoped I had become convinced of the injury I was doing myself by incurring his displeasure. He wrote that he had made up his mind to go to Louisiana, that he should take several slaves with him, and intended I should be one of the number. My mistress would remain where she was, therefore I should have nothing to fear from that quarter. If I merited kindness from him, he assured me that it would be lavishly bestowed. He begged me to think over the matter and answer the following day.

The next morning I was called to carry a pair of scissors to his room. I laid them on the table, with the letter beside them. He thought it was my answer, and did not call me back.

I went as usual to attend my young mistress to and from school. He met me in the street, and ordered me to stop at his office on my way back. When I entered, he showed me his letter, and asked me why I had not answered it. I replied, "I am your daughter's property, and it is in your power to send me, or take me, wherever you please."

He said he was very glad to find me so willing to go, and that we should start early in the autumn.

However that might be, I was determined that I would never go to Louisiana with him.

Summer passed away, and early in the autumn Dr. Flint's eldest son was sent to Louisiana to examine the country, with a view to emigrating. That news did not disturb me. I knew very well that I should not be sent with him. That I had not been taken to the plantation before this time, was owing to the fact that his son was there. He was jealous of his son, and jealousy of the overseer had kept him from punishing me by sending me into the fields to work. Is it strange that I was not proud of these protectors? As for the overseer, he was a man for whom I had less respect than I had for a bloodhound.

Young Mr. Flint did not bring back a favorable report of Louisiana, and I heard no more of that scheme. Soon after this, my lover met me at the corner of the street, and I stopped to speak to him. Looking up, I saw my master watching us from his window. I hurried home, trembling with fear. I was sent for, immediately, to go to his room. He met me with a blow.

"When is mistress to be married?" said he, in a sneering tone. A shower of oaths and imprecations followed. How thankful I was that my lover was a free man, that my tyrant had no power to flog him for speaking to me in the street.

Again and again I revolved in my mind how all this would end. There was no hope that the doctor would consent to sell me on any terms. He had an iron will and was determined to keep me, and to conquer me. My lover was an intelligent and religious man. Even if he could have obtained permission to marry me while I was a slave, the marriage would give him no power to protect me from my master. It would have made him miserable to witness the insults I should have been subjected to. And then, if we had children, I knew they must follow the condition of the mother. What a terrible blight that would be on the heart of a free, intelligent father. For his sake, I felt that I ought not to link his fate with my own unhappy destiny. He was going to Savannah to see about a little property left him by an uncle, and hard as it was to bring my feelings to it, I earnestly entreated him not to come back. I advised him to go to the Free States, where his tongue would not be tied, and where his intelligence would be of more avail to him. He left me, still hoping the day would come when I could be bought. With me the lamp of hope had gone out. The dream of my girlhood was over. I felt lonely and desolate.

Still I was not stripped of all. I still had my good grandmother, and my affectionate brother. When he put his arms round my neck and looked into my eyes, as if to read there the troubles I dared not tell, I felt that I still had something to love. But even that pleasant emotion was chilled by the reflection that he might be torn from me at any moment, by some sudden freak of my master. If he had known how we loved each other, I think he would have exulted in separating us. We often planned together how we could get to the North. But, as William remarked, such things are easier said than done. My movements were very closely watched, and we had no means of getting any money to defray our expenses. As for grandmother, she was strongly opposed to her children's undertaking any such project. She had not forgotten poor Benjamin's sufferings, and she was afraid that if another child tried to escape, he would have a similar or a worse fate To me, nothing seemed more dreadful than my present life. I said to myself, "William must be free. He shall go to the North, and I will follow him." Many a slave sister has formed the same plans.

Slaveholders pride themselves upon being honorable men, but if you were to hear the enormous lies they tell their slaves, you would have small respect for their veracity. I have spoken plain English. Pardon me. I cannot use a milder term. When they visit the North and return home, they tell their slaves of the runaways they have seen, and describe them to be in the most deplorable condition. A slaveholder once told me that he had seen a runaway friend of mine in New York, and that she besought him to take her back to her master, for she was literally dying of starvation, that many days she had only one cold potato to eat, and at other times could get nothing at all. He said he refused to take her, because he knew her master would not thank him for bringing such a miserable wretch to his house. He ended by saying to me, "This is the punishment she brought on herself for running away from a kind master."

This whole story was false. I afterwards stayed with that friend in New York, and found her in comfortable circumstances. She had never thought of such a thing as wishing to go back to slavery. Many of the slaves believe such stories, and think it is not worthwhile to exchange slavery for such a hard kind of freedom. It is difficult to persuade such that freedom could make them useful men, and enable them to protect their wives and children. If those heathens in our Christian land had as much teaching as some Hindus, they would think otherwise. They would know that liberty is more valuable than life. They would begin to understand their own capabilities, and exert themselves to become men and women.

But while the Free States sustain a law which hurls fugitives back into slavery, how can the slaves resolve to become men? There are some who strive to protect wives and daughters from the insults of their masters, but those who have such sentiments have had advantages above the general mass of slaves. They have been partially civilized and Christianized by favorable circumstances. Some are bold enough to utter such sentiments to their masters. Oh, that there were more of them.

Some poor creatures have been so brutalized by the lash that they will sneak out of the way to give their masters free access to their wives and daughters. Do you think this proves the black man to belong to an inferior order of beings? What would you be, if you had been born and brought up a slave, with generations of slaves for ancestors? What makes the black man inferior is the ignorance in which white men compel him to live, it is the torturing whip that lashes manhood out of him, it is the fierce bloodhounds of the South, and the scarcely less cruel human bloodhounds of the North, who enforce the Fugitive Slave Law.

Southern gentlemen indulge in the most contemptuous expressions about the Yankees, while they, on their part, consent to do the vilest work for them, such as the ferocious bloodhounds and the despised negro-hunters are employed to do at home. When Southerners go to the North, they are proud to do them honor, but the northern man is not welcome south of Mason and Dixon's line, unless he suppresses every thought and feeling at variance with their peculiar institution. Nor is it enough to be silent. The masters are not pleased, unless they obtain a greater degree of subservience than that, and they are generally accommodated. Do they respect the northerner for this? I believe not. Even the slaves despise a northern man with Southern principles, and that is the class they generally see. When northerners go to the South to reside, they prove very apt scholars. They soon imbibe the sentiments and disposition of their neighbors, and generally go beyond their teachers. Of the two, they are proverbially the hardest masters.

They seem to satisfy their consciences with the doctrine that God created the Africans to be slaves. What a libel upon the heavenly Father, who *made of one blood all nations of men.* And then who are Africans? Who can measure the amount of Anglo-Saxon blood coursing in the veins of American slaves?

I have spoken of the pains slaveholders take to give their slaves a bad opinion of the North, notwithstanding this, intelligent slaves are aware that they have many friends in the Free States. Even the most ignorant have some confused notions about it. They knew that I could read, and I was often asked if I had seen anything in the newspapers about white folks over in the big North, who were trying to get their freedom for them. Some believe that the abolitionists have already made them free, and that it is established by law, but that their masters prevent the law from going into effect. One woman begged me to get a newspaper and read it over. She said her husband told her that the black people had sent word to "the queen of 'Merica" that they were all slaves, that she didn't believe it, and went to Washington city to see the president about it. They quarreled, she drew her sword upon him, and swore that he should help her to make them all free.

That poor, ignorant woman thought that America was governed by a queen, to whom the President was subordinate. I wish the President was subordinate to Queen Justice.

There was a planter in the country, not far from us, whom I will call Mr. Fitch. He was an ill-bred, uneducated man, but very wealthy. He had six hundred slaves, many of whom he did not know by sight. His extensive plantation was managed by well-paid overseers. There was a jail and a whipping post on his grounds, and whatever cruelties were perpetrated there, they passed without comment. He was so effectually screened by his great wealth that he was called to no account for his crimes, not even for murder.

Various were the punishments resorted to. A favorite one was to tie a rope round a man's body, and suspend him from the ground. A fire was kindled over him, from which was suspended a piece of fat pork. As this cooked, the scalding drops of fat continually fell on the bare flesh. On his own plantation, he required very strict obedience to the eighth commandment. But depredations on the neighbors were allowable, provided the culprit managed to evade detection or suspicion. If a neighbor brought a charge of theft against any of his slaves, he was browbeaten by the master, who assured him that his slaves had enough of everything at home, and had no inducement to steal. No sooner was the neighbor's back turned, than the accused was sought out and whipped for his lack of discretion. If a slave stole from him even a pound of meat or a peck of corn, if detection followed, he was put in chains and imprisoned, and so kept till his form was attenuated by hunger and suffering.

A flood once bore his wine cellar and meat house miles away from the plantation. Some slaves followed, and secured bits of meat and bottles of wine. Two were detected, a ham and some liquor being found in their huts. They were summoned by their master.

No words were used, but a club felled them to the ground. A rough box was their coffin, and their interment was a dog's burial.

Nothing was said. Murder was so common on his plantation that he feared to be alone after nightfall. He might have believed in ghosts.

His brother, if not equal in wealth, was at least equal in cruelty. His bloodhounds were well trained. Their pen was spacious, and a terror to the slaves. They were let loose on a runaway and, if they tracked him, they literally tore the flesh from his bones. When this slaveholder died, his shrieks and groans were so frightful that they appalled his own friends. His last words were, "I am going to hell, bury my money with me."

After death his eyes remained open. To press the lids down, silver dollars were laid on them. These were buried with him. From this circumstance, a rumor went abroad that his coffin was filled with money. Three times his grave was opened, and his coffin taken out. The last time, his body was found on the ground, and a flock of buzzards were pecking at it. He was again interred and a sentinel set over his grave. The perpetrators were never discovered.

Cruelty is contagious in uncivilized communities. Mr. Conant, a neighbor of Mr. Litch, returned from town one evening in a partial state of intoxication. His body servant gave him some offense. He was divested of his clothes, except his shirt, whipped and tied to a large tree in front of the house. It was a stormy night in winter. The wind blew bitterly cold, and the boughs of the old tree crackled under falling sleet. A member of the family, fearing he would freeze to death, begged that he might be taken down, but the master would not relent. He remained there three hours and, when he was cut down, he was more dead than alive. Another slave, who stole a pig from this master, to appease his hunger, was terribly flogged. In desperation, he tried to run away. But at the end of two miles, he was so faint with loss of blood, he thought he was dying. He had a wife, and he longed to see her once more. Too sick to walk, he crept back that long distance on his hands and knees. When he reached his master's, it was night. He had not strength to rise and open the gate. He moaned, and tried to call for help. I had a friend living in the same family. At last his cry reached her. She went out and found the prostrate man at the gate. She ran back to the house for assistance, and two men returned with her. They carried him in, and laid him on the floor. The back of his shirt was one clot of blood. By means of lard, my friend loosened it from the raw flesh. She bandaged him, gave him cool drink, and left him to rest. The master said he deserved a hundred more lashes. When his own labor was stolen from him, he had stolen food to appease his hunger. This was his crime.

Another neighbor was a Mrs. Wade. At no hour of the day was there cessation of the lash on her premises. Her labors began with the dawn, and did not cease till long after nightfall. The barn was her particular place of torture. There she lashed the slaves with the might of a man. An old slave of hers once said to me, "It is hell in missis's house. 'Pears I can never get out. Day and night I prays to."

The mistress died before the old woman and, when dying, entreated her husband not to permit anyone of her slaves to look on her after death. A slave who had nursed her children, and had still a child in her care, watched her chance, and stole with it in her arms to the room where lay her dead mistress. She gazed a while on her, then raised her hand and dealt two blows on her face, saying, as she did so, "The devil has got you now."

She forgot that the child was looking on. She had just begun to talk, and she said to her father, "I did see ma, and mammy did strike ma, so," striking her own face with her little hand.

The master was startled. He could not imagine how the nurse could obtain access to the room where the corpse lay, for he kept the door locked. He questioned her. She confessed that what the child had said was true, and told how she had procured the key.

She was sold to Georgia.

In my childhood I knew a valuable slave named Charity, and loved her, as all children did. Her young mistress married and took her to Louisiana. Her little boy, James, was sold to a good sort of master. He became involved in debt, and James was sold again to a wealthy slaveholder, noted for his cruelty. With this man he grew up to manhood, receiving the treatment of a dog. After a severe whipping, to save himself from further infliction of the lash, with which he was threatened, James took to the woods. He was in a most miserable condition, cut by the cowskin, half-naked, half-starved and without the means of procuring a crust of bread.

Some weeks after his escape, he was captured, tied, and carried back to his master's plantation. This man considered punishment in his jail, on bread and water, after receiving hundreds of lashes, too mild for the poor slave's offense. Therefore he decided, after the overseer should have whipped him to his satisfaction, to have him placed between the screws of the cotton gin, to stay as long as he had been in the woods. This wretched creature was cut with the whip from his head to his feet, then washed with strong brine to prevent the flesh from mortifying, and make it heal sooner than it otherwise would. He was then put into the cotton gin, which was screwed down, only allowing him room to turn on his side when he could not lie on his back. Every morning a slave was sent with a piece of bread and bowl of water, which were placed within reach of the poor fellow. The slave was charged, under penalty of severe punishment, not to speak to him.

Four days passed, and the slave continued to carry the bread and water. On the second morning, he found the bread gone, but the water untouched. When he had been in the press four days and five nights, the slave informed his master that the water had not been used for four mornings, and that a horrible stench came from the gin house. The overseer was sent to examine into it. When the press was unscrewed, the dead body was found partly eaten by rats and vermin. Perhaps the rats that devoured his bread had gnawed him before life was extinct.

Poor Charity. Grandmother and I often asked each other how her affectionate heart would bear the news, if she should ever hear of the murder of her son. We had known her husband, and knew that James was like him in manliness and intelligence. These were the qualities that made it so hard for him to be a plantation slave. They put him into a rough box and buried him with less feeling than would have been manifested for an old house dog. Nobody asked any questions. He was a slave, and the feeling was that the master had a right to do what he pleased with his own property. And what did he care for the value of a slave? He had hundreds of them.

When they had finished their daily toil, they must hurry to eat their little morsels and be ready to extinguish their pine knots before nine o'clock, when the overseer went his patrol rounds. He entered every cabin, to see that men and their wives had gone to bed together, lest the men, from fatigue, should fall asleep in the chimney corner and remain there till the morning horn called them to their daily task. Women are considered of no value, unless they continually increase their owner's stock. They are put on a par with animals. This same master shot a woman through the head, who had run away and been brought back to him. No one called him to account for it. If a slave resisted being whipped, the bloodhounds were unpacked and set upon him to tear his flesh from his bones. The master who did these things was highly educated, and styled a perfect gentleman. He also boasted the name and standing of a Christian, though Satan never had a truer follower.

I could tell of more slaveholders as cruel as those I have described. They are not exceptions to the general rule. I do not say there are no humane slaveholders. Such characters exist notwithstanding the hardening influences around them. But they are like angels' visits — few and far between."

I knew a young lady who was one of these rare specimens. She was an orphan, and inherited as slaves a woman and her six children. Their father was a free man. They had a comfortable home of their own, parents and children living together. The mother and eldest daughter served their mistress during the day and at night returned to their dwelling, which was on the premises. The young lady was very pious, and there was some reality in her religion. She taught her slaves to lead pure lives, and wished them to enjoy the fruit of their own industry. Her religion was not a garb put on for Sunday, and laid aside till Sunday returned again. The eldest daughter of the slave mother was promised in marriage to a free man, and the day before the wedding this good mistress emancipated her, in order that her marriage might have the sanction of law.

Report said that this young lady cherished an unrequited affection for a man who had resolved to marry for wealth. In the course of time a rich uncle of hers died. He left six thousand dollars to his two sons by a colored woman, and the remainder of his property to this orphan niece. The metal soon attracted the magnet. The lady and her weighty purse became his. She offered to manumit her slaves — telling them that her marriage might make unexpected changes in their destiny, and she wished to insure their happiness. They refused to take their freedom, saying that she had always been their best friend and they could not be so happy anywhere as with her. I was not surprised. I had often seen them in their comfortable home, and thought that the whole town did not contain a happier family. They had never felt slavery and, when it was too late, they were convinced of its reality.

When the new master claimed this family as his property, the father became furious, and went to his mistress for protection.

"I can do nothing for you now, Harry," said she. "I no longer have the power I had a week ago. I have succeeded in obtaining the freedom of your wife, but I cannot obtain it for your children."

The unhappy father swore that nobody should take his children from him. He concealed them in the woods for some days, but they were discovered and taken. The father was put in jail, and the two oldest boys sold to Georgia. One little girl, too young to be of service to her master, was left with the wretched mother. The other three were carried to their master's plantation.

The eldest soon became a mother and, when the slaveholder's wife looked at the babe, she wept bitterly. She knew that her own husband had violated the purity she had so carefully inculcated. She had a second child by her master, and then he sold her and his offspring to his brother. She bore two children to the brother, and was sold again.

The next sister went crazy. The life she was compelled to lead drove her mad.

The third one became the mother of five daughters. Before the birth of the fourth the pious mistress died. To the last, she rendered every kindness to the slaves that her unfortunate circumstances permitted. She passed away peacefully, glad to close her eyes on a life which had been made so wretched by the man she loved.

This man squandered the fortune he had received, and sought to retrieve his affairs by a second marriage but, having retired after a night of drunken debauch, he was found dead in the morning. He was called a good master, for he fed and clothed his slaves better than most masters, and the lash was not heard on his plantation so frequently as on many others. Had it not been for slavery, he would have been a better man, and his wife a happier woman.

No pen can give an adequate description of the all-pervading corruption produced by slavery. The slave girl is reared in an atmosphere of licentiousness and fear. The lash and the foul talk of her master and his sons are her teachers. When she is fourteen or fifteen, her owner, or his sons, or the overseer, or perhaps all of them, begin to bribe her with presents. If these fail to accomplish their purpose, she is whipped or starved into submission to their will. She may have had religious principles inculcated by some pious mother or grandmother, or some good mistress, she may have a lover, whose good opinion and peace of mind are dear to her heart, or the profligate men who have power over her may be exceedingly odious to her. But resistance is hopeless.

> *The poor worm*
> *Shall prove her contest vain. Life's little day*
> *Shall pass, and she is gone.*

The slaveholder's sons are of course vitiated, even while boys, by the unclean influences everywhere around them. Nor do the master's daughters always escape. Severe retributions sometimes come upon him for the wrongs he does to the daughters of the slaves. The white daughters early hear their parents quarreling about some female slave. Their curiosity is excited, and they soon learn the cause. They are attended by the young slave girls whom their father has corrupted, and they hear such talk as should never meet youthful ears, or any other ears. They know that the women slaves are subject to their father's authority in all things, and in some cases they exercise the same authority over the men slaves. I have myself seen the master of such a household whose head was bowed down in shame, for it was known in the neighborhood that his daughter had selected one of the meanest slaves on his plantation to be the father of his first grandchild. She did not make her advances to her equals, nor even to her father's more intelligent servants. She selected the most brutalized, over whom her authority could be exercised with less fear of exposure. Her father, half-frantic with rage, sought to revenge himself on the offending black man, but his daughter, foreseeing the storm that would arise, had given him free papers, and sent him out of the State.

In such cases the infant is smothered, or sent where it is never seen by any who know its history. But if the white parent is the father, the offspring are unblushingly reared for the market. If they are girls, I have indicated plainly enough what will be their inevitable destiny.

You may believe what I say, for I write only that whereof I know. I was twenty-one years in that cage of obscene birds. I can testify, from my own experience and observation, that slavery is a curse to the whites as well as to the blacks. It makes the white fathers cruel and sensual, the sons violent and licentious, it contaminates the daughters, and makes the wives wretched. And as for the colored race, it needs an abler pen than mine to describe the extremity of their sufferings, the depth of their degradation.

Yet few slaveholders seem to be aware of the widespread

moral ruin occasioned by this wicked system. Their talk is of blighted cotton crops, not of the blight on their children's souls.

If you want to be fully convinced of the abominations of slavery, go on a Southern plantation, and call yourself a negro trader. Then there will be no concealment, and you will see and hear things that will seem to you impossible among human beings with immortal souls.

After my lover went away, Dr. Flint contrived a new plan. He seemed to have an idea that my fear of my mistress was his greatest obstacle. In the blandest tones, he told me that he was going to build a small house for me, in a secluded place, four miles away from the town. I shuddered, but I was constrained to listen, while he talked of his intention to give me a home of my own, and to make a lady of me. Hitherto, I had escaped my dreaded fate by being in the midst of people. My grandmother had already had high words with my master about me. She had told him pretty plainly what she thought of his character, and there was considerable gossip in the neighborhood about our affairs, to which the open-mouthed jealousy of Mrs. Flint contributed not a little. When my master said he was going to build a house for me, and that he could do it with little trouble and expense, I was in hope that something would happen to frustrate his scheme, but I soon heard that the house was actually begun. I vowed before my Maker that I would never enter it. I would rather toil on the plantation from dawn till dark, rather live and die in jail than drag on, from day to day, through such a living death. I was determined that the master, whom I so hated and loathed, who had blighted the prospects of my youth, and made my life a desert, should not, after my long struggle with him, succeed at last in trampling his victim under his feet. I would do anything, everything, for the sake of defeating him. What could I do? I thought and thought, till I became desperate, and made a plunge into the abyss.

And now, reader, I come to a period in my unhappy life,

which I would gladly forget if I could. The remembrance fills me with sorrow and shame. It pains me to tell you of it, but I have promised to tell you the truth, and I will do it honestly, let it cost me what it may. I will not try to screen myself behind the plea of compulsion from a master, for it was not so. Neither can I plead ignorance or thoughtlessness. For years, my master had done his utmost to pollute my mind with foul images, and to destroy the pure principles inculcated by my grandmother, and the good mistress of my childhood. The influences of slavery had had the same effect on me that they had on other young girls, they had made me prematurely knowing, concerning the evil ways of the world. I knew what I did, and I did it with deliberate calculation.

But, oh, ye happy women, whose purity has been sheltered from childhood, who have been free to choose the objects of your affection, whose homes are protected by law, do not judge the poor desolate slave girl too severely. If slavery had been abolished, I, also, could have married the man of my choice. I could have had a home shielded by the laws, and I should have been spared the painful task of confessing what I am now about to relate, but all my prospects had been blighted by slavery. I wanted to keep myself pure and, under the most adverse circumstances, I tried hard to preserve my self-respect, but I was struggling alone in the powerful grasp of the demon slavery, and the monster proved too strong for me. I felt as if I was forsaken by God and man, as if all my efforts must be frustrated, and I became reckless in my despair.

I have told you that Dr. Flint's persecutions and his wife's jealousy had given rise to some gossip in the neighborhood. Among others, it chanced that a white unmarried gentleman had obtained some knowledge of the circumstances in which I was placed. He knew my grandmother, and often spoke to me in the street. He became interested in me, and asked questions about my master, which I answered in part. He expressed a great deal of sympathy, and a wish to aid me. He constantly sought opportunities to see me, and wrote to me frequently. I was a poor slave girl, only fifteen years old.

So much attention from a superior person was, of course, flattering, for human nature is the same in all. I also felt grateful for his sympathy, and encouraged by his kind words. It seemed to me a great thing to have such a friend. By degrees, a more tender feeling crept into my heart. He was an educated and eloquent gentleman, too eloquent, alas, for the poor slave girl who trusted in him. Of course I saw whither all this was tending. I knew the impassable gulf between us, but to be an object of interest to a man who is not married, and who is not her master, is agreeable to the pride and feelings of a slave, if her miserable situation has left her any pride or sentiment. It seems less degrading to give one's self, than to submit to compulsion. There is something akin to freedom in having a lover who has no control over you, except that which he gains by kindness and attachment. A master may treat you as rudely as he pleases, and you dare not speak, moreover, the wrong does not seem so great with an unmarried man, as with one who has a wife to be made unhappy. There may be sophistry in all this, but the condition of a slave confuses all principles of morality and, in fact, renders the practice of them impossible.

When I found that my master had actually begun to build the lonely cottage, other feelings mixed with those I have described. Revenge, and calculations of interest, were added to flattered vanity and sincere gratitude for kindness. I knew nothing would enrage Dr. Flint so much as to know that I favored another, and it was something to triumph over my tyrant even in that small way. I thought he would revenge himself by selling me, and I was sure my friend, Mr. Sands, would buy me. He was a man of more generosity and feeling than my master, and I thought my freedom could be easily obtained from him. The crisis of my fate now came so near that

I was desperate. I shuddered to think of being the mother of children that should be owned by my old tyrant. I knew that as soon as a new fancy took him, his victims were sold far off to get rid of them, especially if they had children. I had seen several women sold, with his babies at the breast. He never allowed his offspring by slaves to remain long in sight of himself and his wife. Of a man who was not my master I could ask to have my children well supported, and in this case, I felt confident I should obtain the boon. I also felt quite sure that they would be made free. With all these thoughts revolving in my mind, and seeing no other way of escaping the doom I so much dreaded, I made a headlong plunge.

Pity me, and pardon me, O virtuous reader. You never knew what it is to be a slave, to be entirely unprotected by law or custom, to have the laws reduce you to the condition of a chattel, entirely subject to the will of another. You never exhausted your ingenuity in avoiding the snares, and eluding the power of a hated tyrant, you never shuddered at the sound of his footsteps, and trembled within hearing of his voice. I know I did wrong. No one can feel it more sensibly than I do. The painful and humiliating memory will haunt me to my dying day. Still, in looking back, calmly, on the events of my life, I feel that the slave woman ought not to be judged by the same standard as others.

The months passed on. I had many unhappy hours. I secretly mourned over the sorrow I was bringing on my grandmother, who had so tried to shield me from harm. I knew that I was the greatest comfort of her old age, and that it was a source of pride to her that I had not degraded myself, like most of the slaves. I wanted to confess to her that I was no longer worthy of her love, but could not utter the dreaded words.

As for Dr. Flint, I had a feeling of satisfaction and triumph in the thought of telling him. From time to time he told me of his intended arrangements, and I was silent. At last, he came and told me the cottage was completed, and ordered me to go to it. I told him I would never enter it. He said, "I have heard enough of such talk as that. You shall go, if you are carried by force, and you shall remain there."

I replied, "I will never go there. In a few months I shall be a mother."

He stood and looked at me in dumb amazement, and left the house without a word. I thought I should be happy in my triumph over him. But now that the truth was out, and my relatives would hear of it, I felt wretched. Humble as were their circumstances, they had pride in my good character. Now, how could I look them in the face. My self-respect was gone. I had resolved that I would be virtuous, though I was a slave. I had said, "Let the storm beat. I will brave it till I die."

And now, how humiliated I felt.

I went to my grandmother. My lips moved to make confession, but the words stuck in my throat. I sat down in the shade of a tree at her door and began to sew. I think she saw something unusual was the matter with me. The mother of slaves is very watchful. She knows there is no security for her children. After they have entered their teens she lives in daily expectation of trouble. This leads to many questions. If the girl is of a sensitive nature, timidity keeps her from answering truthfully, and this well-meant course has a tendency to drive her from maternal counsels.

Presently, in came my mistress, like a mad woman, and accused me concerning her husband. My grandmother, whose suspicions had been previously awakened, believed what she said. She exclaimed, "Linda. Has it come to this? I had rather see you dead than to see you as you now are. You are a disgrace to your dead mother."

She tore from my fingers my mother's wedding ring and her silver thimble.

"Go away," she exclaimed, "and never come to my house

again."

Her reproaches fell so hot and heavy, that they left me no chance to answer. Bitter tears, such as the eyes never shed but once, were my only answer. I rose from my seat, but fell back again, sobbing. She did not speak to me, but the tears were running down her furrowed cheeks, and they scorched me like fire. She had always been so kind to me. So kind. How I longed to throw myself at her feet, and tell her all the truth. But she had ordered me to go, and never to come there again. After a few minutes, I mustered strength, and started to obey her. With what feelings did I now close that little gate, which I used to open with such an eager hand in my childhood. It closed upon me with a sound I never heard before.

Where could I go? I was afraid to return to my master's. I walked on recklessly, not caring where I went, or what would become of me. When I had gone four or five miles, fatigue compelled me to stop. I sat down on the stump of an old tree. The stars were shining through the boughs above me. How they mocked me, with their bright, calm light. The hours passed by, and as I sat there alone a chilliness and deadly sickness came over me. I sank on the ground. My mind was full of horrid thoughts. I prayed to die, but the prayer was not answered. At last, with great effort I roused myself, and walked some distance further, to the house of a woman who had been a friend of my mother. When I told her why I was there, she spoke soothingly to me, but I could not be comforted. I thought I could bear my shame if I could only be reconciled to my grandmother. I longed to open my heart to her. I thought if she could know the real state of the case, and all I had been bearing for years, she would perhaps judge me less harshly. My friend advised me to send for her. I did so, but days of agonizing suspense passed before she came. Had she utterly forsaken me? No. She came at last. I knelt before her, and told her things that had poisoned my life, how long I had been persecuted, that I saw no way of escape, and in an hour of extremity I had become desperate. She listened in silence. I told her I would bear anything and do anything, if in time I had hopes of obtaining her forgiveness. I begged of her to pity me, for my dead mother's sake. And she did pity me. She did not say, "I forgive you," but she looked at me lovingly, with her eyes full of tears. She laid her old hand gently on my head, and murmured, "Poor child. Poor child."

I returned to my good grandmother's house. She had an interview with Mr. Sands. When she asked him why he could have left her one ewe lamb — whether there were not plenty of slaves who did not care about character — he made no answer, but he spoke kind and encouraging words. He promised to care for my child, and to buy me, be the conditions what they might.

I had not seen Dr. Flint for five days. I had never seen him since I made the avowal to him. He talked of the disgrace I had brought on myself, how I had sinned against my master, and mortified my old grandmother. He intimated that if I had accepted his proposals, he, as a physician, could have saved me from exposure. He even condescended to pity me. Could he have offered wormwood more bitter? He, whose persecutions had been the cause of my sin.

"Linda," said he, "though you have been criminal towards me I feel for you, and I can pardon you if you obey my wishes. Tell me whether the fellow you wanted to marry is the father of your child. If you deceive me, you shall feel the fires of hell."

I did not feel as proud as I had done. My strongest weapon with him was gone. I was lowered in my own estimation, and had resolved to bear his abuse in silence. But when he spoke contemptuously of the lover who had always treated me honorably, when I remembered that but for him I might have been a virtuous, free, and happy wife, I lost my patience.

"I have sinned against God and myself," I replied, "but not against you."

He clinched his teeth, and muttered, "Curse you." He came towards me, with ill-suppressed rage, and exclaimed, "You obstinate girl. I could grind your bones to powder. You have thrown yourself away on some worthless rascal. You are weak-minded and have been easily persuaded by those who don't care a straw for you. The future will settle accounts between us. You are blinded now, but hereafter you will be convinced that your master was your best friend. My lenity towards you is a proof of it. I might have punished you in many ways. I might have had you whipped till you fell dead under the lash. But I wanted you to live, I would have bettered your condition. Others cannot do it. You are my slave. Your mistress, disgusted by your conduct, forbids you to return to the house, therefore I leave you here for the present, but I shall see you often. I will call tomorrow."

He came with frowning brows, that showed a dissatisfied state of mind. After asking about my health, he inquired whether my board was paid, and who visited me. He then went on to say that he had neglected his duty, that as a physician there were certain things that he ought to have explained to me. Then followed talk such as would have made the most shameless blush. He ordered me to stand up before him. I obeyed.

"I command you," said he, "to tell me whether the father of your child is white or black."

I hesitated.

"Answer me this instant," he exclaimed.

I did answer. He sprang upon me like a wolf, and grabbed my arm as if he would have broken it.

"Do you love him?" said he, in a hissing tone.

"I am thankful that I do not despise him," I replied.

He raised his hand to strike me, but it fell again. I don't know what arrested the blow. He sat down, with lips tightly compressed.

At last he spoke.

"I came here," said he, "to make you a friendly proposition, but your ingratitude chafes me beyond endurance. You turn aside all my good intentions towards you. I don't know what it is that keeps me from killing you."

Again he rose, as if he had a mind to strike me.

But he resumed. "On one condition I will forgive your insolence and crime. You must henceforth have no communication of any kind with the father of your child. You must not ask anything from him, or receive anything from him. I will take care of you and your child. You had better promise this at once, and not wait till you are deserted by him. This is the last act of mercy I shall show towards you."

I said something about being unwilling to have my child supported by a man who had cursed it and me also. He rejoined, that a woman who had sunk to my level had no right to expect anything else. He asked, for the last time, would I accept his kindness? I answered that I would not.

"Very well," said he, "then take the consequences of your wayward course. Never look to me for help. You are my slave, and shall always be my slave. I will never sell you, that you may depend upon."

Hope died away in my heart as he closed the door after him. I had calculated that in his rage he would sell me to a slave-trader, and I knew the father of my child was on the watch to buy me.

About this time my uncle Phillip was expected to return from a voyage. The day before his departure I had officiated as bridesmaid to a young friend. My heart was then ill at ease, but my smiling countenance did not betray it. Only a year had passed, but what fearful changes it had wrought. My heart had grown gray in misery. Lives that flash in sunshine, and lives that are born in tears, receive their hue from circumstances. None of us know what a year may bring forth.

I felt no joy when they told me my uncle had come. He wanted to see me, though he knew what had happened. I shrank from him at first, but at last consented that he should come to my room. He received me as he always had done. Oh, how my heart smote me when I felt his tears on my burning cheeks. The words of my grandmother came to my mind: "Perhaps your mother and father are taken from the evil days to come."

My disappointed heart could now praise God that it was so. But why, thought I, did my relatives ever cherish hopes for me? What was there to save me from the usual fate of slave girls? Many more beautiful and more intelligent than I had experienced a similar fate, or a far worse one. How could they hope that I should escape?

My uncle's stay was short, and I was not sorry for it. I was too ill in mind and body to enjoy my friends as I had done.

For some weeks I was unable to leave my bed. I could not have any doctor but my master, and I would not have him sent for. At last, alarmed by my increasing illness, they sent for him. I was very weak and nervous, and as soon as he entered the room, I began to scream. They told him my state was very critical. He had no wish to hasten me out of the world, and he withdrew.

When my babe was born, they said it was premature. It weighed only four pounds, but God let it live. I heard the doctor say I could not survive till morning. I had often prayed for death, but now I did not want to die, unless my child could die too. Many weeks passed before I was able to leave my bed. I was a mere wreck of my former self. For a year there was scarcely a day when I was free from chills and fever. My babe also was sickly. His little limbs were often racked with pain. Dr. Flint continued his visits, to look after my health, and he did not fail to remind me that my child was an addition to his stock of slaves.

I felt too feeble to dispute with him, and listened to his remarks in silence. His visits were less frequent, but his busy spirit could not remain quiet. He employed my brother in his office, and he was made the medium of frequent notes and messages to me. William was a bright lad, and of much use to the doctor. He had learned to put up medicines, to leech, cup, and bleed. He had taught himself to read and spell. I was proud of my brother, and the old doctor suspected as much. One day, when I had not seen him for several weeks, I heard his steps approaching the door. I dreaded the encounter, and hid myself. He inquired for me, of course, but I was nowhere to be found. He went to his office, and despatched William with a note.

The color mounted to my brother's face when he gave it to me, and he said, "Don't you hate me, Linda, for bringing you these things?" I told him I could not blame him, he was a slave, and obliged to obey his master's will.

The note ordered me to come to his office. I went. He demanded to know where I was when he called. I told him I was at home. He flew into a passion and said he knew better. Then he launched out upon his usual themes — my crimes against him, and my ingratitude for his forbearance. The laws were laid down to me anew, and I was dismissed.

I felt humiliated that my brother should stand by and listen to such language as would be addressed only to a slave. Poor boy. He was powerless to defend me, but I saw the tears, which he vainly strove to keep back. This manifestation of feeling irritated the doctor. William could do nothing to please him. One morning he did not arrive at the office so early as usual, and that circumstance afforded his master an opportunity to vent his spleen. He was put in jail. The next day my brother sent a trader to the doctor with a request to be sold. His master was greatly incensed at what he called his insolence. He said he had put him there to reflect upon his bad conduct, and he certainly was not giving any evidence of repentance. For two days he harassed himself to find somebody to do his office work, but everything went wrong without William. He was released, and ordered to take his old stand, with many threats, if he was not careful about his future behavior.

As the months passed on, my boy improved in health. When he was a year old, they called him beautiful. The little vine was taking deep root in my existence, though its clinging fondness excited a mixture of love and pain. When I was most sorely oppressed I found a solace in his smiles. I loved to watch his infant slumbers, but always there was a dark cloud over my enjoyment. I could never forget that he was a slave. Sometimes I wished that he might die in infancy. God tried me. My darling became very ill. The bright eyes grew dull, and the little feet and hands were so icy cold that I thought death had already touched them. I had prayed for his death, but never so earnestly as I now prayed for his life.

My prayer was heard. Alas, what mockery it is for a slave mother to try to pray back her dying child to life. Death is better than slavery. It was a sad thought that I had no name to give my child. His father caressed him and treated him kindly whenever he had a chance to see him. He was not unwilling that he should bear his name, but he had no legal claim to it, and if I had bestowed it upon him, my master would have regarded it as a new crime, a new piece of insolence, and would, perhaps, revenge it on the boy. Oh, the serpent of slavery has many and poisonous fangs.

Not far from this time Nat Turner's insurrection broke out, and the news threw our town into great commotion. Strange that they should be alarmed, when their slaves were 'so contented and happy'. But so it was.

It was always the custom to have a muster every year. On that occasion every white man shouldered his musket. The citizens and the so-called country gentlemen wore military uniforms. The poor whites took their places in the ranks in everyday dress, some without shoes, some without hats. This grand occasion had already passed, and when the slaves were told there was to be another muster, they were surprised and rejoiced. Poor creatures. They thought it was going to be a holiday. I was informed of the true state of affairs, and imparted it to the few I could trust. Most gladly would I have proclaimed it to every slave, but I dared not. All could not be relied on. Mighty is the power of the torturing lash.

By sunrise, people were pouring in from every quarter within twenty miles of the town. I knew the houses were to be searched, and I expected it would be done by country bullies and the poor whites. I knew nothing annoyed them so much as to see colored people living in comfort and respectability, so I made arrangements for them with especial care. I arranged everything in my grandmother's house as neatly as possible. I put white quilts on the beds and decorated some of the rooms with flowers. When all was arranged, I sat down at the window to watch. Far as my eye could reach, it rested on a motley crowd of soldiers. Drums and fifes were discoursing martial music. The men were divided into companies of sixteen, each headed by a captain. Orders were given and the wild scouts rushed in every direction, wherever a colored face was to be found.

It was a grand opportunity for the low whites, who had no negroes of their own, to scourge. They exulted in such a chance to exercise a little brief authority and show their subserviency to the slaveholders, not reflecting that the power which trampled on the colored people also kept themselves in poverty, ignorance and moral degradation.

Those who never witnessed such scenes can hardly believe what I know was inflicted at this time on innocent men, women, and children, against whom there was not the slightest ground for suspicion. Colored people and slaves who lived in remote parts of the town suffered in an especial manner. In some cases the searchers scattered powder and shot among their clothes, and then sent other parties to find them, and bring them forward as proof that they were plotting insurrection. Everywhere men, women and children were whipped till the blood stood in puddles at their feet. Some received five hundred lashes, others were tied hands and feet, and tortured with a bucking paddle, which blisters the skin terribly. The dwellings of the colored people, unless they happened to be protected by some influential white person, who was nigh at hand, were robbed of clothing and everything else the marauders thought worth carrying away. All day long these unfeeling wretches went round, like a troop of demons, terrifying and tormenting the helpless. At night, they formed themselves into patrol bands and went wherever they chose among the colored people, acting out their brutal will. Many women hid themselves in woods and swamps to keep out of their way. If any of the husbands or fathers told of these outrages, they were tied up to the public whipping post and cruelly scourged for telling lies about white men. The consternation was universal. No two people that had the slightest tinge of color in their faces dared to be seen talking together.

I entertained no positive fears about our household, because we were in the midst of white families who would protect us. We were ready to receive the soldiers whenever they came. It was not long before we heard the tramp of feet and the sound of voices. The door was rudely pushed open, and in they tumbled, like a pack of hungry wolves. They snatched at everything within their reach. Every box, trunk, closet and corner underwent a thorough examination. A box in one of the drawers containing some silver change was eagerly pounced upon. When I stepped forward to take it from them, one of the soldiers turned and said angrily, "What are you following us, for? D'you s'pose white folks is come to steal?"

I replied, "You have come to search, but you have searched that box, and I will take it, if you please."

At that moment I saw a white gentleman who was friendly to us, and I called to him and asked him to have the goodness to come in and stay till the search was over. He readily complied. His entrance into the house brought in the captain of the company, whose business it was to guard the outside of the house and see that none of the inmates left it. This officer was Mr. Litch, the wealthy slaveholder whom I mentioned in the account of neighboring planters, as being notorious for his cruelty. He felt above soiling his hands with the search. He merely gave orders and, if a bit of writing was discovered, it was carried to him by his ignorant followers, who were unable to read.

My grandmother had a large trunk of bedding and tablecloths. When that was opened, there was a great shout of surprise, and one exclaimed, "Where'd the damned niggers git all this sheet an' tablecloth?"

My grandmother, emboldened by the presence of our white protector, said, "You may be sure we didn't pilfer 'em from your houses."

"Look here, mammy," said a grim-looking fellow without any coat, "you seem to feel mighty gran' 'cause you got all them 'ere fixens. White folks oughta have 'em all."

His remarks were interrupted by a chorus of voices shouting, "We've got 'em. We've got 'em. This yaller gal's got letters."

There was a general rush for the supposed letter, which, upon examination, proved to be some verses written to me by a friend.

In packing away my things, I had overlooked them. When their captain informed them of their contents, they seemed much disappointed. He inquired of me who wrote them. I told him it was one of my friends.

"Can you read them?" he asked.

When I told him I could, he swore, and raved, and tore the paper into bits.

"Bring me all your letters," said he, in a commanding tone. I told him I had none.

"Don't be afraid," he continued, in an insinuating way. "Bring them all to me. Nobody shall do you any harm." Seeing I did not move to obey him, his pleasant tone changed to oaths and threats. "Who writes to you? Half-free niggers?" inquired he.

I replied, "No, no, most of my letters are from white people. Some request me to burn them after they are read, and some I destroy without reading."

An exclamation of surprise from some of the company put a stop to our conversation. Some silver spoons which ornamented an old-fashioned buffet had just been discovered. My grandmother was in the habit of preserving fruit for many ladies in the town, and of preparing suppers for parties, consequently she had many jars of preserves. The closet that contained these was next invaded, and the contents tasted. One of them, who was helping himself freely, tapped his neighbor on the shoulder, and said, "Well done. Don't wonder the niggers want to kill all the white folks, when they live on good food."

I stretched out my hand to take the jar, saying, "You were not sent here to search for sweetmeats."

"And what were we sent for?" said the captain, bristling up to me.

I evaded the question.

The search of the house was completed, and nothing found to condemn us. They next proceeded to the garden, and knocked about every bush and vine, with no better success. The captain called his men together and, after a short consultation, the order to march was given. As they passed out of the gate, the captain turned back, and pronounced a malediction on the house. He said it ought to be burned to the ground, and each of its inmates receive thirty-nine lashes. We came out of this affair very fortunately, not losing anything except some wearing apparel.

Towards evening the turbulence increased. The soldiers, stimulated by drink, committed still greater cruelties. Shrieks and shouts continually rent the air. Not daring to go to the door, I peeped under the window curtain. I saw a mob dragging along a number of colored people, each white man, with his musket upraised, threatening instant death if they did not stop their shrieks. Among the prisoners was a respectable old colored minister. They had found a few parcels of shot in his house, which his wife had for years used to balance her scales. For this they were going to shoot him on Court House Green. What a spectacle was that for a civilized country. A rabble, staggering under intoxication, assuming to be the administrators of justice.

The better class of the community exerted their influence to save the innocent, persecuted people, and in several instances they succeeded by keeping them shut up in jail till the excitement abated. At last the white citizens found that their own property was not safe from the lawless rabble they had summoned to protect them. They rallied the drunken swarm, drove them back into the country, and set a guard over the town.

The next day, the town patrols were commissioned to search colored people that lived out of the city. The most shocking outrages were committed with perfect impunity. Every day for a fortnight, if I looked out, I saw horsemen with some poor panting negro tied to their saddles, compelled by the lash to keep up with their speed, till they arrived at the jail yard. Those who had been whipped too unmercifully to walk were washed with brine, tossed into a cart and carried to jail. One black man, who had not fortitude to endure scourging, promised to give information about the conspiracy. But it turned out that he knew nothing at all. He had not even heard the name of Nat Turner. The poor fellow had, however, made up a story, which augmented his own sufferings and those of the colored people.

The day patrol continued for some weeks. At sundown a night guard was substituted. Nothing at all was proved against the colored people, bond or free.

The wrath of the slaveholders was somewhat appeased by the capture of Nat Turner. The imprisoned were released. The slaves were sent to their masters, and the free were permitted to return to their ravaged homes. Visiting was strictly forbidden on the plantations. The slaves begged the privilege of again meeting at their little church in the woods, with their burying ground around it. It was built by the colored people, and they had no higher happiness than to meet there and sing hymns together and pour out their hearts in spontaneous prayer. Their request was denied. The church was demolished. They were permitted to attend the white churches, a certain portion of the galleries being appropriated to their use. There, when everybody else had partaken of the communion and the benediction had been pronounced, the minister said, "Come down, now, my colored friends."

They obeyed the summons and partook of the bread and wine in commemoration of the meek and lowly Jesus, who said, "God is your Father, and all ye are brethren."

After the alarm caused by Nat Turner's insurrection had subsided, the slaveholders came to the conclusion that it would be well to give the slaves enough of religious instruction to keep them from murdering their masters. The Episcopal clergyman offered to hold a separate service on Sundays for their benefit. His colored members were very few, and also very respectable — a fact which I presume had some weight with him. The difficulty was to decide on a suitable place for them to worship. The Methodist and Baptist churches admitted them in the afternoon, but their carpets and cushions were not so costly as those at the Episcopal church. It was at last decided that they should meet at the house of a free colored man, who was a member.

I was invited to attend, because I could read. Sunday evening came and, trusting to the cover of night, I ventured out. I rarely ventured out by daylight, for I always went with fear, expecting at every turn to encounter Dr. Flint, who was sure to turn me back or order me to his office to inquire where I got my bonnet, or some other article of dress. When the Rev. Mr. Pike came, there were some twenty persons present. The reverend gentleman knelt in prayer, then seated himself and requested all present who could read, to open their books while he gave out the portions he wished them to repeat or respond to.

His text was, "Servants, be obedient to them that are your masters according to the flesh, with fear and trembling, in singleness of your heart, as unto Christ."

Pious Mr. Pike brushed up his hair till it stood upright and, in deep, solemn tones, began: "Hearken, ye servants! Give strict heed unto my words. You are rebellious sinners. Your hearts are filled with all manner of evil. 'Tis the devil who tempts you. God is angry with you and will surely punish you if you don't forsake your wicked ways. You that live in town are eye-servants behind your master's back. Instead of serving your masters faithfully, which is pleasing in the sight of your heavenly Master, you are idle and shirk your work. God sees you. You tell lies. God hears you. Instead of being engaged in worshipping him, you are hidden away somewhere, feasting on your master's substance, tossing coffee-grounds with some wicked fortune-teller, or cutting cards with another old hag. Your masters may not find you out, but God sees you, and will punish you. Oh, the depravity of your hearts! When your master's work is done, are you quietly together, thinking of the goodness of God to such sinful creatures? No, you are quarreling and tying up little bags of roots to bury under the doorsteps to poison each other with. God sees you. You men steal away to every grog shop to sell your master's corn, that you may buy rum to drink. God sees you. You sneak into the back streets, or among the bushes, to pitch coppers. Although your masters may not find you out, God sees you, and he will punish you. You must forsake your sinful ways, and be faithful servants. Obey your old master and your young master — your old mistress and your young mistress. If you disobey your earthly master, you offend your heavenly Master. You must obey God's commandments. When you go from here, don't stop at the corners of the streets to talk, but go directly home. Let your master and mistress see that you have come."

The benediction was pronounced. We went home, highly amused at brother Pike's gospel teaching, and we determined to hear him again. I went the next Sabbath evening and heard pretty much a repetition of the last discourse. At the close of the meeting, Mr. Pike informed us that he found it very inconvenient to meet at the friend's house, and he should be glad to see us, every Sunday evening, at his own kitchen.

I went home with the feeling that I had heard the Reverend Mr. Pike for the last time. Some of his members repaired to his house, and found that the kitchen sported two tallow candles, the first time, I am sure, since its present occupant owned it, for the servants never had anything but pine knots. It was so long before the reverend gentleman descended from his comfortable parlor that the slaves left, and went to enjoy a Methodist shout. They never seem so happy as when shouting and singing at religious meetings. Many of them are sincere and nearer to the gate of heaven than sanctimonious Mr. Pike and other long-faced Christians, who see wounded Samaritans, and pass by on the other side.

The slaves generally compose their own songs and hymns, and they do not trouble their heads much about the measure. They often sing the following verses:

Old Satan is one busy ole man,
He rolls dem blocks all in my way,
But Jesus is my bosom friend,
He rolls dem blocks away.

If I had died when I was young,
Den how my stam'ring tongue would have sung,
But I am ole, and now I stand
A narrow chance for to tread dat heavenly land.

I well remember one occasion when I attended a Methodist mass meeting. I went with a burdened spirit, and happened to sit next a poor, bereaved mother, whose heart was still heavier than mine. The class leader was the town constable — a man who bought and sold slaves, who whipped his brethren and sisters of the church at the public whipping post, in jail or out of jail. He was ready to perform that Christian office anywhere for fifty cents. This white-faced, black-hearted brother came near us, and said to the stricken woman, "Sister, can't you tell us how the Lord deals with your soul? Do you love him as you did formerly?"

She rose to her feet, and said, in piteous tones, "My Lord and Master, help me. My load is more than I can bear. God has hid himself from me and I am left in darkness and misery." Then, striking her breast, she continued, "I can't tell you what is in here. They've got all my children. Last week they took the last one. God only knows where they've sold her. They let me have her sixteen years, and then — oh! Pray for her brothers and sisters. I've got nothing to live for now. God make my time short."

She sat down, quivering in every limb. I saw that constable

class leader become crimson in the face with suppressed laughter, while he held up his handkerchief, that those who were weeping for the poor woman's calamity might not see his merriment. Then, with assumed gravity, he said to the bereaved mother, "Sister, pray to the Lord that every dispensation of his divine will may be sanctified to the good of your poor needy soul."

The congregation struck up a hymn and sung as though they were as free as the birds that warbled round us:

> *Ole Satan thought he had a mighty aim,*
> *He missed my soul, and caught my sins.*
> *Cry Amen, cry Amen, cry Amen to God.*
>
> *He took my sins upon his back,*
> *Went muttering and grumbling down to hell.*
> *Cry Amen, cry Amen, cry Amen to God.*
>
> *Ole Satan's church is here below.*
> *Up to God's free church I hope to go.*
> *Cry Amen, cry Amen, cry Amen to God.*

Precious are such moments to the poor slaves. If you were to hear them at such times you might think they were happy. But can that hour of singing and shouting sustain them through the dreary week, toiling without wages, under constant dread of the lash?

The Episcopal clergyman, who, ever since my earliest recollection, had been a sort of god among the slaveholders, concluded, as his family was large, that he must go where money was more abundant. A very different clergyman took his place. The change was very agreeable to the colored people, who said, "God has sent us a good man this time." They loved him, and their children followed him for a smile or a kind word. Even the slaveholders felt his influence. He brought to the rectory five slaves. His wife taught them to read and write, and to be useful to her and themselves. As soon as he was settled, he turned his attention to the needy slaves around him. He urged upon his parishioners the duty of having a meeting expressly for them every Sunday, with a sermon adapted to their comprehension. After much argument and importunity, it was finally agreed that they might occupy the gallery of the church on Sunday evenings. Many colored people, hitherto unaccustomed to attend church, now gladly went to hear the gospel preached. The sermons were simple, and they understood them. Moreover, it was the first time they had ever been addressed as human beings. It was not long before his white parishioners began to be dissatisfied. He was accused of preaching better sermons to the negroes than he did to them. He honestly confessed that he bestowed more pains upon those sermons than upon any others, for the slaves were reared in such ignorance that it was a difficult task to adapt himself to their comprehension. Dissensions arose in the parish. Some wanted he should preach to them in the evening, and to the slaves in the afternoon. In the midst of these disputings his wife died, after a very short illness. Her slaves gathered round her dying bed in great sorrow. She said, "I have tried to do you good and promote your happiness. If I have failed, it has not been for want of interest in your welfare. Do not weep for me, but prepare for the new duties that lie before you. I leave you all free. May we meet in a better world." Her liberated slaves were sent away, with funds to establish them comfortably. The colored people will long bless the memory of that truly Christian woman. Soon after her death, her husband preached his farewell sermon. Many tears were shed at his departure.

Years after, he passed through our town and preached to his former congregation. In his afternoon sermon he addressed the colored people. "My friends," said he, "it affords me great happiness to have an opportunity of speaking to you again. For two years I have been striving to do something for the colored people of my own parish, but nothing is yet accomplished. I have not even preached a sermon to them. Try to live according to the word of God, my friends. Your skin is darker than mine, but God judges men by their hearts, not by the color of their skins."

This was strange doctrine from a Southern pulpit. It was very offensive to slaveholders. They said he and his wife had made fools of their slaves, and that he preached like a fool to the negroes.

I knew an old black man, whose pious and childlike trust in God were beautiful to witness. At fifty-three years old he joined the Baptist church. He had a most earnest desire to learn to read. He thought he should know how to serve God better if he could only read the Bible. He came to me and begged me to teach him. He said he could not pay me, for he had no money, but he would bring me nice fruit when the season for it came. I asked him if he didn't know it was contrary to law, and that slaves were whipped and imprisoned for teaching each other to read. This brought tears into his eyes.

"Don't be troubled, Uncle Fred," said I. "I have no thoughts of refusing to teach you. I only told you of the law, that you might know the danger, and be on your guard."

He thought he could plan to come three times a week without being suspected. I selected a quiet nook where no intruder was likely to penetrate, and there I taught him his A, B, C.

Considering his age, his progress was astonishing. As soon as he could spell in two syllables he wanted to spell out words in the Bible. The happy smile that illuminated his face put joy into my heart. After spelling out a few words, he paused and said, "Honey, it 'pears when I can read this good book I shall be nearer to God. White man got all the sense. He can learn easy.

It ain't easy for ole black man like me. I only wants to read this book, so I may know how to live, then I have no fear 'bout dying."

I tried to encourage him by speaking of the rapid progress he had made.

"Have patience, child," he replied. "I learns slow."

I had no need of patience. His gratitude and the happiness I imparted were more than a recompense for all my trouble.

At the end of six months he had read through the New Testament and could find any text in it. One day, when he had recited unusually well, I said, "Uncle Fred, how do you manage to get your lessons so well?"

"Lord bless you, chile," he replied. "You never give me a lesson dat I don't pray to God to help me to understan' what I spells and what I reads. And he does help me, chile. Bless his holy name."

There are thousands, who, like good Uncle Fred, are thirsting for the water of life, but the law forbids it, and the churches withhold it. They send the Bible to heathen abroad, and neglect the heathen at home. I am glad that missionaries go out to the dark corners of the earth, but I ask them not to overlook the dark corners at home. Talk to American slaveholders as you talk to savages in Africa. Tell them it is wrong to traffic in men. Tell them it is sinful to sell their own children, and atrocious to violate their own daughters. Tell them that all men are brethren, and that man has no right to shut out the light of knowledge from his brother. Tell them they are answerable to God for sealing up the fountain of Life from souls that are thirsting for it.

There are men who would gladly undertake such missionary work as this but, alas, their number is small. They are hated by the South, and would be driven from its soil, or dragged to prison to die, as others have been before them. The field is ripe for the harvest, and awaits the reapers. Perhaps the great grandchildren of Uncle Fred may have freely imparted to them the divine treasures, which he sought by stealth, at the risk of the prison and the scourge.

Are doctors of divinity blind, or are they hypocrites? I suppose some are the one, and some the other, but I think if they felt the interest in the poor and the lowly, that they ought to feel, they would not be so easily blinded. A clergyman who goes to the South for the first time has usually some feeling, however vague, that slavery is wrong. The slaveholder suspects this, and plays his game accordingly. He makes himself as agreeable as possible, talks on theology and other kindred topics. The reverend gentleman is asked to invoke a blessing on a table loaded with luxuries. After dinner he walks round the premises, and sees the beautiful groves and flowering vines, and the comfortable huts of favored household slaves. The Southerner invites him to talk with these slaves. He asks them if they want to be free, and they say, "Oh, no, massa." This is sufficient to satisfy him. He comes home to publish a 'South-Side View of Slavery', and to complain of the exaggerations of abolitionists. He assures people that he has been to the South and seen slavery for himself, that it is a beautiful "patriarchal institution," that the slaves don't want their freedom, that they have hallelujah meetings and other religious privileges.

What does he know of the half-starved wretches toiling from dawn till dark on the plantations, of mothers shrieking for their children, torn from their arms by slave-traders, of young girls dragged down into moral filth, of pools of blood around the whipping post, of hounds trained to tear human flesh, of men screwed into cotton gins to die? The slaveholder showed him none of these things, and the slaves dared not tell of them if he had asked them.

There is a great difference between Christianity and religion in the South. If a man goes to the communion table, and pays money into the treasury of the church, no matter if it be the price of blood, he is called religious. If a pastor has offspring by a woman not his wife, the church dismiss him, if she is a white woman, but if she is colored, it does not hinder his continuing to be their good shepherd.

When I was told that Dr. Flint had joined the Episcopal church, I was much surprised. I supposed that religion had a purifying effect on the character of men, but the worst persecutions I endured from him were after he was a communicant. The conversation of the doctor, the day after he had been confirmed, certainly gave me no indication that he had 'renounced the devil and all his works'. In answer to some of his usual talk, I reminded him that he had just joined the church.

"Yes, Linda," said he. "It was proper for me to do so. I am getting on in years, and my position in society requires it. It puts an end to all the damned slang. You would do well to join the church, too, Linda."

"There are sinners enough in it already," rejoined I. "If I could be allowed to live like a Christian, I should be glad."

"You can do what I require, and if you are faithful to me, you will be as virtuous as my wife," he replied.

I answered that the Bible didn't say so.

His voice became hoarse with rage.

"How dare you preach to me about your infernal Bible," he exclaimed. "What right have you, who are my negro, to talk to me about what you would like, and what you wouldn't like? I am your master. You shall obey me."

No wonder the slaves sing:

Ole Satan's church is here below,
Up to God's free church I hope to go.

I had not returned to my master's house since the birth of my child. The old man raved to have me thus removed from his immediate power, but his wife vowed, by all that was good and great, she would kill me if I came back, and he did not doubt her word.

Sometimes he would stay away for a season. Then he would come and renew the old threadbare discourse about his forbearance and my ingratitude. He labored, most unnecessarily, to convince me that I had lowered myself. The venomous old reprobate had no need of descanting on that theme. I felt humiliated enough. My unconscious babe was the ever-present witness of my shame. I listened with silent contempt when he talked about my having forfeited his good opinion, but I shed bitter tears that I was no longer worthy of being respected by the good and pure. Alas, slavery still held me in its poisonous grasp. There was no chance for me to be respectable. There was no prospect of being able to lead a better life.

Sometimes, when my master found that I still refused to accept what he called his kind offers, he would threaten to sell my child.

"Perhaps that will humble you," said he.

Humble me! Was I not already in the dust? His threat lacerated my heart. I knew the law gave him power to fulfill it, for slaveholders have been cunning enough to enact that "the child shall follow the condition of the mother," not of the father, thus taking care that licentiousness shall not interfere with avarice. This reflection made me clasp my innocent babe all the more firmly to my heart. Horrid visions passed through my mind when I thought of his liability to fall into the slave-trader's hands. I wept over him and said, "My child, perhaps they will leave you in some cold cabin to die and then throw you into a hole, as if you were a dog."

When Dr. Flint learned that I was again to be a mother, he was exasperated beyond measure. He rushed from the house and returned with a pair of shears. I had a fine head of hair, and he often railed about my pride of arranging it nicely. He cut every hair close to my head, storming and swearing all the time. I replied to some of his abuse, and he struck me. Some months before, he had pitched me downstairs in a fit of passion, and the injury I received was so serious that I was unable to turn myself in bed for many days. He then said, "Linda, I swear by God I will never raise my hand against you again," but I knew that he would forget his promise.

After he discovered my situation, he was like a restless spirit from the pit. He came every day, and I was subjected to such insults as no pen can describe. I would not describe them if I could, they were too low, too revolting. I tried to keep them from my grandmother's knowledge as much as I could. I knew she had enough to sadden her life, without having my troubles to bear. When she saw the doctor treat me with violence, and heard him utter oaths terrible enough to palsy a man's tongue, she could not always hold her peace. It was natural and motherlike that she should try to defend me, but it only made matters worse.

When they told me my new-born babe was a girl, my heart was heavier than it had ever been before. Slavery is terrible for men, but it is far more terrible for women. Superadded to the burden common to all, they have wrongs, and sufferings, and mortifications peculiarly their own.

Dr. Flint had sworn that he would make me suffer, to my last day, for this new crime against him, as he called it, and as long as he had me in his power he kept his word. On the fourth day after the birth of my babe, he entered my room suddenly and commanded me to rise and bring my baby to him. The nurse who took care of me had gone out of the room to prepare some nourishment, and I was alone. There was no alternative. I rose, took up my babe, and crossed the room to where he sat.

"Now stand there," said he, "till I tell you to go back."

My child bore a strong resemblance to her father, and to the deceased Mrs. Sands, her grandmother. He noticed this, and while I stood before him, trembling with weakness, he heaped upon me and my little one every vile epithet he could think of. Even the grandmother in her grave did not escape his curses. In the midst of his vituperations I fainted at his feet. This recalled him to his senses. He took the baby from my arms, laid it on the bed, dashed cold water in my face, took me up and shook me violently to restore my consciousness before anyone entered the room. Just then my grandmother came in, and he hurried out of the house. I suffered in consequence of this treatment, but I begged my friends to let me die rather than send for the doctor. There was nothing I dreaded so much as his presence. My life was spared, and I was glad for the sake of my little ones. Had it not been for these ties to life, I should have been glad to be released by death, though I had lived only nineteen years.

Always it gave me a pang that my children had no lawful claim to a name. Their father offered his, but, if I had wished to accept the offer, I dared not while my master lived. Moreover, I knew it would not be accepted at their baptism. A Christian name they were at least entitled to, and we resolved to call my boy for our dear good Benjamin, who had gone far away from us.

My grandmother belonged to the church, and she was very desirous of having the children christened. I knew Dr. Flint would forbid it, and I did not venture to attempt it. But chance favored me. He was called to visit a patient out of town, and was obliged to be absent during Sunday.

"Now is the time," said my grandmother, "we will take the children to church, and have them christened."

When I entered the church, recollections of my mother came over me, and I felt subdued in spirit. There she had presented me for baptism, without any reason to feel ashamed. She had been married and had such legal rights as slavery allows to a slave. The vows had at least been sacred to her, and she had never violated them. I was glad she was not alive, to know under what different circumstances her grandchildren were presented for baptism. Why had my lot been so different from my mother's? Her master had died when she was a child, and she remained with her mistress till she married. She was never in the power of any master, and thus she escaped one class of the evil that generally befalls slaves.

When my baby was about to be christened, the former mistress of my father stepped up to me, and proposed to give it her Christian name. To this I added the surname of my father, who had himself no legal right to it, for my grandfather on the paternal side was a white gentleman. What tangled skeins are the genealogies of slavery! I loved my father, but it mortified me to be obliged to bestow his name on my children.

When we left the church, my father's old mistress invited me to go home with her. She clasped a gold chain round my baby's neck. I thanked her for this kindness, but I did not like the emblem. I wanted no chain to be fastened on my daughter, not even if its links were of gold. How earnestly I prayed that she might never feel the weight of slavery's chain, whose iron entereth into the soul.

My children grew fine, and Dr. Flint would often say to me, with an exulting smile, "These brats will bring me a handsome sum of money one of these days."

I thought to myself that, God being my helper, they should never pass into his hands. It seemed to me I would rather see them killed than have them given up to his power. The money for the freedom of myself and my children could be obtained, but I derived no advantage from that circumstance. Dr. Flint loved money, but he loved power more.

After much discussion, my friends resolved on making another trial. There was a slaveholder about to leave for Texas, and he was commissioned to buy me. He was to begin with nine hundred dollars, and go up to twelve. My master refused his offers. "Sir," said he, "she don't belong to me. She is my daughter's property and I have no right to sell her. I mistrust that you come from her paramour. If so, you may tell him that he cannot buy her for any money, neither can he buy her children."

The doctor came to see me the next day. My heart beat quicker as he entered. I never had seen the old man tread with so majestic a step. He seated himself and looked at me with withering scorn. My children had learned to be afraid of him. The little one would shut her eyes and hide her face on my shoulder whenever she saw him, and Benny, who was now nearly five years old, often inquired, "What makes that bad man come here so many times? Does he want to hurt us?" I would clasp the dear boy in my arms, trusting that he would be free before he was old enough to solve the problem. And now, as the doctor sat there so grim and silent, the child left his play and came and nestled up by me.

At last my tormentor spoke.

"So you are left in disgust, are you?" said he. "It is no more than I expected. You remember I told you years ago that you would be treated so. So he is tired of you? Ha! The virtuous madam don't like to hear about it, does she? Ha!"

There was a sting in his calling me virtuous madam. I no longer had the power of answering him as I had formerly done. He continued.

"So it seems you are trying to get up another intrigue. Your new paramour came to me and offered to buy you, but you may be assured you will not succeed. You are mine, and you shall be mine for life. There lives no human being that can take you out of slavery. I would have done it, but you rejected my kind offer."

I told him I did not wish to get up any intrigue, that I had never seen the man who offered to buy me.

"Do you tell me I lie?" exclaimed he, dragging me from my chair. "Will you say again that you never saw that man?"

I answered, "I do say so."

He clinched my arm with a volley of oaths. Ben began to scream, and I told him to go to his grandmother.

Don't you stir a step, you little wretch," said he.

The child drew nearer to me, and put his arms round me, as if he wanted to protect me. This was too much for my enraged master. He caught him up and hurled him across the room. I thought he was dead, and rushed towards him to take him up.

"Not yet," exclaimed the doctor. "Let him lie there till he comes to."

"Let me go. Let me go," I screamed, "or I will raise the whole house."

I struggled and got away, but he clinched me again. Somebody opened the door, and he released me. I picked up my insensible child. When I turned my tormentor was gone. Anxiously I bent over the little form, so pale and still. When the brown eyes at last opened, I don't know whether I was very happy.

All the doctor's former persecutions were renewed. He came morning, noon and night. No jealous lover ever watched a rival more closely than he watched me and the unknown slaveholder, with whom he accused me of wishing to get up an intrigue. When my grandmother was out of the way he searched every room to find him.

In one of his visits, he happened to find a young girl, whom he had sold to a trader a few days previous. His statement was, that he sold her because she had been too familiar with the overseer. She had had a bitter life with him, and was glad to be sold. She had no mother, and no near ties. She had been torn from all her family years before. A few friends had entered into bonds for her safety, if the trader would allow her to spend with them the time that intervened between her sale and the gathering up of his human stock. Such a favor was rarely granted. It saved the trader the expense of board and jail fees, and though the amount was small, it was a weighty consideration in a slave-trader's mind.

Dr. Flint always had an aversion to meeting slaves after he had sold them. He ordered Rose out of the house, but he was no longer her master, and she took no notice of him. For once the crushed Rose was the conqueror. His gray eyes flashed angrily upon her, but that was the extent of his power.

"How came this girl here?" he exclaimed. "What right had you to allow it, when you knew I had sold her?"

I answered "This is my grandmother's house, and Rose came to see her. I have no right to turn anybody out of doors who comes here for honest purposes."

He gave me the blow that would have fallen upon Rose if she had still been his slave. My grandmother's attention had been attracted by loud voices, and she entered in time to see a second blow dealt. She was not a woman to let such an outrage, in her own house, go unrebuked. The doctor undertook to explain that I had been insolent. Her indignant feelings rose higher and higher, and finally boiled over in words.

"Get out of my house," she exclaimed. "Go home, and take care of your wife and children. You will have enough to do without watching my family."

He threw the birth of my children in her face, accused her of sanctioning the life I was leading. She told him I was living with her by compulsion of his wife, that he needn't accuse her, for he was the one to blame, he was the one who had caused all the trouble. She grew more and more excited as she went on.

"I tell you what, Dr. Flint," said she, "you ain't got many more years to live, you'd better be saying your prayers. It will take 'em all, and more too, to wash the dirt off your soul."

"Do you know whom you are talking to?" he exclaimed.

She replied, "Yes, I know very well who I am talking to."

He left the house in a great rage. I looked at my grandmother. Our eyes met. Their angry expression had passed away, but she looked sorrowful and weary — weary of incessant strife. I wondered that it did not lessen her love for me, but if it did she never showed it. She was always kind, always ready to sympathize with my troubles. There might have been peace and contentment in that humble home if it had not been for the demon slavery.

The winter passed undisturbed by the doctor. The beautiful spring came. When Nature resumes her loveliness, the human soul is apt to revive also. My drooping hopes came to life again with the flowers. I was dreaming of freedom again, more for my children's sake than my own. I planned and I planned. Obstacles hit against plans. There seemed no way of overcoming them, and yet I hoped.

Back came the wily doctor. I was not at home when he called. A friend had invited me to a small party, and to gratify her I went. To my great consternation, a messenger came in haste to say that Dr. Flint was at my grandmother's, and insisted on seeing me. They did not tell him where I was, or he would have come and raised a disturbance in my friend's house. They sent me a dark wrapper, I threw it on and hurried home. My speed did not save me, the doctor had gone away in anger. I dreaded the morning, but I could not delay it. It came, warm and bright. At an early hour the doctor came and asked me where I had been last night. I told him. He did not believe me, and sent to my friend's house to ascertain the facts. He came in the afternoon to assure me he was satisfied that I had spoken the truth. He seemed to be in a facetious mood, and I expected some jeers were coming.

"I suppose you need some recreation," said he, "but I am surprised at your being there, among those negroes. It was not the place for you. Are you allowed to visit such people?"

I understood this covert fling at the white gentleman who

was my friend, but I merely replied, "I went to visit my friends. Any company they keep is good enough for me."

He went on to say, "I have seen very little of you of late, but my interest in you is unchanged. When I said I would have no more mercy on you I was rash. I recall my words. Linda, you desire freedom for yourself and your children, and you can obtain it only through me. If you agree to what I am about to propose, you and they shall be free. There must be no communication of any kind between you and their father. I will procure a cottage, where you and the children can live together. Your labor shall be light, such as sewing for my family. Think what is offered you, Linda — a home and freedom. Let the past be forgotten. If I have been harsh with you at times, your willfulness drove me to it. You know I enact obedience from my own children, and I consider you as yet a child."

He paused for an answer, but I remained silent.

"Why don't you speak?" said he. "What more do you wait for?"

"Nothing, sir."

"Then you accept my offer?"

"No, sir."

His anger was ready to break loose, but he succeeded in curbing it, and replied, "You have answered without thought. But I must let you know there are two sides to my proposition, if you reject the bright side, you will be obliged to take the dark one. You must either accept my offer, or you and your children shall be sent to your young master's plantation, there to remain till your young mistress is married, and your children shall fare like the rest of the negro children. I give you a week to consider of it."

He was shrewd, but I knew he was not to be trusted. I told him I was ready to give my answer now.

"I will not receive it now," he replied. "You act too much from impulse. Remember that you and your children can be free a week from today if you choose."

On what a monstrous chance hung the destiny of my children. I knew that my master's offer was a snare, and that if I entered it escape would be impossible. As for his promise, I knew him so well that I was sure if he gave me free papers, they would be so managed as to have no legal value. The alternative was inevitable. I resolved to go to the plantation. But then I thought how completely I should be in his power, and the prospect was appalling. Even if I should kneel before him, and implore him to spare me, for the sake of my children, I knew he would spurn me with his foot, and my weakness would be his triumph.

Before the week expired, I heard that young Mr. Flint was about to be married to a lady of his own stamp. I foresaw the position I should occupy in his establishment. I had once been sent to the plantation for punishment, and fear of the son had induced the father to recall me very soon. My mind was made up, I was resolved that I would foil my master and save my children, or I would perish in the attempt. I kept my plans to myself, I knew that friends would try to dissuade me from them, and I would not wound their feelings by rejecting their advice.

On the decisive day the doctor came, and said he hoped I had made a wise choice.

"I am ready to go to the plantation, sir," I replied.

"Have you thought how important your decision is to your children?" said he.

I told him I had.

"Very well. Go to the plantation, and my curse go with you," he replied. "Your boy shall be put to work, and he shall soon be sold. Your girl shall be raised for the purpose of selling well. Go your own ways."

He left the room with curses, not to be repeated.

As I stood rooted to the spot, my grandmother came and

said, "Linda, child, what did you tell him?"

I answered that I was going to the plantation.

"Must you go?" said she. "Can't something be done to stop it?"

I told her it was useless to try, but she begged me not to give up. She said she would go to the doctor and remind him how long and how faithfully she had served in the family, and how she had taken her own baby from her breast to nourish his wife. She would tell him I had been out of the family so long they would not miss me, that she would pay them for my time, and the money would procure a woman who had more strength for the situation than I had. I begged her not to go, but she persisted in saying, "He will listen to me, Linda."

She went, and was treated as I expected. He coolly listened to what she said, but denied her request. He told her that what he did was for my good, that my feelings were entirely above my situation, and that on the plantation I would receive treatment that was suitable to my behavior.

My grandmother was much cast down. I had my secret hopes, but I must fight my battle alone. I had a woman's pride, and a mother's love for my children. I resolved that out of the darkness of this hour a brighter dawn should rise for them. My master had power and law on his side, I had a determined will. There is might in each.

Early the next morning I left my grandmother's with my youngest child. My boy was ill, and I left him behind. I had many sad thoughts as the old wagon jolted on. Hitherto, I had suffered alone, now, my little one was to be treated as a slave. As we drew near the great house, I thought of the time when I was formerly sent there out of revenge. I wondered for what purpose I was now sent. I could not tell. I resolved to obey orders so far as duty required, but within myself, I determined to make my stay as short as possible.

Mr. Flint was waiting to receive us, and told me to follow

him upstairs to receive orders for the day. My little Ellen was left below in the kitchen. It was a change for her, who had always been so carefully tended. My young master said she might amuse herself in the yard. This was kind of him, since the child was hateful to his sight.

My task was to fit up the house for the reception of the bride. In the midst of sheets, tablecloths, towels, drapery, and carpeting, my head was as busy planning, as were my fingers with the needle. At noon I was allowed to go to Ellen. She had sobbed herself to sleep.

I heard Mr. Flint say to a neighbor, "I've got her down here, and I'll soon take the town notions out of her head. My father is partly to blame for her nonsense. He ought to have broke her in long ago."

The remark was made within my hearing, and it would have been quite as manly to have made it to my face. He had said things to my face which might, or might not, have surprised his neighbor if he had known of them. He was a chip off the old block.

I resolved to give him no cause to accuse me of being too much of a lady so far as work was concerned. I worked day and night, with wretchedness before me. When I lay down beside my child, I felt how much easier it would be to see her die than to see her master beat her about, as I daily saw him beat other little ones. The spirit of the mothers was so crushed by the lash that they stood by, without courage to remonstrate. How much more must I suffer, before I should be 'broke in' to that degree?

I wished to appear as contented as possible. Sometimes I had an opportunity to send a few lines home, and this brought up recollections that made it difficult, for a time, to seem calm and indifferent to my lot. Notwithstanding my efforts, I saw that Mr. Flint regarded me with a suspicious eye.

Ellen broke down under the trials of her new life. Separated from me, with no one to look after her, she wandered about, and in a few days cried herself sick. One day, she sat under the window where I was at work, crying that weary cry which makes a mother's heart bleed. I was obliged to steel myself to bear it. After a while it ceased. I looked out, and she was gone. As it was near noon, I ventured to go down in search of her. The great house was raised two feet above the ground. I looked under it, and saw her about midway, fast asleep. I crept under and drew her out. As I held her in my arms, I thought how well it would be for her if she never woke up, and I uttered my thought aloud. I was startled to hear someone say, "Did you speak to me?" I looked up, and saw Mr. Flint standing beside me. He said nothing further, but turned away, frowning. That night he sent Ellen a biscuit and a cup of sweetened milk. This generosity surprised me. I learned afterwards, that in the afternoon he had killed a large snake, which crept from under the house. I supposed that incident had prompted his unusual kindness.

The next morning the old cart was loaded with shingles for town. I put Ellen into it and sent her to her grandmother. Mr. Flint said I ought to have asked his permission. I told him the child was sick and required attention which I had no time to give. He let it pass, for he was aware that I had accomplished much work in a little time.

I had been three weeks on the plantation, when I planned a visit home. It must be at night, after everybody was in bed. I was six miles from town, and the road was very dreary. I was to go with a young man who, I knew, often stole to town to see his mother. One night, when all was quiet, we started. Fear gave speed to our steps, and we were not long in performing the journey. I arrived at my grandmother's. Her bedroom was on the first floor, and the window was open, the weather being warm. I called out to her and she awoke. She let me in and closed the window, lest some late passer-by should see me. A light was brought, and the whole household gathered round me, some smiling and some crying. I went to look at my children, and thanked God for their happy sleep. The tears fell as I leaned over them. As I moved to leave, Benny stirred. I turned back, and whispered, "Mother is here."

After digging at his eyes with his little fist, they opened, and he sat up in bed, looking at me curiously. Having satisfied himself that it was I, he exclaimed, "Mother, you ain't dead, are you? They didn't cut off your head at the plantation, did they?"

My time was up too soon, my guide was waiting for me. I laid Benny back in his bed and dried his tears with a promise to come again soon. Rapidly we retraced our steps back to the plantation. About halfway we were met by a company of four patrols. Luckily we heard their horses' hoofs before they came in sight, and we had time to hide behind a large tree. They passed, shouting in a manner that indicated a recent carousal. How thankful we were that they had not their dogs with them. We hastened our footsteps.

When we arrived on the plantation we heard the sound of the hand-mill. The slaves were grinding their corn. We were safely in the house before the horn summoned them to their labor. I divided my little parcel of food with my guide, knowing that he had lost the chance of grinding his corn, and must toil all day in the field.

Mr. Flint often took an inspection of the house, to see that no one was idle. The entire management of the work was trusted to me, because he knew nothing about it, and rather than hire a superintendent he contented himself with my arrangements. He had often urged upon his father the necessity of having me at the plantation to take charge of his affairs, and make clothes for the slaves, but the old man knew him too well to consent to that arrangement.

When I had been working a month at the plantation, the great aunt of Mr. Flint came to visit. This was the good old lady who paid fifty dollars for my grandmother for the purpose of making her free when she stood on the auction block. My grandmother loved this old lady, whom we all called Miss Fanny. She often came to take tea with us. On such occasions the table was spread with a snow-white cloth and the china cups and silver spoons were taken from the old-fashioned buffet. There were hot muffins, tea rusks and delicious sweetmeats. My grandmother kept two cows, and the fresh cream was Miss Fanny's delight. She invariably declared that it was the best in town. The old ladies had cosy times together. They would work and chat and sometimes, while talking over old times, their spectacles would get dim with tears, and would have to be taken off and wiped. When Miss Fanny bade us goodbye, her bag was filled with grandmother's best cakes, and she was urged to come again soon.

There had been a time when Dr. Flint's wife came to take tea with us, and when her children were also sent to have a feast of Aunt Marthy's nice cooking. But after I became an object of her jealousy and spite, she was angry with grandmother for giving a shelter to me and my children. She would not even speak to her in the street. This wounded my grandmother's feelings, for she could not retain ill will against the woman whom she had nourished with her milk when a babe.

The doctor's wife would gladly have prevented our intercourse with Miss Fanny if she could have done it, but fortunately she was not dependent on the bounty of the Flints. She had enough to be independent, and that is more than can ever be gained from charity, however lavish it may be.

Miss Fanny was endeared to me by many recollections, and I was rejoiced to see her at the plantation. The warmth of her large, loyal heart made the house seem pleasanter while she was in it.

She stayed a week, and I had many talks with her. She said her principal object in coming was to see how I was treated, and whether anything could be done for me. She inquired whether she could help me in any way. I told her I believed not. She condoled with me in her own peculiar way, saying she wished that I and all my grandmother's family were at rest in our graves, for not until then should she feel any peace about us. The good old soul did not dream that I was planning to bestow peace upon her, with regard to myself and my children, not by death, but by securing our freedom.

Again and again I had traversed those dreary twelve miles to and from the town. All the way I was meditating upon some means of escape for myself and my children. My friends had made every effort that ingenuity could devise to effect our purchase, but all their plans had proved abortive. Dr. Flint was suspicious, determined not to loosen his grasp upon us.

I could have made my escape alone, but it was more for my helpless children than for myself that I longed for freedom. Though the boon would have been precious to me, above all price, I would not have taken it at the expense of leaving them in slavery. Every trial I endured, every sacrifice I made for their sakes, drew them closer to my heart, and gave me fresh courage to beat back the dark waves that rolled and rolled over me in a seemingly endless night of storms.

The six weeks were nearly over, when Mr. Flint's bride was expected to take possession of her new home. The arrangements were all completed, and Mr. Flint said I had done well. We expected to leave home on Saturday and return with his bride the following Wednesday. After receiving various orders from him, I ventured to ask permission to spend Sunday in town. It was granted, for which favor I was thankful. It was the first I had ever asked of him, and I intended it should be the last. It needed more than one night to accomplish the project I had in view, but the whole of Sunday would give me an opportunity.

I spent the Sabbath with my grandmother. A calmer, more

beautiful day never came down out of heaven. To me it was a day of conflicting emotions. Perhaps it was the last day I should ever spend under that dear old sheltering roof. Perhaps these were the last talks I should ever have with the faithful old friend of my whole life. Perhaps it was the last time I and my children should be together. Well, better so, I thought, than that they should be slaves. I knew the doom that awaited my fair baby in slavery, and I determined to save her from it, or perish in the attempt. I went to make this vow at the graves of my poor parents, in the burying-ground of the slaves.

> *There the wicked cease from troubling*
> *There the weary be at rest.*
> *There the prisoners rest together*
> *They hear not the voice of the oppressor*
> *The servant is free from his master.*

I knelt by the graves of my parents, and thanked God, as I had often done before, that they had not lived to witness my trials, or to mourn over my sins. I had received my mother's blessing when she died, and in many an hour of tribulation I had seemed to hear her voice, sometimes chiding me, sometimes whispering loving words into my wounded heart. I have shed many and bitter tears, to think that when I am gone from my children they cannot remember me with such entire satisfaction as I remembered my mother.

The graveyard was in the woods, and twilight was coming on. Nothing broke the death-like stillness except the occasional twitter of a bird. My spirit was overawed by the solemnity of the scene. For more than ten years I had frequented this spot, but never had it seemed to me so sacred as now. A black stump, at the head of my mother's grave, was all that remained of a tree my father had planted. His grave was marked by a small wooden board, bearing his name, the letters of which were nearly obliterated. I knelt down and kissed them, and poured forth a prayer to God for guidance and support in the perilous step I was about to take. As I passed the wreck of the old meeting house where, before Nat Turner's time, the slaves had been allowed to meet for worship, I seemed to hear my father's voice come from it, bidding me not to tarry till I reached freedom or the grave. I rushed on with renovated hopes. My trust in God had been strengthened by that prayer among the graves.

My plan was to conceal myself at the house of a friend and remain there a few weeks till the search was over. My hope was that the doctor would get discouraged and, for fear of losing my value, and also of subsequently finding my children among the missing, he would consent to sell us. I knew somebody would buy us.

I had done all in my power to make my children comfortable during the time I expected to be separated from them. I was packing my things, when grandmother came into the room, and asked what I was doing.

"I am putting my things in order," I replied.

I tried to look and speak cheerfully, but her watchful eye detected something beneath the surface. She drew me towards her, and asked me to sit down. She looked earnestly at me and said, "Linda, do you want to kill your old grandmother? Do you mean to leave your little, helpless children? I am old now, and cannot do for your babies as I once did for you."

I replied that, if I went away, perhaps their father would be able to secure their freedom.

"Ah, my child," said she, "don't trust too much to him. Stand by your own children and suffer with them till death. Nobody respects a mother who forsakes her children. If you leave them, you will never have a happy moment. If you go, you will make me miserable the short time I have to live. You would be taken and brought back, and your sufferings would be dreadful. Remember poor Benjamin. Do give it up, Linda. Try to bear a little longer. Things may turn out better than we expect."

My courage failed me, in view of the sorrow I should bring on that faithful, loving old heart. I promised that I would try longer, and that I would take nothing out of her house without her knowledge.

Whenever the children climbed on my knee or laid their heads on my lap, she would say, "Poor little souls, what would you do without a mother? She don't love you as I do" And she would hug them to her own bosom, as if to reproach me for my want of affection, but she knew all the while that I loved them better than my life. I slept with her that night, and it was the last time. The memory of it haunted me for many a year.

On Monday I returned to the plantation, and busied myself with preparations for the important day. Wednesday came. It was a beautiful day, and the faces of the slaves were as bright as the sunshine. The poor creatures were merry. They were expecting little presents from the bride and hoping for better times under her administration. I had no such hopes for them. I knew that the young wives of slaveholders often thought their authority and importance would be best established and maintained by cruelty. What I had heard of young Mrs. Flint gave me no reason to expect that her rule over them would be less severe than that of the master and overseer. Truly, the colored race are the most cheerful and forgiving people on the face of the earth. That their masters sleep in safety is owing to their superabundance of heart, yet they look upon their sufferings with less pity than they would bestow on those of a horse or a dog.

I stood at the door with others to receive the bridegroom and bride. She was a handsome, delicate-looking girl, her face flushed with emotion at sight of her new home. I thought it likely that visions of a happy future were rising before her. It made me sad, for I knew how soon clouds would come over her sunshine. She examined every part of the house and told me she was delighted with the arrangements I had made. I was afraid old Mrs. Flint had tried to prejudice her against me, and I did my best to please her.

It passed off smoothly for me until dinner time arrived. I did not mind the embarrassment of waiting on a dinner party for the first time in my life half so much as I did the meeting with Dr. Flint and his wife, who would be among the guests. It was a mystery to me why Mrs. Flint had not made her appearance at the plantation during all the time I was putting the house in order. I had not met her, face to face, for five years, and I had no wish to see her now. She was a praying woman and, doubtless, considered my present position a special answer to her prayers. Nothing could please her better than to see me humbled and trampled upon. I was just where she would have me — in the power of a hard, unprincipled master. She did not speak to me when she took her seat at table, but her satisfied, triumphant smile when I handed her plate, was more eloquent than words. The old doctor was not so quiet in his demonstrations. He ordered me here and there and spoke with peculiar emphasis when he said "your mistress."

I was drilled like a disgraced soldier. When all was over, and the last key turned, I sought my pillow, thankful that God had appointed a season of rest for the weary.

The next day my new mistress began her housekeeping. I was not exactly appointed maid of all work, but I was to do whatever I was told. Monday evening came. It was always a busy time. On that night the slaves received their weekly allowance of food. Three pounds of meat, a peck of corn and perhaps a dozen herring were allowed to each man. Women received a pound and a half of meat, a peck of corn and the same number of herring. Children over twelve years old had half the allowance of the women. The meat was cut and weighed by the foreman of the field hands and piled on planks before the meat house. Then the second foreman went behind the building, and when the first foreman called out, "Who takes this piece of meat?" he answered by calling somebody's name. This method was resorted to as means of preventing partiality in distributing the meat. The young mistress came out to see how things were done on her plantation, and she soon gave a specimen of her character. Among those in waiting for their allowance was a very old slave, who had faithfully served the Flint family through three generations. When he hobbled up to get his bit of meat, the mistress said he was too old to have any allowance, that when niggers were too old to work they ought to be fed on grass. Poor old man. He suffered much before he found rest in the grave.

My mistress and I got along very well together. At the end of a week old Mrs. Flint made us another visit, and was closeted a long time with her daughter-in-law. I had my suspicions what was the subject of the conference. The old doctor's wife had been informed that I could leave the plantation on one condition, and she was very desirous to keep me there. If she had trusted me, as I deserved to be trusted by her, she would have had no fears of my accepting that condition When she entered her carriage to return home, she said to young Mrs. Flint, "Don't neglect to send for them as quick as possible."

My heart was on the watch all the time, and I at once concluded that she spoke of my children. The doctor came the next day, and as I entered the room to spread the tea table, I heard him say, "Don't wait any longer. Send for them tomorrow."

I saw through the plan. They thought my children's being there would fetter me to the spot, and that it was a good place to break us all in to abject submission to our lot as slaves. After the doctor left, a gentleman called, who had always manifested friendly feelings towards my grandmother and her family. Mr. Flint carried him over the plantation to show him the results of labor performed by men and women who were unpaid, miserably clothed, and half-famished.

The cotton crop was all they thought of. It was duly admired, and the gentleman returned with specimens to show his friends. I was ordered to carry water to wash his hands. As I did so, he said, "Linda, how do you like your new home?"

I told him I liked it as well as I expected.

He replied, "They don't think you are contented, and tomorrow they are going to bring your children to be with you. I am sorry for you, Linda. I hope they will treat you kindly."

I hurried from the room, unable to thank him. My suspicions were correct. My children were to be brought to the plantation to be 'broke in'.

To this day I feel grateful to the gentleman who gave me this timely information. It nerved me to immediate action.

Mr. Flint was hard pushed for house servants. Rather than lose me he had restrained his malice. I did my work faithfully, though not, of course, with a willing mind. They were evidently afraid I should leave them. Mr. Flint wished that I should sleep in the great house instead of the servants' quarters. His wife agreed to the proposition, but said I mustn't bring my bed into the house, because it would scatter feathers on her carpet. I knew when I went there that they would never think of such a thing as furnishing a bed of any kind for me and my little one. I therefore carried my own bed, and now I was forbidden to use it. I did as I was ordered. But now that I was certain my children were to be put in their power, in order to give them a stronger hold on me, I resolved to leave them that night. I remembered the grief this step would bring upon my dear old grandmother, and nothing less than the freedom of my children would have induced me to disregard her advice. I went about my evening work with trembling steps. Mr. Flint twice called from his chamber door to inquire why the house was not locked up. I replied that I had not done my work.

"You have had time enough to do it," said he. "Take care how you answer me."

I shut all the windows, locked all the doors and went up to the third story, to wait till midnight. How long those hours seemed, and how fervently I prayed that God would not forsake me in this hour of utmost need. I was about to risk everything on the throw of a die, and if I failed, what would become of me and my poor children? They would be made to suffer for my fault.

At half past twelve I stole softly downstairs. I stopped on the second floor, thinking I heard a noise. I felt my way down into the parlor and looked out of the window. The night was so intensely dark that I could see nothing. I raised the window very softly and jumped out. Large drops of rain were falling, and the darkness bewildered me. I dropped on my knees and breathed a short prayer to God for guidance and protection. I groped my way to the road and rushed towards the town with almost lightning speed. I arrived at my grandmother's house, but dared not see her. She would say, "Linda, you are killing me," and I knew that would unnerve me.

I tapped softly at the window of a room occupied by a woman who had lived in the house several years. I knew she was a faithful friend and could be trusted with my secret. I tapped several times before she heard me. At last she raised the window.

I whispered, "Sally, I have run away. Let me in, quick."

She opened the door softly, and said in low tones, "For God's sake, don't. Your grandmother is trying to buy you and the children. Mr. Sands was here last week. He told her he was going away on business, but he wanted her to go ahead about buying you and the children, and he would help her all he could. Don't run away, Linda. Your grandmother is all bowed down with trouble now."

I replied, "Sally, they are going to carry my children to the plantation tomorrow, and they will never sell them to anybody so long as they have me in their power. Now, would you advise me to go back?"

"No, chile, no," answered she. "When they finds you is gone, they won't want the plague of the children. But where is you going to hide? They knows every inch of this house."

I told her I had a hiding place, and that was all it was best for her to know. I asked her to go into my room as soon as it was light and take all my clothes out of my trunk, and pack them in hers, for I knew Mr. Flint and the constable would be there early to search my room. I feared the sight of my children would be too much for my full heart, but I could not go out into the uncertain future without one last look. I bent over the bed where lay my little Benny and baby Ellen. Poor little ones. Fatherless and motherless! Memories of their father came over me. He wanted to be kind to them, but they were not all to him, as they were to my womanly heart. I knelt and prayed for the innocent little sleepers. I kissed them lightly, and turned away.

As I was about to open the street door, Sally laid her hand on my shoulder, and said, "Linda, is you gwine all alone? Let me call your uncle."

"No, Sally," I replied, "I want no one to be brought into trouble on my account."

I went forth into the darkness and rain. I ran on till I came to the house of the friend who was to conceal me.

Early the next morning Mr. Flint was at my grandmother's inquiring for me. She told him she had not seen me, and supposed I was at the plantation. He watched her face narrowly, and said, "Don't you know anything about her running off?" She assured him that she did not. He went on to say, "Last night she ran off without the least provocation. We had treated her very kindly. My wife liked her. She will soon be found and brought back. Are her children with you?" When told that they were, he said, "I am very glad to hear that. If they are here, she cannot be far off. If I find out that any of my niggers have had anything to do with this damned business, I'll give 'em five hundred lashes." As he started to go to his father's, he turned round and added, persuasively, "Let her be brought back, and she shall have her children to live with her."

The tidings made the old doctor rave and storm at a furious rate. It was a busy day for them. My grandmother's house was searched from top to bottom. As my trunk was empty, they concluded I had taken my clothes with me. Before ten o'clock, every vessel northward bound was thoroughly examined, and the law against harboring fugitives was read to all on board. At night a watch was set over the town. Knowing how distressed my grandmother would be, I wanted to send her a message, but it could not be done. Everyone who went in or out of her house was closely watched. The doctor said he would take my children, unless she became responsible for them, which of course she willingly did. The next day was spent in searching. Before night, the following advertisement was posted at every corner, and in every public place for miles round:

$300 REWARD!

Ran away from the subscriber, an intelligent, bright, mulatto girl, named Linda, 21 years of age. Five feet four inches high. Dark eyes, and black hair inclined to curl, but it can be made straight. Has a decayed spot on a front tooth. She can read and write, and in all probability will try to get to the Free States. All persons are forbidden, under penalty of the law to harbor or employ said slave. $150 will be given to whoever takes her in the State, and $300 if taken out of the State and delivered to me, or lodged in jail.

  DR. FLINT

The search for me was kept up with more perseverance than I

had anticipated. I began to think that escape was impossible. I was in great anxiety lest I should implicate the friend who harbored me. I knew the consequences would be frightful. Much as I dreaded being caught, even that seemed better than causing an innocent person to suffer for kindness to me. A week had passed in terrible suspense, when my pursuers came into such close vicinity that I concluded they had tracked me to my hiding place. I flew out of the house, and concealed myself in a thicket of bushes. There I remained in an agony of fear for two hours. Suddenly, a reptile of some kind seized my leg. In my fright, I struck a blow which loosened its hold, but I could not tell whether I had killed it. It was so dark, I could not see what it was, I only knew it was something cold and slimy. The pain I felt soon indicated that the bite was poisonous. I was compelled to leave my place of concealment, and I groped my way back into the house. The pain had become intense, and my friend was startled by my look of anguish. I asked her to prepare a poultice of warm ashes and vinegar, and I applied it to my leg, which was already much swollen. The application gave me some relief, but the swelling did not abate. The dread of being disabled was greater than the physical pain I endured. My friend asked an old woman, who doctored among the slaves, what was good for the bite of a snake or a lizard. She told her to steep a dozen coppers in vinegar overnight, and apply the cankered vinegar to the inflamed part.

I had succeeded in cautiously conveying some messages to my relatives. They were harshly threatened, and despairing of my having a chance to escape, they advised me to return to my master, ask his forgiveness, and let him make an example of me. But such counsel had no influence with me. When I started upon this hazardous undertaking, I had resolved that, come what would, there should be no turning back. *Give me liberty, or give me death,* was my motto. When my friend contrived to make known to my relatives the painful situation I had been in

for twenty-four hours, they said no more about my going back
to my master. Something must be done, and that speedily, but
where to turn for help, they knew not.

God in his mercy raised up *a friend in need.*

Among the ladies who were acquainted with my
grandmother, was one who had known her from childhood,
and always been very friendly to her. She had also known my
mother and her children, and felt interested for them. At this
crisis of affairs she called to see my grandmother, as she not
infrequently did. She observed the sad and troubled expression
of her face and asked if she knew where Linda was and
whether she was safe.

My grandmother shook her head, without answering.

"Come, Aunt Martha," said the kind lady, "tell me all about
it. Perhaps I can do something to help you."

The husband of this lady held many slaves, and bought and
sold slaves. She also held a number in her own name, but she
treated them kindly and would never allow any of them to be
sold. She was unlike the majority of slaveholders' wives. My
grandmother looked earnestly at her. Something in the
expression of her face said 'Trust me', and she did trust her. She
listened attentively to the details of my story, and sat thinking
for a while. At last she said, "Aunt Martha, I pity you both. If
you think there is any chance of Linda's getting to the Free
States, I will conceal her for a time. But first you must solemnly
promise that my name shall never be mentioned. If such a thing
should become known, it would ruin me and my family. No
one in my house must know of it, except the cook. She is so
faithful that I would trust my own life with her, and I know she
likes Linda. It is a great risk, but I trust no harm will come of it.
Get word to Linda to be ready as soon as it is dark, before the
patrols are out. I will send the housemaids on errands, and
Betty shall go to meet Linda."

The place where we were to meet was designated and

agreed upon. My grandmother was unable to thank the lady for this noble deed. Overcome by her emotions, she sank on her knees and sobbed like a child.

I received a message to leave my friend's house at such an hour, and go to a certain place where a friend would be waiting for me. As a matter of prudence no names were mentioned. I had no means of conjecturing who I was to meet, or where I was going. I did not like to move thus blindfolded, but I had no choice. It would not do for me to remain where I was. I disguised myself, summoned up courage to meet the worst, and went to the appointed place. My friend Betty was there, she was the last person I expected to see. We hurried along in silence. The pain in my leg was so intense that it seemed as if I should drop, but fear gave me strength. We reached the house and entered unobserved. Her first words were: "Honey, now you is safe. Dem devils ain't coming to search this house. When I get you into missis' safe place, I will bring some nice hot supper. I specs you need it."

Betty's vocation led her to think eating the most important thing in life. She did not realize that my heart was too full for me to care much about supper.

The mistress came to meet us, and led me upstairs to a small room over her own sleeping apartment.

"You will be safe here, Linda," said she, "I keep this room to store away things that are out of use. The girls are not accustomed to be sent to it, and they will not suspect anything unless they hear some noise. I always keep it locked. Betty shall take care of the key. But you must be very careful, for my sake as well as your own, and you must never tell my secret, for it would ruin me and my family. I will keep the girls busy in the morning, that Betty may have a chance to bring your breakfast, but it will not do for her to come to you again till night. I will come to see you sometimes. Keep up your courage. I hope this state of things will not last long."

Betty came with the 'nice hot supper', and the mistress hastened downstairs to keep things straight till she returned. How my heart overflowed with gratitude! Words choked in my throat, but I could have kissed the feet of my benefactress. For that deed of Christian womanhood, may God forever bless her.

I went to sleep that night with the feeling that I was for the present the most fortunate slave in town. Morning came and filled my little cell with light. I thanked the heavenly Father for this safe retreat. Opposite my window was a pile of feather beds. On the top of these I could lie perfectly concealed, and command a view of the street through which Dr. Flint passed to his office. Anxious as I was, I felt a gleam of satisfaction when I saw him. Thus far I had outwitted him, and I triumphed over it. Who can blame slaves for being cunning? They are constantly compelled to resort to it. It is the only weapon of the weak and oppressed against the strength of their tyrants.

I was daily hoping to hear that my master had sold my children, for I knew who was on the watch to buy them. But Dr. Flint cared even more for revenge than he did for money. My brother William, and the good aunt who had served in his family twenty years, and my little Benny, and Ellen, who was a little over two years old, were thrust into jail, as a means of compelling my relatives to give some information about me. He swore my grandmother should never see one of them again till I was brought back. They kept these facts from me for several days. When I heard that my little ones were in a loathsome jail, my first impulse was to go to them. I was encountering dangers for the sake of freeing them, and must I be the cause of their death? The thought was agonizing. My benefactress tried to soothe me by telling me that my aunt would take good care of the children while they remained in jail. But it added to my pain to think that the good old aunt who had always been so kind to her sister's orphan children, should be shut up in prison for no other crime than loving them. I suppose my friends feared a reckless movement on my part, knowing as they did that my life was bound up in my children. I received a note from my brother William. It was scarcely legible, and ran thus:

Wherever you are, dear sister, I beg of you not to come here. We are all much better off than you are. If you come, you will ruin us all. They would force you to tell where you had been, or they would kill you. Take the advice of your friends, if not for the sake of me and your children, at least for the sake of those you would ruin.

Poor William. He also must suffer for being my brother. I took his advice and kept quiet.

My aunt was taken out of jail at the end of a month because Mrs. Flint could not spare her any longer. She was tired of being her own housekeeper. It was quite too fatiguing to order her dinner and eat it too. My children remained in jail, where brother William did all he could for their comfort. Betty went to see them sometimes, and brought me tidings. She was not permitted to enter the jail, but William would hold them up to the grated window while she chatted with them. When she repeated their prattle, and told me how they wanted to see their ma, my tears would flow. Old Betty would exclaim, "Lawd, chile, what you crying 'bout? Dem young uns will kill you dead. Don't be so chicken-hearted. If you does, you will never git thro' this world."

Good old soul. She had gone through the world childless. She had never had little ones to clasp their arms round her neck, she had never seen their soft eyes looking into hers, no sweet little voices had called her mother, she had never pressed her own infants to her heart, with the feeling that even in fetters there was something to live for. How could she realize my feelings?

Betty's husband loved children dearly, and wondered why God had denied them to him. He expressed great sorrow when he came to Betty with the tidings that Ellen had been taken out of jail and carried to Dr. Flint's. She had the measles a short time before they carried her to jail, and the disease had left her eyes affected. The doctor had taken her home to attend to them. My children had always been afraid of the doctor and his wife. They had never been inside of their house. Poor little Ellen cried all day to be carried back to prison. The instincts of childhood are true. She knew she was loved in the jail. Her screams and sobs annoyed Mrs. Flint. Before night she called one of the slaves, and said, "Here, Bill, carry this brat back to the jail. I can't stand her noise. If she would be quiet I should like to keep the little minx. She would make a handy waiting-maid for my daughter by and by. But if she stayed here, with her white face, I suppose I should either kill her or spoil her. I hope the doctor will sell them as far as wind and water can carry them. As for their mother, her ladyship will find out yet what she gets by running away. She hasn't so much feeling for her children as a cow has for its calf. If she had, she would have come back long ago, to get them out of jail and save all this expense and trouble. The good-for-nothing hussy! When she is caught, she shall stay in jail, in irons, for six months, and then be sold to a sugar plantation. I shall see her broke in yet. What do you stand there for, Bill? Why don't you go off with the brat? Mind, now, that you don't let any of the niggers speak to her in the street."

When these remarks were reported to me, I smiled at Mrs. Flint's saying that she should either kill my child or spoil her. I thought to myself there was very little danger of the latter. I have always considered it as one of God's special providences that Ellen screamed till she was carried back to jail.

That same night Dr. Flint was called to a patient, and did not return till near morning. Passing my grandmother's, he saw a light in the house, and thought to himself, "Perhaps this has something to do with Linda." He knocked, and the door was opened. "What calls you up so early?" said he. "I saw your light, and I thought I would just stop and tell you that I have found out where Linda is. I know where to put my hands on her, and I shall have her before twelve o'clock."

When he had turned away, my grandmother and my uncle looked anxiously at each other. They did not know whether or not it was merely one of the doctor's tricks to frighten them. In their uncertainty, they thought it was best to have a message conveyed to my friend Betty. Unwilling to alarm her mistress, Betty resolved to dispose of me herself. She came to me, and told me to rise and dress quickly. We hurried downstairs and across the yard, into the kitchen. She locked the door, and lifted up a plank in the floor. A buffalo skin and a bit of carpet were spread for me to lie on, and a quilt thrown over me. "Stay there," said she, "till I sees if they know 'bout you. They say they will put their hands on you afore twelve o'clock. If they did know where you are, they won't know now. They'll be disappointed this time. Dat's all I got to say. If they comes rummagin 'mong my things, they'll get one blessed saucing from this 'ere nigger."

In my shallow bed I had but just room enough to bring my hands to my face to keep the dust out of my eyes, for Betty walked over me twenty times in an hour, passing from the dresser to the fireplace. When she was alone, I could hear her pronouncing anathemas over Dr. Flint and all his tribe, every now and then saying, with a chuckling laugh, "This nigger's too cute for 'em this time."

When the housemaids were about she had sly ways of drawing them out, that I might hear what they would say. She would repeat stories she had heard about my being in this or that place. To which they would answer that I was not fool enough to be staying round there, that I was in Philadelphia or New York by now. When all were in bed and asleep, Betty raised the plank and said, "Come out, chile, come out. They don't know nothing 'bout you. 'Twas only white folks' lies, to scarer the niggers."

Some days after this adventure I had a much worse fright. As I sat very still in my retreat above stairs, cheerful visions floated through my mind. I thought Dr. Flint would soon get discouraged and would be willing to sell my children, when he lost all hopes of making them the means of my discovery. Suddenly I heard a voice that chilled my blood. The sound was too familiar to me, too dreadful for me not to recognize at once my old master. He was in the house. I at once concluded he had come to seize me. I looked round in terror: There was no way of escape. The voice receded. I supposed the constable was with him, and they were searching the house. In my alarm I did not forget the trouble I was bringing on my generous benefactress. It seemed as if I were born to bring sorrow on all who befriended me, and that was the bitterest drop in the bitter cup of my life. After a while I heard approaching footsteps, the key was turned in my door. I braced myself against the wall to keep from falling. I ventured to look up, and there stood my kind benefactress alone. I was too much overcome to speak, and sunk down upon the floor.

"I thought you would hear your master's voice," she said, "and knowing you would be terrified, I came to tell you there is nothing to fear. You may even indulge in a laugh at the old gentleman's expense. He is so sure you are in New York, that he came to borrow five hundred dollars to go in pursuit of you. My sister had some money to loan on interest. He has obtained it, and proposes to start for New York tonight. So, for the present, you see you are safe. The doctor will merely lighten his pocket hunting after the bird he has left behind."

The doctor came back from New York, of course without accomplishing his purpose. He had expended considerable money, and was rather disheartened. My brother and the children had now been in jail two months, and that also was some expense. My friends thought it was a favorable time to work on his discouraged feelings. Mr. Sands sent a speculator to offer him nine hundred dollars for my brother William, and eight hundred for the two children. These were high prices, as slaves were then selling, but the offer was rejected. If it had been merely a question of money, the doctor would have sold any boy of Benny's age for two hundred dollars, but he could not bear to give up the power of revenge. But he was hard pressed for money, and he revolved the matter in his mind. He knew that if he could keep Ellen till she was fifteen, he could sell her for a high price, but I presume he reflected that she might die, or might be stolen away. At all events, he came to the conclusion that he had better accept the slave-trader's offer. Meeting him in the street, he inquired when he would leave town.

"Today, at ten o'clock," he replied.

"Ah, do you go so soon?" said the doctor, "I have been reflecting upon your proposition, and I have concluded to let you have the three negroes if you will say nineteen hundred dollars."

After some parley, the trader agreed to his terms. He wanted the bill of sale drawn up and signed immediately, as he had a great deal to attend to during the short time he remained in town. The doctor went to the jail and told William he would take him back into his service if he would promise to behave himself, but he replied that he would rather be sold.

"And you shall be sold, you ungrateful rascal," exclaimed the doctor. In less than an hour the money was paid, the papers were signed, sealed, and delivered, and my brother and children were in the hands of the trader.

It was a hurried transaction. After it was over, the doctor's characteristic caution returned. He went back to the speculator, and said, "Sir, I have come to lay you under obligations of a thousand dollars not to sell any of those negroes in this State."

"You come too late," replied the trader, "our bargain is

closed."

He had, in fact, already sold them to Mr. Sands, but he did not mention it. The doctor required him to put irons on "that rascal, Bill," and to pass through the back streets when he took his gang out of town. The trader was privately instructed to concede to his wishes.

My good old aunt went to the jail to bid the children goodbye, supposing them to be the speculator's property, and that she should never see them again. As she held Benny in her lap, he said, "Aunt Nancy, I want to show you something." He led her to the door and showed her a long row of marks, saying, "Uncle Will taught me to count. I have made a mark for every day I have been here, and it is sixty days. It is a long time, and the speculator is going to take me and Ellen away. He's a bad man. It's wrong for him to take grandmother's children. I want to go to my mother."

My grandmother was told that the children would be restored to her, but she was requested to act as if they were really to be sent away. Accordingly, she made up a bundle of clothes and went to the jail. When she arrived, she found William handcuffed among the slave gang, and the children in the trader's cart. The scene seemed too much like reality. She was afraid there might have been some deception or mistake. She fainted, and was carried home.

When the wagon stopped at the hotel, several gentlemen came out and proposed to purchase William, but the trader refused their offers, without stating that he was already sold. And now came the trying hour for that drove of human beings, driven away like cattle, to be sold they knew not where. Husbands were torn from wives, parents from children, never to look upon each other again this side the grave. There was wringing of hands and cries of despair.

Dr. Flint had the supreme satisfaction of seeing the wagon leave town, and Mrs. Flint had the gratification of supposing that my children were going "as far as wind and water would carry them."

According to agreement, my uncle followed the wagon some miles, until they came to an old farm house. There the trader took the irons from William, and as he did so, he said, "You are a damned clever fellow. I should like to own you myself. Them gentlemen that wanted to buy you said you was a bright, honest chap, and I must git you a good home. I guess your old master will swear tomorrow, and call himself an old fool for selling the children. I reckon he'll never git their mammy back agin. I expect she's made tracks for the North. Goodbye, old boy. Remember, I have done you a good turn. You must thank me by coaxing all the pretty gals to go with me next fall. That's going to be my last trip. This trading in niggers is a bad business for a fellow that's got any heart. Move on, you fellows."

And the gang went on, God alone knows where.

Much as I despise and detest the class of slave-traders, whom I regard as the vilest wretches on earth, I must do this man the justice to say that he seemed to have some feeling. He took a fancy to William in the jail, and wanted to buy him. When he heard the story of my children, he was willing to aid them in getting out of Dr. Flint's power, even without charging the customary fee.

My uncle procured a wagon and carried William and the children back to town. Great was the joy in my grandmother's house. The curtains were closed, and the candles lighted. The happy grandmother cuddled the little ones to her bosom. They hugged her, and kissed her, and clapped their hands, and shouted. She knelt down and poured forth one of her heartfelt prayers of thanksgiving to God. The father was present for a while, and though such a parental relation as existed between him and my children takes slight hold of the hearts or consciences of slaveholders, it must be that he experienced some moments of pure joy in witnessing the happiness he had imparted.

I had no share in the rejoicings of that evening. The events of the day had not come to my knowledge. I will tell you something that happened to me, though you will perhaps think it illustrates the superstition of slaves. I sat in my usual place on the floor near the window, where I could hear much that was said in the street without being seen. The family had retired for the night, and all was still. I sat there thinking of my children, when I heard a low strain of music. A band of serenaders were under the window, playing *Home, Sweet Home*. I listened till the sounds did not seem like music, but like the moaning of children. It seemed as if my heart would burst. I rose from my sitting posture, and knelt. A streak of moonlight was on the floor before me, and in the midst of it appeared the forms of my two children. They vanished, but I had seen them distinctly. Some will call it a dream, others a vision.

I know not how to account for it, but it made a strong impression on my mind, and I felt certain something had happened to my little ones.

I had not seen Betty since morning. Now I heard her softly turning the key. As soon as she entered, I clung to her, and begged her to let me know whether my children were dead or whether they were sold, for I had seen their spirits in my room, I was sure something had happened to them.

"Lawd, chile," said she, putting her arms round me, "you's got the highsterics. I'll sleep with you tonight, 'cause you'll make a noise and ruin missis. Something has stirred you up mightily. When you is done crying, I'll talk with you.

"The children is well, and mighty happy. I seen 'em myself. Does dat satisfy you?

There, chile, be still, somebody will hear you." I tried to obey her. She lay down, and was soon sound asleep, but no sleep would come to my eyelids.

At dawn, Betty was up and off to the kitchen. The hours passed on, and the vision of the night kept constantly recurring to my thoughts. After a while I heard the voices of two women in the entry. In one of them I recognized the housemaid. The other said to her, "Did you know Linda Brent's children was sold to the speculator yesterday. They say ole massa Flint was mighty glad to see 'em drove out of town, but they say they've come back agin. I 'spect it's all their daddy's doings. They say he's bought William too. Lawd, how it will take hold of old massa Flint. I'm going roun' to Aunt Marthy's to see 'bout it."

I bit my lips till the blood came to keep from crying out. Were my children with their grandmother, or had the speculator carried them off? The suspense was dreadful. Would Betty never come and tell me the truth about it? At last she came, and I eagerly repeated what I had overheard. Her face was one broad, bright smile.

"Lawd, you foolish thing," said she. I'm gwine to tell you all 'bout it. The gals is eating their breakfast, and missis told me to let her tell you but, poor creature, t'aint right to keep you waitin'. Brother, children, all is bought by the daddy. I'se laugh more than nuff, thinking 'bout ole massa Flint. Lawd, how he will swear! He's got ketched this time. Anyhow, I must be going, or dem gals will come and ketch me."

Betty went off laughing, and I said to myself, "Can it be true that my children are free? I have not suffered for them in vain. Thank God."

Great surprise was expressed when it was known that my children had returned to their grandmother's. The news spread through the town, and many a kind word was bestowed on the little ones.

Dr. Flint went to my grandmother's to ascertain who was the owner of my children, and she informed him.

"I expected as much," said he. "I am glad to hear it. I have had news from Linda lately, and I shall soon have her. You need never expect to see her free. She shall be my slave as long as I live, and when I am dead she shall be the slave of my children. If I ever find out that you or Phillip had anything to do with her running off I'll kill him. And if I meet William in the street, and he presumes to look at me, I'll flog him within an inch of his life. Keep those brats out of my sight."

As he turned to leave, my grandmother said something to remind him of his own doings. He looked back upon her, as if he would have been glad to strike her to the ground.

I had my season of joy and thanksgiving. It was the first time since my childhood that I had experienced any real happiness. I heard of the old doctor's threats, but they no longer had the same power to trouble me. The darkest cloud that hung over my life had rolled away. Whatever slavery might do to me, it could not shackle my children. If I fell a sacrifice, my little ones were saved. It was well for me that my simple heart believed all that had been promised for their welfare. It is always better to trust than to doubt.

The doctor, more exasperated than ever, again tried to revenge himself on my relatives. He arrested uncle Phillip on the charge of having aided my flight. He was carried before a court, and swore truly that he knew nothing of my intention to escape and that he had not seen me since I left my master's plantation. The doctor then demanded that he should give bail for five hundred dollars that he would have nothing to do with me. Several gentlemen offered to be security for him, but Mr. Sands told him he had better go back to jail, and he would see that he came out without giving bail.

The news of his arrest was carried to my grandmother, who conveyed it to Betty. In the kindness of her heart, she again stowed me away under the floor, and as she walked back and forth, in the performance of her culinary duties, she talked apparently to herself, but with the intention that I should hear what was going on. I hoped that my uncle's imprisonment

would last but few days, still I was anxious. I thought it likely
Dr. Flint would do his utmost to taunt and insult him, and I was
afraid my uncle might lose control of himself, and retort in
some way that would be construed into a punishable offense. I
was well aware that in court his word would not be taken
against any white man's.

The search for me was renewed. Something had excited
suspicions that I was in the vicinity. They searched the house I
was in. I heard their steps and their voices. At night, when all
were asleep, Betty came to release me from my place of
confinement. The fright I had undergone, the constrained
posture, and the dampness of the ground, made me ill for
several days. My uncle was soon after taken out of prison, but
the movements of all my relatives, and of all our friends, were
very closely watched.

We all saw that I could not remain where I was much longer.
I had already stayed longer than was intended, and I knew my
presence must be a source of perpetual anxiety to my kind
benefactress. During this time, my friends had laid many plans
for my escape, but the extreme vigilance of my persecutors
made it impossible to carry them into effect.

One morning, I was much startled by hearing somebody
trying to get into my room. Several keys were tried, but none
fitted. I instantly conjectured it was one of the housemaids, and
I concluded she must either have heard some noise in the room
or have noticed the entrance of Betty. When my friend came, at
her usual time, I told her what had happened.

"I knows who it was," said she. " 'Pend upon it, 'twas dat
Jenny. Dat nigger always got the devil in her."

I suggested that she might have seen or heard something
that excited her curiosity.

"Chile," exclaimed Betty, "she ain't seen nothin', nor heard
nothin'. She only 'spects something. Dat's all. She wants to find
out who has cut and made my gowns. But she won't never

know. I'll git missis to fix her."

I reflected a moment and said, "Betty, I must leave here tonight."

"Do as you think best, poor chile," she replied. "I'se mighty 'fraid dat 'ere nigger will pop on you some time."

She reported the incident to her mistress, and received orders to keep Jenny busy in the kitchen till she could see my uncle Phillip. He told her he would send a friend for me that very evening. She told him she hoped I was going to the North, for it was very dangerous for me to remain anywhere in the vicinity. Alas, it was not an easy thing for one in my situation to go to the North. In order to leave the coast quite clear for me, she went into the country to spend the day with her brother, and took Jenny with her. She was afraid to come and bid me goodbye, but she left a kind message with Betty. I heard her carriage roll from the door, and I never again saw her who had so generously befriended the poor trembling fugitive. Though she was a slaveholder, to this day my heart blesses her!

I had not the slightest idea where I was going. Betty brought me a suit of sailor's clothes — jacket, trousers, and tarpaulin hat. She gave me a small bundle, saying I might need it where I was going. In cheery tones, she exclaimed, "I'se so glad you is gwine to free parts. Don't forget old Betty. P'raps I'll come 'long by and by."

I tried to tell her how grateful I felt for all her kindness, but she interrupted me.

"I don't want no thanks, honey. I'se glad I could help you, and I hope the good Lord will open the path for you. I'se gwine with you to the lower gate. Put your hands in your pockets, and walk rickety, like the sailors."

I performed to her satisfaction. At the gate I found Peter, a young colored man, waiting for me. I had known him for years. He had been an apprentice to my father, and had always borne a good character. I was not afraid to trust to him. Betty bade me a hurried goodbye, and we walked off.

"Take courage, Linda," said my friend Peter. "I've got a dagger, and no man shall take you from me, unless he passes over my dead body."

It was a long time since I had taken a walk out of doors, and the fresh air revived me. It was also pleasant to hear a human voice speaking to me above a whisper. I passed several people whom I knew, but they did not recognize me in my disguise. I prayed internally that, for Peter's sake, as well as my own, nothing might occur to bring out his dagger. We walked on till we came to the wharf.

My aunt Nancy's husband was a seafaring man, and it had been deemed necessary to let him into our secret. He took me into his boat, rowed out to a vessel not far distant, and hoisted me on board. We three were the only occupants of the vessel. I now ventured to ask what they proposed to do with me. They said I was to remain on board till near dawn, and then they would hide me in Snaky Swamp, till my uncle Phillip had prepared a place of concealment for me. If the vessel had been bound north, it would have been of no avail to me, for it would certainly have been searched. About four o'clock, we were again seated in the boat, and rowed three miles to the swamp. My fear of snakes had been increased by the venomous bite I had received, and I dreaded to enter this hiding place. But I was in no situation to choose, and I gratefully accepted the best that my poor, persecuted friends could do for me.

Peter landed first, and with a large knife cut a path through bamboos and briers of all descriptions. He came back, took me in his arms, and carried me to a seat made among the bamboos. Before we reached it, we were covered with hundreds of mosquitoes. In an hour's time they had so poisoned my flesh that I was a pitiful sight to behold. As the light increased, I saw snake after snake crawling round us. I had been accustomed to the sight of snakes all my life, but these were larger than any I had ever seen. To this day, I shudder when I remember that morning. As evening approached, the number of snakes increased so much that we were continually obliged to thrash them with sticks to keep them from crawling over us.

The bamboos were so high and so thick that it was impossible to see beyond a very short distance. Just before it became dark we procured a seat nearer to the entrance of the swamp, being fearful of losing our way back to the boat. It was not long before we heard the paddle of oars and the low whistle, which had been agreed upon as a signal. We made haste to enter the boat, and were rowed back to the vessel. I passed a wretched night, for the heat of the swamp, the mosquitoes, and the constant terror of snakes, had brought on a burning fever. I had just dropped asleep, when they came and told me it was time to go back to that horrid swamp. I could scarcely summon courage to rise. But even those large, venomous snakes were less dreadful to my imagination than the white men in that community called civilized. This time Peter took a quantity of tobacco to burn, to keep off the mosquitos. It produced the desired effect on them, but gave me nausea and severe headache. At dark we returned to the vessel. I had been so sick during the day, that Peter declared I should go home that night, if the devil himself was on patrol. They told me a place of concealment had been provided for me at my grandmother's. I could not imagine how it was possible to hide me in her house, every nook and corner of which was known to the Flint family. They told me to wait and see. We were rowed ashore, and went boldly through the streets to my grandmother's. I wore my sailor's clothes, and had blackened my face with charcoal. I passed several people whom I knew. The father of my children came so near that I brushed against his arm, but he had no idea who it was.

"You must make the most of this walk," said my friend Peter, "for you may not have another very soon."

I thought his voice sounded sad. It was kind of him to conceal from me what a dismal hole was to be my home for a long, long time.

A small shed had been added to my grandmother's house years ago. Some boards were laid across the joists at the top, and between these boards and the roof was a very small garret, never occupied by anything but rats and mice. It was a pent roof, covered with nothing but shingles, according to the Southern custom for such buildings. The garret was only nine feet long and seven wide. The highest part was three feet high, and sloped down abruptly to the loose floorboards. There was no admission for either light or air. My uncle Phillip, who was a carpenter, had very skillfully made a concealed trap-door, which communicated with the storeroom. He had been doing this while I was waiting in the swamp. The storeroom opened upon a piazza. To this hole I was conveyed as soon as I entered the house. The air was stifling, the darkness total. A bed had been spread on the floor. I could sleep quite comfortably on one side, but the slope was so sudden that I could not turn on the other without hitting the roof. The rats and mice ran over my bed, but I was weary, and I slept such sleep as the wretched may, when a tempest has passed over them.

Morning came. I knew it only by the noises I heard, for in my small den day and night were all the same. I suffered for air even more than for light. But I was not comfortless. I heard the voices of my children. There was joy and there was sadness in the sound. It made my tears flow. How I longed to speak to them. I was eager to look on their faces, but there was no hole, no crack through which I could peep. This continued darkness was oppressive. It seemed horrible to sit or lie in a cramped position day after day, without one gleam of light. Yet I would have chosen this, rather than my lot as a slave, though white people considered it an easy one, and it was so compared with the fate of others. I was never cruelly overworked, I was never lacerated with the whip from head to foot, I was never so beaten and bruised that I could not turn from one side to the other, I never had my heelstrings cut to prevent my running away, I was never chained to a log and forced to drag it about, while I toiled in the fields from morning till night, I was never branded with hot iron, or torn by bloodhounds. On the contrary, I had always been kindly treated, and tenderly cared for, until I came into the hands of Dr. Flint. I had never wished for freedom till then. But though my life in slavery was comparatively devoid of hardships, God pity the woman who is compelled to lead such a life.

My food was passed up to me through the trap-door my uncle had contrived, and my grandmother, my uncle Phillip, and aunt Nancy would seize such opportunities as they could, to mount up there and chat with me at the opening. But of course this was not safe in the daytime. It must all be done in darkness. It was impossible for me to move in an erect position, but I crawled about my den for exercise. One day I hit my head against something, and found it was a gimlet. My uncle had left it sticking there when he made the trap-door. I was as rejoiced as Robinson Crusoe could have been at finding such a treasure. It put a lucky thought into my head. I said to myself, "Now I will have some light. Now I will see my children."

I did not dare to begin my work during the daytime, for fear of attracting attention. But I groped round, and having found the side next the street, where I could frequently see my children, I stuck the gimlet in and waited for evening. I bored three rows of holes, one above another, then I bored out the interstices between. I thus succeeded in making one hole about an inch long and an inch broad. I sat by it till late into the night, to enjoy the little whiff of air that floated in. In the morning I watched for my children. The first person I saw in the street was Dr. Flint. I had a shuddering, superstitious feeling that it was a bad omen. Several familiar faces passed by. At last I heard the merry laugh of children, and presently two sweet little faces were looking up at me, as though they knew I was there, and were conscious of the joy they imparted. How I longed to tell them I was there.

My condition was now a little improved. But for weeks I was tormented by hundreds of little red insects, fine as a needle's point, that pierced through my skin, and produced an intolerable burning. The good grandmother gave me herb teas and cooling medicines, and finally I got rid of them. The heat of my den was intense, for nothing but thin shingles protected me from the scorching summer's sun. But I had my consolations. Through my peeping hole I could watch the children, and when they were near enough, I could hear their talk.

Aunt Nancy brought me all the news she could hear at Dr. Flint's. From her I learned that the doctor had written to New York to a colored woman, who had been born and raised in our neighborhood, and had breathed his contaminating atmosphere. He offered her a reward if she could find out anything about me. I know not what was the nature of her reply, but he soon after started for New York in haste, saying to his family that he had business of importance to transact. I peeped at him as he passed on his way to the steamboat. It was a satisfaction to have miles of land and water between us, even for a little while, and it was a still greater satisfaction to know that he believed me to be in the Free States. My little den seemed less dreary than it had done. He returned, as he did from his former journey to New York, without obtaining any satisfactory information. When he passed our house next morning, Benny was standing at the gate. He had heard them say that he had gone to find me, and he called out, "Dr. Flint, did you bring my mother home? I want to see her."

The doctor stamped his foot at him in a rage, and exclaimed, "Get out of the way, you little damned rascal. If you don't, I'll cut off your head."

Benny ran terrified into the house, saying, "You can't put me in jail again. I don't belong to you now."

It was well that the wind carried the words away from the doctor's ear. I told my grandmother of it, when we had our next conference at the trap-door, and begged of her not to allow the children to be impertinent to the irascible old man.

Autumn came, with a pleasant abatement of heat. My eyes had become accustomed to the dim light, and by holding my book or work in a certain position near the aperture I contrived to read and sew. That was a great relief to the tedious monotony of my life. But when winter came, the cold penetrated through the thin shingle roof, and I was dreadfully chilled. The winters there are not so long or so severe as in northern latitudes, but the houses are not built to shelter from cold, and my little den was peculiarly comfortless. The kind grandmother brought me bedclothes and warm drinks. Often I was obliged to lie in bed all day to keep comfortable, but with all my precautions, my shoulders and feet were frostbitten. Oh, those long, gloomy days, with no object for my eye to rest upon, and no thoughts to occupy my mind, except the dreary past and the uncertain future. I was thankful when there came a day sufficiently mild for me to wrap myself up and sit at the loophole to watch the passers-by. Southerners have the habit of stopping and talking in the streets, and I heard many conversations not intended to meet my ears. I heard slavehunters planning how to catch some poor fugitive. Several times I heard allusions to Dr. Flint, myself, and the history of my children, who, perhaps, were playing near the gate. One would say, "I wouldn't move my little finger to catch her, as old Flint's property," Another would say, "I'll catch any nigger for the reward. A man ought to have what belongs to him, if he is a damned brute." The opinion was often expressed that I was in the Free States. Very rarely did anyone suggest that I might be in the vicinity. Had the least suspicion rested on my grandmother's house, it would have been burned to the ground. But it was the last place they thought of. Yet there was no place where slavery existed that could have afforded me so good a place of concealment.

Dr. Flint and his family repeatedly tried to coax and bribe my children to tell something they had heard said about me. One day the doctor took them into a shop and offered them some bright little silver pieces and gay handkerchiefs if they would tell where their mother was. Ellen shrank away from him, and would not speak, but Benny spoke up, and said, "Dr. Flint, I don't know where my mother is. I guess she's in New York, and when you go there again, I wish you'd ask her to come home, for I want to see her. But if you put her in jail, or tell her you'll cut her head off, I'll tell her to go right back."

Christmas was approaching. Grandmother brought me materials, and I busied myself making some new garments and little playthings for my children. Were it not that hiring day is near at hand, and many families are fearfully looking forward to the probability of separation in a few days, Christmas might be a happy season for the poor slaves. Even slave mothers try to gladden the hearts of their little ones on that occasion. Benny and Ellen had their Christmas stockings filled. Their imprisoned mother could not have the privilege of witnessing their surprise and joy. But I had the pleasure of peeping at them as they went into the street with their new suits on. I heard Benny ask a little playmate whether Santa Claus brought him anything.

"Yes," replied the boy, "but Santa Claus ain't a real man. It's the children's mothers that put things into the stockings."

"No, that can't be," replied Benny, "for Santa Claus brought Ellen and me these new clothes, and my mother has been gone this long time."

How I longed to tell him that his mother made those

garments, and that many a tear fell on them while she worked.

Every child rises early on Christmas morning to see the Johnkannus. Without them, Christmas would be shorn of its greatest attraction. They consist of companies of slaves from the plantations, generally of the lower class. Two athletic men, in calico wrappers, have a net thrown over them, covered with all manner of bright-colored stripes. Cows' tails are fastened to their backs, and their heads are decorated with horns. A box, covered with sheepskin, is called the gumbo box. A dozen beat on this, while others strike triangles and jawbones, to which bands of dancers keep time. For a month previous they are composing songs, which are sung on this occasion. These companies, of a hundred each, turn out early in the morning, and are allowed to go round till twelve o'clock, begging for contributions. Not a door is left unvisited where there is the least chance of obtaining a penny or a glass of rum. They do not drink while they are out, but carry the rum home in jugs, to have a carousal. These Christmas donations frequently amount to twenty or thirty dollars. It is seldom that any white man or child refuses to give them a trifle. If he does, they regale his ears with the following song:

> Poor massa, so they say,
> Down in the heel, so they say,
> Got no money, so they say,
> Not one shilling, so they say,
> God A'mighty bless you, so they say.

Christmas is a day of feasting, both for white and colored people. Slaves who are lucky enough to have a few shillings are sure to spend them for good eating. Many a turkey and pig is captured. Those who cannot obtain these cook a possum or a raccoon, from which savory dishes can be made. My grandmother raised poultry and pigs for sale, and it was her established custom to have both a turkey and a pig roasted for Christmas dinner.

On this occasion, I was warned to keep extremely quiet, because two guests had been invited. One was the town constable, and the other was a free colored man, who tried to pass himself off for white, and who was always ready to do any mean work for the sake of currying favor with white people. My grandmother had a motive for inviting them. She managed to take them all over the house. All the rooms on the lower floor were thrown open for them to pass in and out, and after dinner, they were invited upstairs to look at a fine mockingbird my uncle had just brought home. There, too, the rooms were all thrown open, that they might look in. When I heard them talking on the piazza, my heart almost stood still. I knew this colored man had spent many nights hunting for me. Everybody knew he had the blood of a slave father in his veins, but for the sake of passing himself off for white, he was ready to kiss the slaveholders' feet. How I despised him. As for the constable, he wore no false colors. The duties of his office were despicable, but he was superior to his companion, inasmuch as he did not pretend to be what he was not. Any white man, who could raise money enough to buy a slave, would have considered himself degraded by being a constable, but the office enabled its possessor to exercise authority. If he found any slave out after nine o'clock, he could whip him as much as he liked, and that was a privilege to be coveted. When the guests were ready to depart, my grandmother gave each of them some of her nice pudding as a present for their wives. Through my peephole I saw them go out of the gate, and I was glad when it closed after them. So passed the first Christmas in my den.

When spring returned, and I took in the little patch of green the aperture commanded, I asked myself how many more summers and winters I must be condemned to spend thus. I

longed to draw in a plentiful draught of fresh air, to stretch my
cramped limbs, to have room to stand erect, to feel the earth
under my feet again. My relatives were constantly on the
lookout for a chance of escape, but none offered that seemed
practicable, and even tolerably safe. The hot summer came
again, and made the turpentine drop from the thin roof over
my head.

During the long nights I was restless for want of air, and I
had no room to toss and turn. There was but one compensation,
the atmosphere was so stifled that even mosquitos would not
condescend to buzz in it. With all my detestation of Dr. Flint, I
could hardly wish him a worse punishment, either in this
world or that which is to come, than to suffer what I suffered in
one single summer. Yet the laws allowed him to be out in the
free air, while I, guiltless of crime, was pent up here, as the only
means of avoiding the cruelties the laws allowed him to inflict
upon me. I don't know what kept life within me. Again and
again, I thought I should die before long, but I saw the leaves
of another autumn whirl through the air, and felt the touch of
another winter. In summer the most terrible thunderstorms
were acceptable, for the rain came through the roof, and I rolled
up my bed that it might cool the hot boards under it. Later in
the season, storms sometimes wet my clothes through and
through, and that was not comfortable when the air grew chilly.
Moderate storms I could keep out by filling the chinks with
oakum.

But uncomfortable as my situation was, I had glimpses of
things out of doors which made me thankful for my wretched
hiding place. One day I saw a slave pass our gate, muttering,
"It's his own, and he can kill it if he will."

My grandmother told me that woman's history. Her
mistress had that day seen her baby for the first time and in the
lineaments of its fair face she saw a likeness to her husband.
She turned the bondwoman and her child out of doors, and

forbade her ever to return. The slave went to her master, and told him what had happened. He promised to talk with her mistress and make it all right. The next day she and her baby were sold to a Georgia trader.

Another time I saw a woman rush wildly by, pursued by two men. She was a slave, the wet nurse of her mistress's children. For some trifling offense her mistress ordered her to be stripped and whipped. To escape the degradation and the torture, she rushed to the river, jumped in, and ended her wrongs in death.

Senator Brown of Mississippi could not be ignorant of many such facts as these, for they are of frequent occurrence in every Southern State. Yet he stood up in the Congress of the United States, and declared that slavery was "a great moral, social, and political blessing, a blessing to the master, and a blessing to the slave."

I suffered much more during the second winter than I did during the first. My limbs were benumbed by inaction, and the cold filled them with cramp. I had a very painful sensation of coldness in my head, even my face and tongue stiffened, and I lost the power of speech. Of course it was impossible, under the circumstances, to summon any physician. My brother William came and did all he could for me. Uncle Phillip also watched tenderly over me, and poor grandmother crept up and down to inquire whether there were any signs of returning life. I was restored to consciousness by the dashing of cold water in my face, and found myself leaning against my brother's arm, while he bent over me with streaming eyes. He afterwards told me he thought I was dying, for I had been in an unconscious state sixteen hours. I next became delirious, and was in great danger of betraying myself and my friends. To prevent this, they stupefied me with drugs. I remained in bed six weeks, weary in body and sick at heart. How to get medical advice was the question. William finally went to a doctor, and described himself as having all my pains and aches. He returned with herbs, roots, and ointment. He was especially charged to rub on the ointment by a fire, but how could a fire be made in my little den? Charcoal in a furnace was tried, but there was no outlet for the gas, and it nearly cost me my life. Afterwards coals, already kindled, were brought up in an iron pan, and placed on bricks. I was so weak, and it was so long since I had enjoyed the warmth of a fire, that those few coals actually made me weep. I think the medicines did me some good, but my recovery was very slow.

Dark thoughts passed through my mind as I lay there day after day. I tried to be thankful for my little cell, dismal as it was, and even to love it, as part of the price I had paid for the redemption of my children. Sometimes I thought God was a compassionate Father, who would forgive my sins for the sake of my sufferings. At other times, it seemed to me there was no justice or mercy in the divine government. I asked why the curse of slavery was permitted to exist, and why I had been so persecuted and wronged from youth upward. These things took the shape of mystery, which is to this day not so clear to my soul as I trust it will be hereafter.

In the midst of my illness, grandmother broke down under the weight of anxiety and toil. The idea of losing her, who had always been my best friend and a mother to my children, was the sorest trial I had yet had. How earnestly I prayed that she might recover. How hard it seemed, that I could not tend upon her, who had so long and so tenderly watched over me.

One day the screams of a child nerved me with strength to crawl to my peephole, and I saw my son covered with blood. A fierce dog, usually kept chained, had seized and bitten him. A doctor was sent for, and I heard the groans and screams of my child while the wounds were being sewed up. What torture to a mother's heart, to listen to this and be unable to go to him.

But childhood is like a day in spring, alternately shower and sunshine. Before night Benny was bright and lively, threatening the destruction of the dog, and great was his delight when the doctor told him the next day that the dog had bitten another boy and been shot. Benny recovered from his wounds, but it was long before he could walk.

When my grandmother's illness became known, many ladies, who were her customers, called to bring her some little comforts, and to inquire whether she had everything she wanted. Aunt Nancy one night asked permission to watch with her sick mother, and Mrs. Flint replied, "I don't see any need of your going. I can't spare you." But when she found other ladies in the neighborhood were so attentive, not wishing to be outdone in Christian charity, she also sallied forth, in magnificent condescension, and stood by the bedside of her who had loved her in her infancy, and who had been repaid by such grievous wrongs. She seemed surprised to find her so ill, and scolded uncle Phillip for not sending for Dr. Flint. She herself sent for him immediately, and he came. Secure as I was in my retreat, I should have been terrified if I had known he was so near me. He pronounced my grandmother in a very critical situation, and said if her attending physician wished it, he would visit her. Nobody wished to have him coming to the house at all hours, and we were not disposed to give him a chance to make out a long bill.

As Mrs. Flint went out, Sally told her the reason Benny was lame was that a dog had bitten him.

"I'm glad of it," replied she. "I wish it had killed him. It would be good news to send to his mother. Her day will come. The dogs will grab her yet."

With these Christian words, she and her husband departed and, to my great satisfaction, returned no more.

I heard from uncle Phillip, with feelings of unspeakable joy and gratitude, that the crisis was passed and grandmother would live. I could now say from my heart, "God is merciful. He has spared me the anguish of feeling that I caused her death."

The summer had nearly ended when Dr. Flint made a third visit to New York in search of me. Two candidates were running for Congress, and he returned in season to vote. The father of my children was the Whig candidate. The doctor had hitherto been a staunch Whig, but now he exerted all his energies for the defeat of Mr. Sands. He invited large parties of men to dine in the shade of his trees, and supplied them with plenty of rum and brandy. If any poor fellow drowned his wits in the bowl and, in the openness of his convivial heart, proclaimed that he did not mean to vote the Democratic ticket, he was shoved into the street without ceremony.

The doctor expended his liquor in vain. Mr. Sands was elected, an event which occasioned me some anxious thoughts.

He had not emancipated my children, and if he should die they would be at the mercy of his heirs. Two little voices that frequently met my ear seemed to plead with me not to let their father depart without striving to make their freedom secure. Years had passed since I had spoken to him. I had not even seen him since the night I passed him, unrecognized, in my disguise of a sailor. I supposed he would call before he left, to say something to my grandmother concerning the children, and I resolved what course to take.

The day before his departure for Washington I made arrangements, towards evening, to get from my hiding place into the storeroom below. I found myself so stiff and clumsy that it was with great difficulty I could hitch from one resting place to another. When I reached the storeroom my ankles gave way under me, and I sank exhausted on the floor. It seemed as if I could never use my limbs again. But the purpose I had in view roused all the strength I had. I crawled on my hands and knees to the window and, screened behind a barrel, I waited for his coming. The clock struck nine, and I knew the steamboat would leave between ten and eleven. My hopes were failing. But presently I heard his voice, saying to someone, "Wait for me a moment. I wish to see Aunt Martha."

When he came out, as he passed the window, I said, "Stop one moment, and let me speak for my children."

He started, hesitated, and then passed on, and went out of the gate. I closed the shutter I had partially opened, and sank down behind the barrel. I had suffered much, but seldom had I experienced a keener pang than I then felt. Had my children, then, become of so little consequence to him? And had he so little feeling for their wretched mother that he would not listen a moment while she pleaded for them? Painful memories were so busy within me, that I forgot I had not hooked the shutter, till I heard someone opening it. I looked up. He had come back.

"Who called me?" said he, in a low tone.

"I did," I replied.

"Oh, Linda," said he, "I knew your voice, but I was afraid to answer, lest my friend should hear me. Why do you come here? Is it possible you risk yourself in this house? They are mad to allow it. I shall expect to hear that you are all ruined."

I did not wish to implicate him by letting him know my place of concealment, so I merely said, "I thought you would come to bid grandmother goodbye, and so I came here to speak a few words to you about emancipating my children. Many changes may take place during the six months you are gone to Washington, it does not seem right for you to expose them to the risk of such changes. I want nothing for myself, all I ask is that you will free my children, or authorize some friend to do it, before you go."

He promised he would do it, and also expressed a readiness to make any arrangements whereby I could be purchased.

I heard footsteps approaching, and closed the shutter

hastily. I wanted to crawl back to my den, without letting the family know what I had done, for I knew they would deem it very imprudent. But he stepped back into the house to tell my grandmother that he had spoken with me at the storeroom window, and to beg of her not to allow me to remain in the house overnight. He said it was the height of madness for me to be there, that we should certainly all be ruined. Luckily, he was in too much of a hurry to wait for a reply, or the dear old woman would surely have told him all.

I tried to go back to my den, but found it more difficult to go up than I had to come down. Now that my mission was fulfilled, the little strength that had supported me through it was gone, and I sank helpless on the floor. My grandmother, alarmed at the risk I had run, came into the storeroom in the dark, and locked the door behind her. "Linda," she whispered, "where are you?"

"I am here by the window," I replied. "I couldn't have him go away without emancipating the children. Who knows what may happen?"

"Come, come, child," said she, "it won't do for you to stay here another minute. You've done wrong, but I can't blame you, poor thing."

I told her I could not return without assistance, and she must call my uncle. Uncle Phillip came. Pity prevented him from scolding me. He carried me back to my dungeon, laid me tenderly on the bed, gave me some medicine and asked me if there was anything more he could do. Then he went. I was left with my own thoughts, starless as the midnight darkness around me.

My friends feared I should become a cripple for life, and I was so weary of my long imprisonment that, had it not been for the hope of serving my children, I should have been thankful to die. For their sakes I was willing to bear on.

Dr. Flint had not given me up. Every now and then he

would say to my grandmother that I would yet come back and voluntarily surrender myself, and that when I did, I could be purchased by my relatives, or anyone who wished to buy me. I knew his cunning nature too well not to perceive that this was a trap laid for me, and so all my friends understood it. I resolved to match my cunning against his cunning. In order to make him believe that I was in New York, I resolved to write him a letter dated from that place. I sent for my friend Peter, and asked him if he knew any trustworthy seafaring person, who would carry such a letter to New York and put it in the post office there. He said he knew one that he would trust with his own life to the ends of the world. I reminded him that it was a hazardous thing for him to undertake. He said he knew it, but he was willing to do anything to help me. I expressed a wish for a New York paper, to ascertain the names of some of the streets. He ran his hand into his pocket, and said, "Here is half a one, that was round a cap I bought from a peddler yesterday."

I told him the letter would be ready the next evening. He bade me goodbye, adding, "Keep up your spirits, Linda, brighter days will come by and by."

My uncle Phillip kept watch over the gate until our brief interview was over. Early the next morning, I seated myself near the little aperture to examine the newspaper. It was a piece of the *New York Herald.* For once, the paper that systematically abuses the colored people was made to render them a service. Having obtained what information I wanted concerning streets and numbers, I wrote two letters, one to my grandmother, the other to Dr. Flint. I reminded him how he, a gray-headed man, had treated a helpless child, who had been placed in his power, and what years of misery he had brought upon her. To my grandmother, I expressed a wish to have my children sent to me in the North, where I could teach them to respect themselves, and set them a virtuous example, which a slave mother was not allowed to do in the South. I asked her to direct her answer to a certain street in Boston, as I did not live in New York, though I went there sometimes. I dated these letters ahead, to allow for the time it would take to carry them, and sent a memorandum of the date to the messenger.

When my friend came for the letters, I said, "God bless and reward you, Peter, for this disinterested kindness. Pray be careful. If you are detected, both you and I will have to suffer dreadfully. I have not a relative who would dare to do it for me."

He replied, "You may trust to me, Linda. I don't forget that your father was my best friend, and I will be a friend to his children so long as God lets me live."

It was necessary to tell my grandmother what I had done, in order that she might be ready for the letter, and prepared to hear what Dr. Flint might say about my being in the North. She was sadly troubled. She felt sure mischief would come of it. I also told my plan to Aunt Nancy, in order that she might report to us what was said at Dr. Flint's house. I whispered it to her through a crack, and she whispered back, "I hope it will succeed. I shan't mind being a slave all my life, if I can only see you and the children free."

I had directed that my letters should be put into the New York post office on the 20th of the month. On the evening of the 24th my aunt came to say that Dr. Flint and his wife had been talking in a low voice about a letter he had received, and that when he went to his office he promised to bring it when he came to tea. So I concluded I should hear my letter read the next morning. I told my grandmother Dr. Flint would be sure to come, and asked her to have him sit near a certain door, and leave it open, that I might hear what he said.

The next morning I took my station within sound of that door, and remained motionless as a statue. It was not long before I heard the gate slam, and the well-known footsteps enter the house. He seated himself in the chair that was placed for him, and said, "Well, Martha, I've brought you a letter from Linda. She has sent me a letter, also. I know exactly where to find her, but I don't choose to go to Boston for her. I had rather she would come back of her own accord, in a respectable manner. Her uncle Phillip is the best person to go for her. With him, she would feel perfectly free to act. I am willing to pay his expenses going and returning. She shall be sold to her friends. Her children are free, at least I suppose they are, and when you obtain her freedom, you'll make a happy family. I suppose, Martha, you have no objection to my reading to you the letter Linda has written to you."

He broke the seal, and I heard him read it. The old villain! He had suppressed the letter I wrote to grandmother, and prepared a substitute of his own, the purport of which was as follows:

Dear Grandmother,
I have long wanted to write to you, but the disgraceful manner in which I left you and my children made me ashamed to do it. If you knew how much I have suffered since I ran away, you would pity and forgive me. I have purchased freedom at a dear rate. If any arrangement could be made for me to return to the South without being a slave, I would gladly come. If not, I beg of you to send my children to the North. I cannot live any longer without them. Let me know in time, and I will meet them in New York or Philadelphia, whichever place best suits my uncle's convenience.
Write as soon as possible to your unhappy daughter.
    LINDA

"It is very much as I expected it would be," said the old hypocrite, rising to go. "You see, the foolish girl has repented of her rashness and wants to return. We must help her to do it, Martha. Talk with Phillip about it. If he will go for her, she will trust him and come back. I should like an answer tomorrow.

Good morning, Martha."

As he stepped out on the piazza, he stumbled over my little girl.

"Ah, Ellen, is that you?" he said, in his most gracious manner. "I didn't see you. How do you do?"

"Pretty well, sir," she replied. "I heard you tell grandmother that my mother is coming home. I want to see her."

"Yes, Ellen, I am going to bring her home very soon," rejoined he, "and you shall see her as much as you like, you little curly-headed nigger."

This was as good as a comedy to me who had heard it all, but grandmother was frightened and distressed because the doctor wanted my uncle to go for me.

The next evening Dr. Flint called to talk the matter over. My uncle told him that from what he had heard of Massachusetts, he judged he should be mobbed if he went there after a runaway slave.

"All stuff and nonsense, Phillip," replied the doctor. "Do you suppose I want you to kick up a row in Boston? The business can all be done quietly. Linda writes that she wants to come back. You are her relative, and she would trust you. The case would be different if I went. She might object to coming with me, and the damned abolitionists, if they knew I was her master, would not believe me, if I told them she had begged to go back. They would get up a row, and I should not like to see Linda dragged through the streets like a common negro. She has been very ungrateful to me for all my kindness, but I forgive her, and want to act the part of a friend towards her. I have no wish to hold her as my slave. Her friends can buy her as soon as she arrives here."

Finding that his arguments failed to convince my uncle, the doctor let the cat out of the bag by saying that he had written to the mayor of Boston, to ascertain whether there was a person of my description at the street and number from which my letter was dated. He had omitted this date in the letter he had made up to read to my grandmother. If I had dated from New York, the old man would probably have made another journey to that city. But even in that dark region, where knowledge is so carefully excluded from the slave, I had heard enough about Massachusetts to come to the conclusion that slaveholders did not consider it a comfortable place to go to in search of a runaway. That was before the Fugitive Slave Law was passed, before Massachusetts had consented to become a 'nigger hunter' for the South.

My grandmother, who had become skittish by seeing her family always in danger, came to me with a very distressed countenance, and said, "What will you do if the mayor of Boston sends him word that you haven't been there? Then he will suspect the letter was a trick, and maybe he'll find out something about it, and we shall all get into trouble. Oh Linda, I wish you had never sent the letters."

"Don't worry yourself, grandmother," said I. "The mayor of Boston won't trouble himself to hunt niggers for Dr. Flint. The letters will do good in the end. I shall get out of this dark hole some time or other."

"I hope you will, child," replied the good, patient old friend. "You have been here a long time, almost five years, but whenever you do go, it will break your old grandmother's heart. I should be expecting every day to hear that you were brought back in irons and put in jail. God help you, poor child. Let us be thankful that some time or other we shall go where the wicked cease from troubling, and the weary are at rest."

My heart responded, *Amen.*

The fact that Dr. Flint had written to the mayor of Boston convinced me that he believed my letter to be genuine, and of course that he had no suspicion of my being anywhere in the vicinity. It was a great object to keep up this delusion, for it made me and my friends feel less anxious, and it would be very convenient whenever there was a chance to escape. I resolved, therefore, to continue to write letters from the North from time to time.

Two or three weeks passed, and as no news came from the mayor of Boston, grandmother began to listen to my entreaty to be allowed to leave my cell, sometimes, and exercise my limbs to prevent my becoming a cripple. I was allowed to slip down into the small storeroom, early in the morning, and remain there a little while. The room was all filled up with barrels, except a small open space under my trap-door. This faced the door, the upper part of which was of glass, and purposely left uncurtained, that the curious might look in. The air of this place was close, but it was so much better than the atmosphere of my cell, that I dreaded to return. I came down as soon as it was light, and remained till eight o'clock, when people began to be about, and there was danger that someone might come on the piazza. I had tried various applications to bring warmth and feeling into my limbs, but without avail. They were so numb and stiff that it was a painful effort to move, and had my enemies come upon me during the first mornings I tried to exercise them a little in the small unoccupied space of the storeroom, it would have been impossible for me to have escaped.

I missed the company and kind attentions of my brother William, who had gone to Washington with his master, Mr. Sands. We received several letters from him, written without any allusion to me, but expressed in such a manner that I knew he did not forget me. I disguised my hand, and wrote to him in the same manner. It was a long session, and when it closed, William wrote to inform us that Mr. Sands was going to the North, to be gone some time, and that he was to accompany him. I knew that his master had promised to give him his freedom, but no time had been specified. Would William trust to a slave's chances? I remembered how we used to talk together in our young days, about obtaining our freedom, and I thought it very doubtful whether he would come back to us.

Grandmother received a letter from Mr. Sands, saying that William had proved a most faithful servant, and he would also say a valued friend, that no mother had ever trained a better boy. He said he had travelled through the Northern States and Canada, and though the abolitionists had tried to decoy him away, they had never succeeded. He ended by saying they should be at home shortly.

We expected letters from William, describing the novelties of his journey, but none came. In time, it was reported that Mr. Sands would return late in the autumn, accompanied by a bride. Still no letters from William. I felt almost sure I should never see him again on Southern soil, but had he no word of comfort to send to his friends at home, to the poor captive in her dungeon? My thoughts wandered through the dark past, and over the uncertain future. Alone in my cell where no eye but God's could see me, I wept bitter tears. How earnestly I prayed to him to restore me to my children, and enable me to be a useful woman and a good mother.

At last the day arrived for the return of the travelers. Grandmother had made loving preparations to welcome her absent boy back to the old hearthstone. When the dinner table was laid, William's plate occupied its old place. The stage coach went by empty. My grandmother waited dinner. She thought perhaps he was necessarily detained by his master. In my prison I listened anxiously, expecting every moment to hear my dear brother's voice and footstep. In the course of the afternoon a lad was sent by Mr. Sands to tell grandmother that William did not return with him, that the abolitionists had decoyed him away. But he begged her not to feel troubled about it, for he felt confident she would see William in a few days. As soon as he had time to reflect he would come back, for he could never expect to be so well off in the North as he had been with him.

If you had seen the tears and heard the sobs, you would have thought the messenger had brought tidings of death instead of freedom. Poor old grandmother felt that she should never see her darling boy again. And I was selfish. I thought more of what I had lost than of what my brother had gained. A new anxiety began to trouble me. Mr. Sands had expended a good deal of money, and would naturally feel irritated by the loss he had incurred. I greatly feared this might injure the prospects of my children, who were now becoming valuable property. I longed to have their emancipation made certain. The more so because their master and father was now married. I was too familiar with slavery not to know that promises made to slaves, though with kind intentions, and sincere at the time, depend upon many contingencies for their fulfillment.

Much as I wished William to be free, the step he had taken made me sad and anxious. The following Sabbath was calm and clear, so beautiful that it seemed like a Sabbath in the eternal world. My grandmother brought the children out on the piazza, that I might hear their voices. She thought it would comfort me in my despondency, and it did. They chatted merrily, as only children can. Benny said, "Grandmother, do you think Uncle Will has gone for good? Won't he ever come back again? Maybe he'll find mother. If he does, won't she be glad to see him. Why don't you and uncle Phillip, and all of us, go and live where mother is? I should like it, wouldn't you, Ellen?"

"Yes, I should like it," replied Ellen, "but how could we find her? Do you know the place, grandmother? I don't remember how mother looked — do you, Benny?"

Benny was just beginning to describe me when they were interrupted by an old slave woman, a near neighbor, named Aggie. This poor creature had witnessed the sale of her children, and seen them carried off to parts unknown, without any hopes of ever hearing from them again. She saw that my grandmother had been weeping, and she said, in a sympathizing tone, "What's the matter, Aunt Marthy?"

"Aggie," she replied, "it seems as if I shouldn't have any of my children or grandchildren left to hand me a drink when I'm dying, and lay my old body in the ground. My boy didn't come back with Mr. Sands. He stayed in the North."

Poor old Aggie clapped her hands for joy.

"Is dat what you's crying for?" she exclaimed. "Get down on your knees and thank the Lord. I don't know where my poor children is, and I never 'spect to know. You don't know where poor Linda's gone to, but you do know where her brother is. He's in free parts, and dat's the right place. Don't murmur at the Lord's doings, but git down on your knees and thank him for his goodness."

My selfishness was rebuked by what poor Aggie said. She rejoiced over the escape of one who was merely her fellow bondman, while his own sister was only thinking what his good fortune might cost her children. I knelt and prayed God to forgive me, and I thanked him from my heart, that one of my family was saved from the grasp of slavery.

It was not long before we received a letter from William. He wrote that Mr. Sands had always treated him kindly, and that he had tried to do his duty to him faithfully. But ever since he was a boy, he had longed to be free, and he had already gone through enough to convince him he had better not lose the chance that offered. He concluded by saying, "Don't worry about me, dear grandmother. I shall think of you always, and it will spur me on to work hard and try to do right. When I have earned money enough to give you a home, perhaps you will come to the North, and we can all live happy together."

Mr. Sands told my uncle Phillip the particulars about William's leaving him. He said, "I trusted him as if he were my own brother, and treated him as kindly. The abolitionists talked to him in several places, but I had no idea they could tempt him. However, I don't blame William. He's young and inconsiderate, and those Northern rascals decoyed him. I must confess the scamp was very bold about it. I met him coming down the steps of the Astor House with his trunk on his shoulder, and I asked him where he was going. He said he was going to change his old trunk. I told him it was rather shabby, and asked if he didn't need some money. He said, "No," thanked me, and went off. He did not return so soon as I expected, but I waited patiently. At last I went to see if our trunks were packed, ready for our journey. I found them locked, and a sealed note on the table informed me where I could find the keys. The fellow even tried to be religious. He wrote that he hoped God would always bless me, and reward me for my kindness, that he was not unwilling to serve me, but he wanted to be a free man, and that if I thought he did wrong, he hoped I would forgive him. I intended to give him his freedom in five years. He might have trusted me. He has shown himself ungrateful, but I shall not go for him, or send for him. I feel confident that he will soon return to me."

I afterwards heard an account of the affair from William himself. He had not been urged away by abolitionists. He needed no information they could give him about slavery to stimulate his desire for freedom. He looked at his hands, and remembered that they were once in irons. What security had he that they would not be so again? Mr. Sands was kind to him, but he might indefinitely postpone the promise he had made to give him his freedom. He might come under pecuniary embarrassments, and his property be seized by creditors, or he might die, without making any arrangements in his favor. He had too often known such accidents to happen to slaves who had kind masters, and he wisely resolved to make sure of the present opportunity to own himself. He was scrupulous about taking any money from his master on false pretenses, so he sold his best clothes to pay for his passage to Boston. The slaveholders pronounced him a base, ungrateful wretch, for thus requiting his master's indulgence. What would they have done under similar circumstances?

When Dr. Flint's family heard that William had deserted Mr. Sands, they chuckled greatly over the news. Mrs. Flint made her usual manifestations of Christian feeling, by saying, "I'm glad of it. I hope he'll never get him again. I like to see people paid back in their own coin. I reckon Linda's children will have to pay for it. I should be glad to see them in the speculator's hands again, for I'm tired of seeing those little niggers march about the streets."

Mrs. Flint proclaimed her intention of informing Mrs. Sands who was the father of my children. She likewise proposed to tell her what an artful devil I was, that I had made a great deal of trouble in her family, that when Mr. Sands was in the North, she didn't doubt that I had followed him in disguise and persuaded William to run away. She had some reason to entertain such an idea, for I had written from the North, from time to time, and I dated my letters from various places. Many of them fell into Dr. Flint's hands, as I expected they would, and he must have come to the conclusion that I travelled about a good deal. He kept a close watch over my children thinking they would eventually lead to my detection.

A new and unexpected trial was in store for me. One day, when Mr. Sands and his wife were walking in the street, they met Benny. The lady took a fancy to him, and exclaimed, "What a pretty little negro. Whom does he belong to?"

Benny did not hear the answer, but he came home very indignant with the stranger lady, because she had called him a negro. A few days afterwards, Mr. Sands called on my grandmother and told her he wanted her to take the children to his house. He said he had informed his wife of his relation to them, and told her they were motherless, and she wanted to see them.

When he had gone, my grandmother came and asked what I would do. The question seemed a mockery. What could I do? They were Mr. Sands's slaves, and their mother was a slave, whom he had represented to be dead. Perhaps he thought I was. I was too much pained and puzzled to come to any decision, and the children were carried without my knowledge.

Mrs. Sands had a sister from Illinois staying with her. This lady, who had no children of her own, was so much pleased with Ellen, that she offered to adopt her, and bring her up as she would a daughter. Mrs. Sands wanted to take Benjamin. When grandmother reported this to me, I was tried almost beyond endurance. Was this all I was to gain by what I had suffered for the sake of having my children free? True, the prospect seemed fair, but I know too well how lightly slaveholders held such parental relations. If pecuniary troubles should come, or if the new wife required more money than could conveniently be spared, my children might be thought of as a convenient means of raising funds. I had no trust in slavery. Never should I know peace till my children were emancipated with all due formalities of law.

I was too proud to ask Mr. Sands to do anything for my own benefit, but I could bring myself to become a suppliant for my children. I resolved to remind him of the promise he had made me, and to throw myself upon his honor for the performance of it. I persuaded my grandmother to go to him and tell him I was not dead, and that I earnestly entreated him to keep the promise he had made me, that I had heard of the recent proposals concerning my children and did not feel easy to accept them, that he had promised to emancipate them, and it was time for him to redeem his pledge. I knew there was some risk in thus betraying that I was in the vicinity, but what will not a mother do for her children?

He received the message with surprise, and said, "The children are free. I have never intended to claim them as slaves.

Linda may decide their fate. In my opinion, they had better be sent to the North. I don't think they are quite safe here. Dr. Flint boasts that they are still in his power. He says they were his daughter's property, and as she was not of age when they were sold, the contract is not legally binding."

So, then, after all I had endured for their sakes, my poor children were between two fires, between my old master and their new master. And I was powerless. There was no protecting arm of the law for me to invoke. Mr. Sands proposed that Ellen should go, for the present, to some of his relatives, who had moved to Brooklyn. It was promised that she should be well taken care of, and sent to school. I consented to it, as the best arrangement I could make for her. My grandmother, of course, negotiated it all, and Mrs. Sands knew of no other person in the transaction. She proposed that they should take Ellen with them to Washington, and keep her till they had a good chance of sending her, with friends to Brooklyn. She had an infant daughter. I had had a glimpse of it, as the nurse passed with it in her arms. It was not a pleasant thought to me, that the bondwoman's child should tend her free-born sister, but there was no alternative.

Ellen was made ready for the journey. How it tried my heart to send her away, so young, alone, among strangers. Without a mother's love to shelter her from the storms of life, almost without memory of a mother. I doubted whether she and Benny would have for me the natural affection that children feel for a parent. I thought to myself that I might perhaps never see my daughter again, and I had a great desire that she should look upon me, before she went, that she might take my image with her in her memory. It seemed to me cruel to have her brought to my dungeon. It was sorrow enough for her young heart to know that her mother was a victim of slavery, without seeing the wretched hiding place to which it had driven her. I begged permission to pass the last night in one of the open chambers, with my little girl. They thought I was crazy to think of trusting such a young child with my perilous secret. I told them I had watched her character, and I felt sure she would not betray me, that I was determined to have an interview, and if they would not facilitate it, I would take my own way to obtain it. They remonstrated against the rashness of such a proceeding, but finding they could not change my purpose, they yielded. I slipped through the trap-door into the storeroom, and my uncle kept watch at the gate, while I passed into the piazza and went upstairs, to the room I used to occupy. It was more than five years since I had seen it, and how the memories eroded on me. There I had taken shelter when my mistress drove me from her house, there came my old tyrant to mock, insult and curse me, there my children were first laid in my arms, there I had watched over them, each day with a deeper and sadder love, there I had knelt to God, in anguish of heart, to forgive the wrong I had done. How vividly it all came back. And after this long, gloomy interval, I stood there such a wreck.

In the midst of these meditations, I heard footsteps on the stairs. The door opened, and my uncle Phillip came in, leading Ellen by the hand. I put my arms round her and said, "Ellen, my dear child, I am your mother."

She drew back a little, and looked at me, then, with sweet confidence, she laid her cheek against mine, and I folded her to the heart that had been so long desolated.

She was the first to speak. Raising her head, she said, inquiringly, "You really are my mother?"

I told her I really was, that during all the long time she had not seen me, I had loved her most tenderly, and that now she was going away, I wanted to see her and talk with her, that she might remember me.

With a sob in her voice, she said, "I'm glad you've come to see me, but why didn't you ever come before? Benny and I have wanted so much to see you. He remembers you, and sometimes he tells me about you. Why didn't you come home when Dr. Flint went to bring you?"

I answered, "I couldn't come before, dear. But now that I am with you, tell me whether you like to go away."

"I don't know," said she, crying. "Grandmother says I ought not to cry, that I am going to a good place, where I can learn to read and write, and that by and by I can write her a letter. But I shan't have Benny or grandmother, or Uncle Phillip, or anybody to love me. Can't you go with me, dear mother?"

I told her I couldn't go now, but sometimes I would come to her, and then she and Benny and I would live together, and have happy times.

She wanted to run and bring Benny to see me now. I told her he was going to the North, before long, with Uncle Phillip, and then I would come to see him before he went away. I asked if she would like to have me stay all night and sleep with her.

"Yes," she replied. Then, turning to her uncle, she said, pleadingly, "May I stay? Please, Uncle. She is my own mother."

He laid his hand on her head, and said, solemnly, "Ellen, this is the secret you have promised grandmother never to tell. If you ever speak of it to anybody, they will never let you see your grandmother again, and your mother can never come to Brooklyn."

"Uncle," she replied, "I will never tell."

He told her she might stay with me. When he had gone, I took her in my arms and told her I was a slave, and that was the reason she must never say she had seen me. I exhorted her to be a good child, to try to please the people where she was going, and that God would raise her up friends. I told her to say her prayers, and remember always to pray for her poor mother, and that God would permit us to meet again. She wept, and I did not check her tears. Perhaps she would never again have a chance to pour her tears into a mother's bosom. All night she nestled in my arms, and I had no inclination to slumber. The moments were too precious to lose any of them. Once, when I thought she was asleep, I kissed her forehead softly, and she said, "I am not asleep, dear mother."

Before dawn they came to take me back to my den. I drew aside the window curtain, to take a last look of my child. The moonlight shone on her face. I bent over her, as I had done years before, that wretched night when I ran away. I hugged her close to my throbbing heart. Tears, too sad for such young eyes to shed, flowed down her cheeks as she gave her last kiss, and whispered in my ear, "Mother, I will never tell."

And she never did.

When I got back to my den, I threw myself on the bed and wept there alone in the darkness. It seemed as if my heart would burst. When the time for Ellen's departure drew nigh, I could hear neighbors and friends saying to her, "Goodbye, Ellen. I hope your poor mothe. will find you. Won't you be glad to see her?"

She replied, "Yes, ma'am."

They little dreamed of the heavy secret that weighed down her young heart. She was an affectionate child, but naturally very reserved, except with those she loved, and I felt secure that my secret would be safe with her. I heard the gate close behind her, with such feelings as only a slave mother can experience.

During the day my meditations were very sad. Sometimes I feared I had been very selfish not to give up all claim to her and let her be adopted by Mrs. Sands's sister. It was my experience of slavery that decided me against it. I feared that circumstances might arise that would cause her to be sent back. I felt confident that I should go to New York myself, and then I should be able to watch over her, and in some degree protect her.

Dr. Flint's family knew nothing of the proposed

arrangement till after Ellen was gone, and the news displeased them greatly. Mrs. Flint called on Mrs. Sands's sister to inquire into the matter. She expressed her opinion very freely as to the respect Mr. Sands showed for his wife, and for his own character, in acknowledging those "young niggers." And as for sending Ellen away, she pronounced it to be just as much stealing as it would be for him to come and take a piece of furniture out of her parlor. She said her daughter was not of age to sign the bill of sale, and the children were her property, and when she became of age, or was married, she could take them, wherever she could lay hands on them.

Miss Emily Flint, the little girl to whom I was bequeathed, was now in her sixteenth year. Her mother considered it all right and honorable for her, or her future husband, to steal my children, but she did not understand how anybody could hold up their heads in respectable society, after they had purchased their own children, as Mr. Sands had done.

Dr. Flint said very little. Perhaps he thought that Benny would be less likely to be sent away if he kept quiet. One of my letters, that fell into his hands, was dated from Canada, and he seldom spoke of me now. This state of things enabled me to slip down in the storeroom more frequently, where I could stand upright, and move my limbs more freely.

Days, weeks, and months passed, and there came no news of Ellen. I sent a letter to Brooklyn, written in my grandmother's name, to inquire whether she had arrived there. Answer was returned that she had not. I wrote to her in Washington, but no notice was taken of it. There was one person there, who ought to have had some sympathy with the anxiety of the child's friends at home, but the links of such relations as he had formed with me are easily broken and cast away as rubbish. Yet how protectingly and persuasively he once talked to the poor, helpless slave girl. And how entirely I trusted him. But now suspicions darkened my mind. Was my child dead, or had they deceived me, and sold her?

If the secret memoirs of many members of Congress should be published, curious details would be unfolded. I once saw a letter from a member of Congress to a slave, who was the mother of six of his children. He wrote to request that she should send her children away from the great house before his return, as he expected to be accompanied by friends. The woman could not read, and was obliged to employ another to read the letter. The existence of the colored children did not trouble this gentleman, it was only the fear that friends might recognize in their features a resemblance to him.

At the end of six months, a letter came to my grandmother, from Brooklyn. It was written by a young lady in the family, and announced that Ellen had just arrived. It contained the following message from her: *I do try to do just as you told me to, and I pray for you every night and morning.*

I understood that these words were meant for me, and they were a balsam to my heart. The writer closed her letter by saying, *Ellen is a nice little girl, and we shall like to have her with us. My cousin, Mr. Sands, has given her to me, to be my little waiting-maid. I shall send her to school, and I hope some day she will write to you herself.*

This letter perplexed and troubled me. Had my child's father merely placed her there till she was old enough to support herself? Or had he given her to his cousin, as a piece of property? If the last idea was correct, his cousin might return to the South at any time, and hold Ellen as a slave. I tried to put away from me the painful thought that such a foul wrong would have been done to us. I said to myself, "Surely there must be some justice in man," then I remembered, with a sigh, how slavery perverted all the natural feelings of the human heart. It gave me a pang to look on my light-hearted boy. He believed himself free, to have him brought under the yoke of slavery would be more than I could bear. How I longed to have him safely out of the reach of its power.

I have mentioned my great-aunt, who was a slave in Dr. Flint's family, and who had been my refuge during the shameful persecutions I suffered from him. This aunt had been married at twenty years of age, that is, as far as slaves can marry. She had the consent of her master and mistress, and a clergyman performed the ceremony. But it was a mere form, without any legal value. Her master or mistress could annul it any day they pleased. She had always slept on the floor in the entry, near Mrs. Flint's chamber door, that she might be within call. When she was married, she was told she might have the use of a small room in an out-house. Her mother and her husband furnished it. He was a seafaring man, and was allowed to sleep there when he was at home. But on the wedding evening, the bride was ordered to her old post on the entry floor.

Mrs. Flint, at that time, had no children, but she was expecting to be a mother, and if she should want a drink of water in the night, what could she do without her slave to bring it? So my aunt was compelled to lie at her door, until one midnight she was forced to leave, to give premature birth to a child. In a fortnight, she was required to resume her place on the entry floor, because Mrs. Flints' baby needed her attentions. She kept her station there through summer and winter, until she had given premature birth to six children, and all the while she was employed as night nurse to Mrs. Flint's children. Finally, toiling all day and being deprived of rest at night, completely broke down her constitution, and Dr. Flint declared it was impossible she could ever become the mother of a living child. The fear of losing so valuable a servant by death, now induced them to allow her to sleep in her little room in the out-house, except when there was sickness in the family. She afterwards had two feeble babes, one of whom died in a few days, and the other in four weeks. I well remember her patient sorrow as she held the last dead baby in her arms. "I wish it could have lived," she said, "it is not the will of God that any of my children should live. But I will try to be fit to meet their little spirits in Heaven."

Aunt Nancy was housekeeper and waiting-maid in Dr. Flint's family. Indeed, she was the factotum of the household. Nothing went on well without her. She was my mother's twin sister and, as far as was in her power, she supplied a mother's place to us orphans. I slept with her the whole time I lived in my old master's house, and the bond between us was very strong. When my friends tried to discourage me from running away, she always encouraged me. When they thought I had better return and ask my master's pardon, because there was no possibility of escape, she sent me word never to yield. She said if I persevered I might, perhaps, gain the freedom of my children, and even if I perished in doing it, that was better than to leave them to groan under the same persecutions that had blighted my own life. After I was shut up in my dark cell, she stole away whenever she could to bring me news and say something cheering. How often did I kneel down to listen to her words of consolation, whispered through a crack.

"I am old, and have not long to live," she used to say, "and I could die happy if I could only see you and the children free. You must pray to God, Linda, as I do for you, that he will lead you out of this darkness."

I would beg her not to worry herself on my account, that there was an end of all suffering sooner or later, and that whether I lived in chains or in freedom, I should always remember her as the good friend who had been the comfort of my life. A word from her always strengthened me, and not me only. The whole family relied upon her judgment and were guided by her advice.

I had been in my cell six years when my grandmother was summoned to the bedside of this, her last remaining daughter.

She was very ill, and they said she would die. Grandmother had not entered Dr. Flint s house for several years. They had treated her cruelly, but she thought nothing of that now. She was grateful for permission to watch by the deathbed of her child. They had always been devoted to each other, and now they sat looking into each other's eyes, longing to speak of the secret that had weighed so much on the hearts of both. My aunt had been stricken with paralysis. She lived but two days, and the last day she was speechless. Before she lost the power of utterance, she told her mother not to grieve if she could not speak to her, that she would try to hold up her hand, to let her know that all was well with her. Even the hard-hearted doctor was a little softened when he saw the dying woman try to smile on the aged mother, who was kneeling by her side. His eyes moistened for a moment, as he said she had always been a faithful servant, and they should never be able to replace her. Mrs. Flint took to her bed, quite overcome by the shock.

While my grandmother sat alone with the dead, the doctor came in, leading his youngest son, who had always been a great pet with Aunt Nancy, and was much attached to her. "Martha," said he, "Aunt Nancy loved this child, and when he comes where you are, I hope you will be kind to him, for her sake."

She replied, "Your wife was my foster-child, Dr. Flint, the foster-sister of my poor Nancy, and you little know me if you think I can feel anything but good will for her children."

"I wish the past could be forgotten, and that we might never think of it," said he, "and that Linda would come to take her aunt's place. She would be worth more to us than all the money that could be paid for her. I wish it for your sake also, Martha. Now that Nancy is taken away from you, she would be a great comfort to your old age."

He knew he was touching a tender chord. Almost choking with grief, my grandmother replied, "It was not I that drove Linda away. My grandchildren are gone, and of my nine children only one is left. God help me!"

To me, the death of this kind relative was an inexpressible sorrow. I knew that she had been slowly murdered, and I felt that my troubles had helped to finish the work. After I heard of her illness, I listened constantly to hear what news was brought from the great house, and the thought that I could not go to her made me utterly miserable. At last, as Uncle Phillip came into the house, I heard someone inquire, "How is she?"

He answered, "She is dead."

My little cell seemed whirling round, and I knew nothing more till I opened my eyes and found Uncle Phillip bending over me. I had no need to ask any questions. He whispered, "Linda, she died happy."

I could not weep. My fixed gaze troubled him.

"Don't look so," he said. "Don't add to my poor mother's trouble. Remember how much she had to bear, and that we ought to do all we can to comfort her."

Ah, yes, that blessed old grandmother, who for seventy-three years had borne the pelting storms of a slave-mother's life. She did indeed need consolation.

Mrs. Flint had rendered her poor foster-sister childless, apparently without any compunction, and with cruel selfishness had ruined her health by years of incessant, unrequited toil and broken rest. But now she became very sentimental. I suppose she thought it would be a beautiful illustration of the attachment existing between slaveholder and slave, if the body of her old worn-out servant was buried at her feet. She sent for the clergyman and asked if he had any objection to burying Aunt Nancy in the doctor's family burial place. No colored person had ever been allowed interment in the white people's burying-ground, and the minister knew that all the deceased of our family reposed together in the old graveyard of the slaves. He therefore replied, "I have no objection to complying with your wish, but perhaps Aunt

Nancy's mother may have some choice as to where her remains shall be deposited."

It had never occurred to Mrs. Flint that slaves could have any feelings. When my grandmother was consulted, she at once said she wanted Nancy to lie with all the rest of her family, and where her own old body would be buried. Mrs. Flint graciously complied with her wish, though she said it was painful to her to have Nancy buried away from her. She might have added with touching pathos, "I was so long used to sleep with her lying near me, on the entry floor."

My uncle Phillip asked permission to bury his sister at his own expense, and slaveholders are always ready to grant such favors to slaves and their relatives. The arrangements were very plain, but perfectly respectable. She was buried on the Sabbath, and Mrs. Flint's minister read the funeral service. There was a large concourse of colored people, bond and free, and a few white persons who had always been friendly to our family. Dr. Flint's carriage was in the procession, and when the body was deposited in its humble resting place, the mistress dropped a tear and returned to her carriage, probably thinking she had performed her duty nobly.

It was talked of by the slaves as a mighty grand funeral. Northern travelers, passing through the place, might have described this tribute of respect to the humble dead as a beautiful feature in the 'patriarchal institution', a touching proof of the attachment between slaveholders and their servants. Tender-hearted Mrs. Flint would have confirmed this impression, with handkerchief at her eyes.

We could have told them a different story. We could have given them a chapter of wrongs and sufferings that would have touched their hearts, if they had any hearts to feel for the colored people. We could have told them how the poor old slave mother had toiled, year after year, to earn eight hundred dollars to buy her son Phillip's right to his own earnings, and how that same Phillip paid the expenses of the funeral, which they regarded as doing so much credit to the master. We could also have told them of a poor, blighted young creature, shut up in a living grave for years, to avoid the tortures that would be inflicted on her if she ventured to come out and look on the face of her departed friend.

All this, and much more, I thought of, as I sat at my loophole, waiting for the family to return from the grave, sometimes weeping, sometimes falling asleep, dreaming strange dreams of the dead and the living.

It was sad to witness the grief of my bereaved grandmother. She had always been strong to bear, and now, as ever, religious faith supported her. But her dark life had become still darker, and age and trouble were leaving deep traces on her withered face. She had four places to knock for me to come to the trap-door, and each place had a different meaning. She now came oftener than she had done, and talked to me of her dead daughter, while tears trickled slowly down her furrowed cheeks. I said all I could to comfort her, but it was a sad reflection that, instead of being able to help her, I was a constant source of anxiety and trouble. The poor old back was fitted to its burden. It bent under it, but did not break.

I hardly expect that the reader will credit me, when I affirm that I lived in that little dismal hole, almost deprived of light and air, and with no space to move my limbs, for nearly seven years. But it is a fact, and to me a sad one, even now, for my body still suffers from the effects of that long imprisonment, to say nothing of my soul.

Members of my family, now living in New York and Boston, can testify to the truth of what I say.

Countless were the nights that I sat late at the little loophole scarcely large enough to give me a glimpse of one twinkling star.

There, I heard the patrols and slave-hunters conferring

together about the capture of runaways, well knowing how rejoiced they would be to catch me.

Season after season, year after year, I peeped at my children's faces, and heard their sweet voices, with a heart yearning all the while to say, "Your mother is here." Sometimes it appeared to me as if ages had rolled away since I entered upon that gloomy, monotonous existence. At times, I was stupefied and listless, at other times I became very impatient to know when these dark years would end, and I should again be allowed to feel the sunshine, and breathe the pure air.

After Ellen left us, this feeling increased. Mr. Sands had agreed that Benny might go to the North whenever his uncle Phillip could go with him, and I was anxious to be there also, to watch over my children and protect them so far as I was able. Moreover, I was likely to be drowned out of my den if I remained much longer, for the slight roof was getting badly out of repair, and uncle Phillip was afraid to remove the shingles, lest someone should get a glimpse of me. When storms occurred in the night, they spread mats and bits of carpet, which in the morning appeared to have been laid out to dry, but to cover the roof in the daytime might have attracted attention. Consequently, my clothes and bedding were often drenched, a process by which the pains and aches in my cramped and stiffened limbs were greatly increased. I revolved various plans of escape in my mind, which I sometimes imparted to my grandmother, when she came to whisper with me at the trap-door. The kind-hearted old woman had an intense sympathy for runaways.

She had known too much of the cruelties inflicted on those who were captured. Her memory always flew back at once to the sufferings of her bright and handsome son, Benjamin, the youngest and dearest of her flock. So, whenever I alluded to the subject, she would groan out, "Don't think of it, child. You'll break my heart."

I had no good old Aunt Nancy now to encourage me, but my brother William and my children were continually beckoning me to the North.

And now I must go back a few months in my story.

I have stated that the first of January was the time for selling slaves, or leasing them out to new masters. If time were counted by heart-throbs, the poor slaves might reckon years of suffering during that festival so joyous to the free. On the New Year's Day preceding my aunt's death, one of my friends, named Fanny, was to be sold at auction, to pay her master's debts. My thoughts were with her during all the day, and at night I anxiously inquired what had been her fate. I was told that she had been sold to one master, and her four little girls to another master, far distant, that she had escaped from her purchaser, and was not to be found. Her mother was the old Aggie I have spoken of. She lived in a small tenement belonging to my grandmother, and built on the same lot with her own house. Her dwelling was searched and watched, and that brought the patrols so near me that I was obliged to keep very close in my den. The hunters were somehow eluded, and not long afterwards Benny accidentally caught sight of Fanny in her mother's hut. He told his grandmother, who charged him never to speak of it, explaining to him the frightful consequences, and he never betrayed the trust. Aggie little dreamed that my grandmother knew where her daughter was concealed, and that the stooping form of her old neighbor was bending under a similar burden of anxiety and fear, but these dangerous secrets deepened the sympathy between the two old persecuted mothers.

My friend Fanny and I remained many weeks hidden within call of each other, but she was unconscious of the fact. I longed to have her share my den, which seemed a more secure retreat than her own, but I had brought so much trouble on my grandmother, that it seemed wrong to ask her to incur greater risks. My restlessness increased. I had lived too long in bodily pain and anguish of spirit. Always I was in dread that by some accident, or some contrivance, slavery would succeed in snatching my children from me. This thought drove me nearly frantic, and I determined to steer for the North star at all hazards. At this crisis, Providence opened an unexpected way for me to escape. My friend Peter came one evening and asked to speak with me.

"Your day has come, Linda," said he. "I have found a chance for you to go to the Free States. You have a fortnight to decide."

The news seemed too good to be true, but Peter explained his arrangements, and told me all that was necessary was for me to say I would go. I was going to answer him with a joyful "yes", when the thought of Benny came to my mind. I told him the temptation was exceedingly strong, but I was terribly afraid of Dr. Flint's alleged power over my child, and that I could not go and leave him behind. Peter remonstrated earnestly. He said such a good chance might never occur again, that Benny was free, and could be sent to me, and that for the sake of my children's welfare I ought not to hesitate a moment. I told him I would consult with Uncle Phillip.

My uncle rejoiced in the plan, and bade me go by all means. He promised, if his life was spared, that he would either bring or send my son to me as soon as I reached a place of safety. I resolved to go, but thought nothing had better be said to my grandmother till very near the time of departure. But my uncle thought she would feel it more keenly if I left her so suddenly.

"I will reason with her," said he, "and convince her how necessary it is, not only for your sake, but for hers also. You cannot be blind to the fact that she is sinking under her burdens."

I was not blind to it. I knew that my concealment was an

ever-present source of anxiety, and that the older she grew the more nervously fearful she was of discovery. My uncle talked with her, and finally succeeded in persuading her that it was absolutely necessary for me to seize the chance so unexpectedly offered.

The anticipation of being a free woman proved almost too much for my weak frame. The excitement stimulated me, and at the same time bewildered me. I made busy preparations for my journey, and for my son to follow me. I resolved to have an interview with him before I went, that I might give him cautions and advice, and tell him how anxiously I should be waiting for him in the North.

Grandmother stole up to me as often as possible to whisper words of counsel. She insisted upon my writing to Dr. Flint, as soon as I arrived in the Free States, and asking him to sell me to her. She said she would sacrifice her house, and all she had in the world, for the sake of having me safe with my children in any part of the world. If she could only live to know that she could die in peace. I promised the dear old faithful friend that I would write to her as soon as I arrived, and put the letter in a safe way to reach her, but in my own mind I resolved that not another cent of her hard earnings should be spent to pay rapacious slaveholders for what they called their property. And even if I had not been unwilling to buy what I had already a right to possess, common humanity would have prevented me from accepting the generous offer, at the expense of turning my aged relative out of house and home, when she was trembling on the brink of the grave.

I was to escape in a vessel, but I forbear to mention any further particulars. I was in readiness, but the vessel was unexpectedly detained several days. Meantime, news came to town of a most horrible murder committed on a fugitive slave, named James. Charity, the mother of this unfortunate young man, had been an old acquaintance of ours. I have told the shocking particulars of his death, in my description of some of the neighboring slaveholders. My grandmother, always nervously sensitive about runaways, was terribly frightened. She felt sure that a similar fate awaited me, if I did not desist from my enterprise. She sobbed, and groaned, and entreated me not to go. Her excessive fear was somewhat contagious, and my heart was not proof against her extreme agony. I was grievously disappointed, but I promised to relinquish my project.

When my friend Peter was apprised of this, he was both disappointed and vexed. He said, that judging from our past experience, it would be a long time before I had such another chance to throw away. I told him it need not be thrown away, that I had a friend concealed nearby, who would be glad enough to take the place that had been provided for me. I told him about poor Fanny, and the kind-hearted, noble fellow, who never turned his back upon anybody in distress, white or black, expressed his readiness to help her.

Aggie was much surprised when she found that we knew her secret. She was rejoiced to hear of such a chance for Fanny, and arrangements were made for her to go on board the vessel the next night. They both supposed that I had long been in the North, therefore my name was not mentioned in the transaction. Fanny was carried on board at the appointed time, and stowed away in a very small cabin. This accommodation had been purchased at a price that would pay for a voyage to England. But when one proposes to go to fine old England, they stop to calculate whether they can afford the cost of the pleasure, while in making a bargain to escape from slavery, the trembling victim is ready to say, "Take all I have, only don't betray me."

The next morning I peeped through my loophole, and saw that it was dark and cloudy. At night I received news that the wind was ahead, and the vessel had not sailed. I was exceedingly anxious about Fanny, and Peter too, who was running a tremendous risk at my instigation. Next day the wind and weather remained the same.

Poor Fanny had been half-dead with fright when they carried her on board, and I could readily imagine how she must be suffering now. Grandmother came often to my den, to say how thankful she was I did not go. On the third morning she knocked for me to come down to the storeroom. The poor old sufferer was breaking down under her weight of trouble. She was easily flurried now. I found her in a nervous, excited state, but I was not aware that she had forgotten to lock the door behind her, as usual. She was exceedingly worried about the detention of the vessel. She was afraid all would be discovered, and then Fanny, and Peter, and I, would all be tortured to death, and Phillip would be utterly ruined, and her house would be torn down. Poor Peter. If he should die such a horrible death as the poor slave James had lately done, and all for his kindness in trying to help me, how dreadful it would be for us all. Alas, the thought was familiar to me, and had sent many a sharp pang through my heart. I tried to suppress my own anxiety, and speak soothingly to her. She brought in some allusion to Aunt Nancy, the dear daughter she had recently buried, and then she lost all control of herself. As she stood there, trembling and sobbing, a voice from the piazza called out, "Where is you, Aunt Marthy?"

Grandmother was startled, and in her agitation opened the door, without thinking of me. In stepped Jenny, the mischievous housemaid who had tried to enter my room when I was concealed in the house of my white benefactress.

"I's been huntin' everywhere for you, Aunt Marthy," said she. "My missis wants you to send her some crackers."

I had slunk down behind a barrel, which entirely screened me, but I imagined that Jenny was looking directly at the spot, and my heart beat violently. My grandmother immediately thought of what she had done, and went out quickly with Jenny to count the crackers, locking the door behind her. She returned to me, in a few minutes, the perfect picture of despair.

"Poor child," she exclaimed, "my carelessness has ruined you. The boat ain't gone yet. Get ready immediately, and go with Fanny. I ain't got another word to say against it now, for there's no telling what may happen this day."

Uncle Phillip was sent for, and he agreed with his mother in thinking that Jenny would inform Dr. Flint in less than twenty-four hours. He advised getting me on board the boat, if possible, if not, I had better keep very still in my den, where they could not find me without tearing the house down. He said it would not do for him to move in the matter, because suspicion would be immediately excited, but he promised to communicate with Peter. I felt reluctant to apply to him again, having implicated him too much already, but there seemed to be no alternative.

Vexed as Peter had been by my indecision, he was true to his generous nature, and said at once that he would do his best to help me, trusting I should show myself a stronger woman this time.

He immediately proceeded to the wharf, and found that the wind had shifted, and the vessel was slowly beating down stream. On some pretext of urgent necessity, he offered two boatmen a dollar apiece to catch up with her. He was of lighter complexion than the boatmen he hired, and when the captain saw them coming so rapidly, he thought officers were pursuing his vessel in search of the runaway slave he had on board. They hoisted sails, but the boat gained upon them, and the indefatigable Peter sprang on board.

The captain at once recognized him. Peter asked him to go below, to speak about a bad bill he had given him. When he told his errand, the captain replied, "Why, the woman's here already, and I've put her where you or the devil would have a tough job to find her."

"But it is another woman I want to bring," said Peter. "She is in great distress, too, and you shall be paid anything within reason, if you'll stop and take her."

"What's her name?" inquired the captain.

"Linda," he replied.

"That's the name of the woman already here," rejoined the captain. "By George! I believe you mean to betray me."

"Oh!" exclaimed Peter, "God knows I wouldn't harm a hair of your head. I am too grateful to you. But there really is another woman in great danger. Do have the humanity to stop and take her."

After a while they came to an understanding. Fanny, not dreaming I was anywhere about in that region, had assumed my name, though she called herself Johnson.

"Linda is a common name," said Peter, "and the woman I want to bring is Linda Brent."

The captain agreed to wait at a certain place till evening, being handsomely paid for his detention.

Of course, the day was an anxious one for us all. But we concluded that if Jenny had seen me, she would be too wise to let her mistress know of it, and that she probably would not get a chance to see Dr. Flint's family till evening, for I knew very well what were the rules in that household. I afterwards believed that she did not see me, for nothing ever came of it, and she was one of those base characters that would have jumped to betray a suffering fellow being for the sake of thirty pieces of silver.

I made all my arrangements to go on board as soon as it was dusk. The intervening time I resolved to spend with my son. I had not spoken to him for seven years, though I had been under the same roof, and seen him every day, when I was well enough to sit at the loophole. I did not dare to venture beyond the storeroom, so they brought him there, and locked us up together, in a place concealed from the piazza door. It was an agitating interview for both of us. After we had talked and wept together for a little while, he said, "Mother, I'm glad you're going away. I wish I could go with you. I knew you was here, and I have been so afraid they would come and catch you."

I was greatly surprised, and asked him how he had found it out.

He replied, "I was standing under the eaves, one day, before Ellen went away, and I heard somebody cough, up over the wood shed. I don't know what made me think it was you, but I did think so. I missed Ellen, the night before she went away, and grandmother brought her back into the room in the night, and I thought maybe she'd been to see you, before she went, for I heard grandmother whisper to her, 'Now go to sleep, and remember never to tell'."

I asked him if he ever mentioned his suspicions to his sister. He said he never did, but after he heard the cough, if he saw her playing with other children on that side of the house, he always tried to coax her round to the other side, for fear they would hear me cough, too. He said he had kept a close lookout for Dr. Flint, and if he saw him speak to a constable, or a patrol, he always told grandmother. I now recollected that I had seen him manifest uneasiness when people were on that side of the house, and I had at the time been puzzled to conjecture a motive for his actions. Such prudence may seem extraordinary in a boy of twelve years, but slaves, being surrounded by mysteries, deceptions and dangers, early learn to be suspicious and watchful, and prematurely cautious and cunning. He had never asked a question of grandmother, or uncle Phillip, and I had often heard him chime in with other children, when they spoke of my being in the North.

I told him I was now really going to the Free States, and if he was a good, honest boy, and a loving child to his dear old grandmother, the Lord would bless him, and bring him to me, and we and Ellen would live together. He began to tell me that grandmother had not eaten anything all day. While he was speaking, the door was unlocked, and she came in with small bag of money, which she wanted me to take. I begged her to keep a part of it, at least, to pay for Benny's being sent to the North, but she insisted, while her tears were falling fast, that I should take the whole.

"You may be sick among strangers," she said, "and they would send you to the poor house to die."

Ah, that good grandmother!

For the last time I went up to my nook. Its desolate appearance no longer chilled me, for the light of hope had risen in my soul. Yet, even with the blessed prospect of freedom before me, I felt very sad at leaving forever that old homestead where I had been sheltered so long by my dear old grandmother, where I had dreamed my first young dream of love, and where, after that had faded away, my children came to twine themselves so closely round my desolate heart. As the hour approached for me to leave, I again descended to the storeroom. My grandmother and Benny were there. She took me by the hand, and said, "Linda, let us pray."

We knelt down together, with my child pressed to my heart, and my other arm round the faithful, loving old friend I was about to leave forever. On no other occasion has it ever been my lot to listen to so fervent a supplication for mercy and protection. It thrilled through my heart, and inspired me with trust in God.

Peter was waiting for me in the street. I was soon by his side, faint in body, but strong of purpose. I did not look back upon the old place, though I felt that I should never see it again.

I never could tell how we reached the wharf. My brain was all of a whirl, and my limbs tottered under me. At an appointed place we met my uncle Phillip, who had started before us on a different route, that he might reach the wharf first, and give us timely warning if there was any danger. A rowboat was in readiness. As I was about to step in, I felt something pull me gently, and turning round I saw Benny, looking pale and anxious. He whispered in my ear, "I've been peeping into the doctor's window, and he's at home. Goodbye, mother. Don't cry, I'll come."

He hastened away. I clasped the hand of my good uncle, to whom I owed so much, and of Peter, the brave, generous friend who had volunteered to run such terrible risks to secure my safety. To this day I remember how his bright face beamed with joy when he told me he had discovered a safe method for me to escape. Yet that intelligent, enterprising, noble-hearted man was a chattel, liable by the laws of a country that calls itself civilized, to be sold with horses and pigs.

We parted in silence. Our hearts were all too full for words!

Swiftly the boat glided over the water. After a while, one of the sailors said, "Don't be down-hearted madam. We will take you safely to your husband."

At first I could not imagine what he meant, but I had presence of mind to think that it probably referred to something the captain had told him, so I thanked him, and said I hoped we should have pleasant weather.

When I entered the vessel the captain came forward to meet me. He was an elderly man, with a pleasant countenance. He showed me to a little box of a cabin, where sat my friend Fanny. She gazed on me in utter astonishment, and exclaimed, "Linda, can this be you, or is it your ghost?"

When we were locked in each other's arms, my over-wrought feelings could no longer be restrained. My sobs reached the ears of the captain, who came and very kindly reminded us that, for his safety, as well as our own, it would be prudent for us not to attract any attention. He said that when there was a sail in sight he wished us to keep below, but at other times, he had no objection to our being on deck. He assured us that he would keep a good lookout, and if we acted prudently, he thought we should be in no danger. He had represented us as women going to meet our husbands. We thanked him, and promised to observe carefully all the directions he gave us.

Fanny and I now talked by ourselves, low and quietly, in our little cabin. She told me of the sufferings she had gone through in making her escape, and of her terrors while she was concealed in her mother's house. Above all, she dwelt on the agony of separation from all her children on that dreadful auction day. She could scarcely credit me, when I told her of the place where I had passed nearly seven years.

"We have the same sorrows," said I.

"No," replied she, "you are going to see your children soon, there is no hope that I shall ever even hear from mine."

The vessel was soon under way, but we made slow progress. The wind was against us. I should not have cared for this, if we had been out of sight of the town, but until there were miles of water between us and our enemies, we were filled with constant apprehensions that the constables would come on board. Neither could I feel quite at ease with the captain and his men. I was an entire stranger to that class of people, and I had heard that sailors were rough, and sometimes cruel. We were so completely in their power that if they were bad men, our situation would be dreadful. Now that the captain was paid for our passage, might he not be tempted to make more money by giving us up to those who claimed us as property? I was naturally of a confiding disposition, but slavery had made me suspicious of everybody. Fanny did not share my distrust of the captain or his men. She said she was afraid at first, but she had been on board three days while the vessel lay in the dock, and nobody had betrayed her, or treated her otherwise than kindly.

The captain soon came to advise us to go on deck for fresh

air. His friendly and respectful manner, combined with Fanny's testimony, reassured me, and we went with him. He placed us in a comfortable seat, and occasionally entered into conversation. He told us he was a Southerner by birth, and had spent the greater part of his life in the slave States, and that he had recently lost a brother who traded in slaves. "But," said he, "it is a pitiable and degrading business, and I always felt ashamed to acknowledge my brother in connection with it."

As we passed Snaky Swamp he pointed to it and said "There is a slave territory that defies all the laws."

I thought of the terrible days I had spent there. It made me feel very dismal as I looked at it.

I shall never forget that night. The balmy air of spring was so refreshing. And how shall I describe my sensations when we were fairly sailing on Chesapeake Bay. Oh, the beautiful sunshine, the exhilarating breeze! I could enjoy them without fear or restraint. I had never realized what grand things air and sunlight are till I had been deprived of them.

Ten days after we left land we were approaching Philadelphia. The captain said we should arrive there in the night, but he thought we had better wait till morning, and go on shore in broad daylight, as the best way to avoid suspicion.

I replied, "You know best. But will you stay on board and protect us?"

He saw that I was suspicious, and he said he was sorry, now that he had brought us to the end of our voyage, to find I had so little confidence in him. Ah, if he had ever been a slave he would have known how difficult it was to trust a white man. He assured us that we might sleep through the night without fear, that he would take care we were not left unprotected. Be it said to the honor of this captain, Southerner as he was, that if Fanny and I had been white ladies, and our passage lawfully engaged, he could not have treated us more respectfully. My intelligent friend, Peter, had rightly estimated the character of the man to whose honor he had entrusted us.

The next morning I was on deck as soon as the day dawned. I called Fanny to see the sun rise, for the first time in our lives, on free soil, for such I then believed it to be. We watched the reddening sky, and saw the great orb come up slowly out of the water, as it seemed. Soon the waves began to sparkle, and everything caught the beautiful glow. Before us lay the city of strangers. We looked at each other, and the eyes of both were moistened with tears. We had escaped from slavery, and we supposed ourselves to be safe from the hunters. But we were alone in the world, and we had left dear ties behind us, ties cruelly sundered by the demon slavery.

I had heard that the poor slave had many friends in the North. I trusted we should find some of them. Meantime, we would take for granted that all were friends, till they proved to the contrary. I sought out the kind captain, thanked him for his attentions, and told him I should never cease to be grateful for the service he had rendered us. I gave him a message to the friends I had left at home, and he promised to deliver it. We were placed in a rowboat, and in about fifteen minutes were landed on a wood wharf in Philadelphia. As I stood looking round, the friendly captain touched me on the shoulder, and said, "There is a respectable-looking colored man behind you. I will speak to him about the New York trains, and tell him you wish to go directly on." I thanked him, and asked him to direct me to some shops where I could buy gloves and veils. He did so, and said he would talk with the colored man till I returned. I made what haste I could. Constant exercise on board the vessel, and frequent rubbing with salt water, had nearly restored the use of my limbs. The noise of the great city confused me, but I found the shops, and bought some double veils and gloves for Fanny and myself. The shopman told me they were so many levies. I had never heard the word before, but I did not tell him so. I thought if he knew I was a stranger he might ask me where I came from. I gave him a gold piece, and when he returned the change, I counted it, and found out how much a levy was.

I made my way back to the wharf, where the captain introduced me to the colored man, as the Rev. Jeremiah Durham, minister of Bethel church. He took me by the hand, as if I had been an old friend. He told us we were too late for the morning train to New York, and must wait until the evening, or the next morning. He invited me to go home with him, assuring me that his wife would give me a cordial welcome, and for my friend he would provide a home with one of his neighbors. I thanked him for so much kindness to strangers, and told him if I must be detained, I should like to hunt up some people who formerly went from our part of the country. Mr. Durham insisted that I should dine with him, and then he would assist me in finding my friends. The sailors came to bid us goodbye. I shook their hardy hands, with tears in my eyes. They had all been kind to us, and they had rendered us a greater service than they could possibly conceive of.

I had never seen so large a city, or been in contact with so many people in the streets. It seemed as if those who passed looked at us with an expression of curiosity. My face was so blistered and peeled, by sitting on deck, in wind and sunshine, that I thought they could not easily decide to what nation I belonged.

Mrs. Durham met me with a kindly welcome, without asking any questions. I was tired, and her friendly manner was a sweet refreshment. God bless her! I was sure that she had comforted other weary hearts before I received her sympathy. She was surrounded by her husband and children, in a home made sacred by protecting laws. I thought of my own children, and sighed.

After dinner Mr. Durham went with me in quest of the friends I had spoken of. They went from my native town, and I anticipated much pleasure in looking on familiar faces. They were not at home, and we retraced our steps through streets delightfully clean. On the way, Mr. Durham observed that I had spoken to him of a daughter I expected to meet, that he was surprised, for I looked so young he had taken me for a single woman. He was approaching a subject on which I was extremely sensitive. He would ask about my husband next, I thought, and if I answered him truly what would he think of me? I told him I had two children, one in New York the other in the South. He asked some further questions, and I frankly told him some of the most important events of my life. It was painful for me to do it, but I would not deceive him. If he was desirous of being my friend, I thought he ought to know how far I was worthy of it.

"Excuse me, if I have tried your feelings," said he. "I did not question you from idle curiosity. I wanted to understand your situation, in order to know whether I could be of any service to you, or your little girl. Your straightforward answers do you credit, but don't answer everybody so openly. It might give some heartless people a pretext for treating you with contempt."

That word contempt burned me like coals of fire. I replied, "God alone knows how I have suffered, and He, I trust, will forgive me. If I am permitted to have my children, I intend to be a good mother, and to live in such a manner that people cannot treat me with contempt."

"I respect your sentiments," said he. "Place your trust in God, and be governed by good principles, and you will not fail to find friends."

When we reached home, I went to my room, glad to shut out the world for a while. The words he had spoken made an indelible impression upon me. They brought up great shadows from the mournful past. In the midst of my meditations I was startled by a knock at the door. Mrs. Durham entered, her face all beaming with kindness, to say that there was an anti-slavery friend downstairs, who would like to see me. I overcame my dread of encountering strangers, and went with her. Many questions were asked concerning my experiences, and my escape from slavery, but I observed how careful they all were not to say anything that might wound my feelings. How gratifying this was, can be fully understood only by those who have been accustomed to be treated as if they were not included within the pale of human beings. The anti-slavery friend had come to inquire into my plans, and to offer assistance, if any was needed. Fanny was comfortably established, for the present, with a friend of Mr. Durham. The Anti-Slavery Society agreed to pay her expenses to New York. The same was offered to me, but I declined to accept it, telling them that my grandmother had given me sufficient to pay for my expenses to the end of my journey. We were urged to remain in Philadelphia a few days, until some suitable escort could be found for us. I gladly accepted the proposition, for I had a dread of meeting slaveholders, and some dread also of railroads. I had never entered a railroad car in my life, and it seemed to me quite an important event.

That night I sought my pillow with feelings I had never carried to it before. I verily believed myself to be a free woman. I was wakeful for a long time, and I had no sooner fallen asleep, than I was roused by fire bells. I jumped up, and hurried on my clothes. Where I came from, everybody hastened to dress themselves on such occasions. The white people thought a great fire might be used as a good opportunity for insurrection, and that it was best to be in readiness, and the colored people were ordered out to labor in extinguishing the flames. There was but one engine in our town, and colored women and children were often required to drag it to the river's edge and fill it. Mrs. Durham's daughter slept in the same room with me, and seeing that she slept through all the din, I thought it was my duty to wake her. "What's the matter?" said she, rubbing her eyes.

"They're screaming fire in the streets, and the bells are ringing," I replied.

"What of that?" said she, drowsily. "We are used to it. We never get up, unless the fire is very near. What good would it do?"

I was quite surprised that it was not necessary for us to go and help fill the engine. I was an ignorant child, just beginning to learn how things went on in great cities.

At daylight, I heard women crying fresh fish, berries, radishes, and various other things. All this was new to me. I dressed myself at an early hour and sat at the window to watch that unknown tide of life. Philadelphia seemed to me a wonderfully great place. At the breakfast table, my idea of going out to drag the engine was laughed over, and I joined in the mirth.

I went to see Fanny, and found her so well contented among her new friends that she was in no haste to leave. I was also very happy with my kind hostess. She had had advantages for education, and was vastly my superior. Every day, almost every hour, I was adding to my little stock of knowledge. She took me out to see the city as much as she deemed prudent. One day she took me to an artist's room and showed me the portraits of some of her children. I had never seen any paintings of colored people before, and they seemed to me beautiful.

At the end of five days, one of Mrs. Durham's friends offered to accompany us to New York the following morning. As I held the hand of my good hostess in a parting clasp, I longed to know whether her husband had repeated to her what I had told him. I supposed he had, but she never made any allusion to it. I presume it was the delicate silence of womanly sympathy.

When Mr. Durham handed us our tickets, he said, "I am afraid you will have a disagreeable ride, but I could not procure tickets for the first class cars."

Supposing I had not given him money enough, I offered more.

"Oh, no," said he, "They could not be had for any money. They don't allow colored people to go in the first class cars."

This was the first chill to my enthusiasm about the Free States. Colored people were allowed to ride in a filthy box, behind white people, in the South, but there they were not required to pay for the privilege. It made me sad to find how the North aped the customs of slavery.

We were stowed away in a large, rough car, with windows on each side, too high for us to look out without standing up. It was crowded with people, apparently of all nations. There were plenty of beds and cradles, containing screaming and kicking babies. Every other man had a cigar or pipe in his mouth, and jugs of whiskey were handed round freely. The fumes of the whiskey and the dense tobacco smoke were sickening to my senses, and my mind was equally nauseated by the coarse jokes and ribald songs around me. It was a very disagreeable ride. Since that time there has been some improvement in these matters.

When we arrived in New York, I was half-crazed by the crowd of coachmen calling out, "Carriage, ma'am?" We bargained with one to take us to Sullivan Street for twelve shillings. A burly Irishman stepped up and said, "I'll take ye for six shillings." The reduction of half the price was an object to us, and we asked if he could take us right away. "Troth an' I will, ladies," he replied.

I noticed that the hackmen smiled at each other, and I inquired whether his conveyance was decent. "Yes, it's decent it is, ma'am. Devil a bit would I be after takin' ladies in a cab that was not decent."

We gave him our checks. He went for the baggage, and soon reappeared, saying, "This way, if you please, ladies."

We followed, and found our trunks on a truck, and we were invited to take our seats on them. We told him that was not what we bargained for, and he must take the trunks off. He swore they should not be touched till we had paid him six shillings. In our situation it was not prudent to attract attention, and I was about to pay him what he required, when a man nearby shook his head for me not to do it. After a great ado we got rid of the Irishman, and had our trunks fastened on a hack. We had been recommended to a boarding-house in Sullivan Street, and thither we drove. There Fanny and I separated. The Anti-Slavery Society provided a home for her, and I afterwards heard of her in prosperous circumstances. I sent for an old friend from my part of the country, who had for some time been doing business in New York. He came immediately. I told him I wanted to go to my daughter, and asked him to aid me in procuring an interview.

I cautioned him not to let it be known to the family that I had just arrived from the South, because they supposed I had been in the North seven years. He told me there was a colored woman in Brooklyn who came from the same town I did, and I had better go to her house and have my daughter meet me there. I accepted the proposition thankfully, and he agreed to escort me to Brooklyn. We crossed Fulton ferry, went up Myrtle Avenue and stopped at the house he designated. I was just about to enter, when two girls passed. My friend called my attention to them. I turned, and recognized in the eldest, Sarah, the daughter of a woman who used to live with my grandmother, but who had left the South years ago.

Surprised and rejoiced at this unexpected meeting, I threw my arms round her, and inquired concerning her mother.

"You take no notice of the other girl," said my friend.

I turned, and there stood my Ellen! I pressed her to my

heart, then held her away from me to take a look at her. She had changed a good deal in the two years since I parted from her. Signs of neglect could be discerned by eyes less observing than a mother's.

My friend invited us all to go into the house, but Ellen said she had been sent on an errand, which she would do as quickly as possible, and go home and ask Mrs. Hobbs to let her come and see me. It was agreed that I should send for her the next day. Her companion, Sarah, hastened to tell her mother of my arrival. When I entered the house, I found the mistress of it absent, and I waited for her return.

Before I saw her, I heard her saying, "Where is Linda Brent? I used to know her father and mother."

Soon Sarah came with her mother. So there was quite a company of us, all from my grandmother's neighborhood. These friends gathered round me and questioned me eagerly. They laughed, cried, and shouted. They thanked God that I had got away from my persecutors and was safe. It was a day of great excitement. How different from the silent days I had passed in my dreary den.

The next morning was Sunday. My first waking thoughts were occupied with the note I was to send to Mrs. Hobbs, the lady with whom Ellen lived. That I had recently come into that vicinity was evident, otherwise I should have sooner inquired for my daughter.

It would not do to let them know I had just arrived from the South, for that would involve the suspicion of my having been harbored there, and might bring trouble, if not ruin, on several people.

I like a straightforward course, and am always reluctant to resort to subterfuge. So far as my ways have been crooked, I charge them all upon slavery. It was that system of violence and wrong which now left me no alternative but to enact a falsehood. I began my note by stating that I had recently arrived from Canada, and was very desirous to have my daughter come to see me. She came and brought a message from Mrs. Hobbs, inviting me to her house, and assuring me that I need not have any fears. The conversation I had with my child did not leave my mind at ease. When I asked if she was well treated, she answered yes, but there was no heartiness in the tone, and it seemed to me that she said it from an unwillingness to have me troubled on her account. Before she left me, she asked very earnestly, "Mother, when will you take me to live with you?" It made me sad to think that I could not give her a home till I went to work and earned the means, and that might take me a long time. When she was placed with Mrs. Hobbs, the agreement was that she should be sent to school. She had been there two years, and was now nine years old, and she scarcely knew her letters. There was no excuse for this, for there were good public schools in Brooklyn, to which she could have been sent without expense.

She stayed with me till dark and I went home with her. I was received in a friendly manner by the family, and all agreed in saying that Ellen was a useful, good girl. Mrs. Hobbs looked me coolly in the face, and said, "I suppose you know that my cousin, Mr. Sands, has given her to my eldest daughter. She will make a nice waiting-maid for her when she grows up."

I did not answer a word. How could she, who knew by experience the strength of a mother's love, and who was perfectly aware of the relation Mr. Sands bore to my children, look me in the face while she thrust such a dagger into my heart?

I was no longer surprised that they had kept her in such a state of ignorance. Mr. Hobbs had formerly been wealthy, but he had failed, and afterwards obtained a subordinate situation in the Custom House. Perhaps they expected to return to the South some day, and Ellen's knowledge was quite sufficient for a slave's condition. I was impatient to go to work and earn money, that I might change the uncertain position of my children. Mr. Sands had not kept his promise to emancipate them. I had also been deceived about Ellen. What security had I with regard to Benjamin? I felt that I had none.

I returned to my friend's house in an uneasy state of mind. In order to protect my children, it was necessary that I should own myself. I called myself free, and sometimes felt so, but I knew I was insecure. I sat down that night and wrote a civil letter to Dr. Flint, asking him to state the lowest terms on which he would sell me, and as I belonged by law to his daughter, I wrote to her also, making a similar request.

Since my arrival in the North I had not been unmindful of my dear brother William. I had made diligent inquiries for him, and having heard of him in Boston, I went thither. When I arrived there, I found he had gone to New Bedford. I wrote to that place, and was informed he had gone on a whaling voyage and would not return for some months. I went back to New York to get employment near Ellen. I received an answer from Dr. Flint, which gave me no encouragement. He advised me to return and submit myself to my rightful owners, and then any request I might make would be granted. I lent this letter to a friend, who lost it, otherwise I would present a copy to my readers.

My greatest anxiety now was to obtain employment. My health was greatly improved, though my limbs continued to trouble me with swelling whenever I walked much. The greatest difficulty in my way was that those who employed strangers required a recommendation. In my peculiar position, I could of course obtain no certificates from the families I had so faithfully served.

One day an acquaintance told me of a lady who wanted a nurse for her baby. I immediately applied for the situation. The lady told me she preferred to have one who had been a mother, and accustomed to the care of infants. I told her I had nursed two babes of my own. She asked me many questions but, to my great relief, did not require a recommendation from my former employers.

She told me she was an English woman, and that was a pleasant circumstance to me, because I had heard they had less prejudice against color than Americans entertained. It was agreed that we should try each other for a week. The trial proved satisfactory to both parties, and I was engaged for a month.

The heavenly Father had been most merciful to me in leading me to this place. Mrs. Bruce was a kind and gentle lady, and proved a true and sympathizing friend. Before the stipulated month expired, the necessity of passing up and downstairs frequently, caused my limbs to swell so painfully, that I became unable to perform my duties. Many ladies would have thoughtlessly discharged me, but Mrs. Bruce made arrangements to save me steps, and employed a physician to attend upon me. I had not yet told her that I was a fugitive slave. She noticed that I was often sad, and kindly inquired the cause. I spoke of being separated from my children, and from relatives who were dear to me, but I did not mention the constant feeling of insecurity which oppressed my spirits. I longed for someone to confide in, but I had been so deceived by white people that I had lost all confidence in them. If they spoke kind words to me, I thought it was for some selfish purpose. I had entered this family with the distrustful feelings I had brought with me out of slavery, but ere six months had passed, I found that the gentle deportment of Mrs. Bruce and the smiles of her lovely baby were thawing my chilled heart. My narrow mind also began to expand under the influences of her intelligent conversation and the opportunities for reading, which were gladly allowed me whenever I had leisure from my duties. I gradually became more energetic and more cheerful.

The old feeling of insecurity, especially with regard to my

children, often threw its dark shadow across my sunshine. Mrs.
Bruce offered me a home for Ellen, but pleasant as it would
have been, I did not dare to accept it, for fear of offending the
Hobbs family. Their knowledge of my precarious situation
placed me in their power, and I felt that it was important for me
to keep on the right side of them till, by dint of labor and
economy, I could make a home for my children. I was far from
feeling satisfied with Ellen's situation. She was not well cared
for. She sometimes came to New York to visit me, but she
generally brought a request from Mrs. Hobbs that I should buy
her a pair of shoes, or some article of clothing. This was
accompanied by a promise of payment when Mr. Hobbs's
salary at the Custom House became due, but somehow or other
the payday never came. Thus many dollars of my earnings
were expended to keep my child comfortably clothed. That,
however, was a slight trouble, compared with the fear that their
pecuniary embarrassments might induce them to sell my
precious young daughter. I knew they were in constant
communication with Southerners, and had frequent
opportunities to do it.

I have stated that when Dr. Flint put Ellen in jail, at two
years old, she had an inflammation of the eyes, occasioned by
measles. This disease still troubled her, and kind Mrs. Bruce
proposed that she should come to New York for a while, to be
under the care of Dr. Elliott, a well known physician. It did not
occur to me that there was anything improper in a mother's
making such a request, but Mrs. Hobbs was very angry and
refused to let her go. Situated as I was, it was not politic to insist
upon it. I made no complaint, but I longed to be entirely free to
act a mother's part towards my children. The next time I went
over to Brooklyn, Mrs. Hobbs, as if to apologize for her anger,
told me she had employed her own physician to attend to
Ellen's eyes, and that she had refused my request because she
did not consider it safe to trust her in New York. I accepted the

explanation in silence, but she had told me that my child belonged to her daughter, and I suspected that her real motive was a fear of my conveying her property away from her. Perhaps I did her injustice, but my knowledge of Southerners made it difficult for me to feel otherwise.

Sweet and bitter were mixed in the cup of my life, and I was thankful that it had ceased to be entirely bitter. I loved Mrs. Bruce's baby. When it laughed and crowed in my face, and twined its little tender arms confidingly about my neck, it made me think of the time when Benny and Ellen were babies, and my wounded heart was soothed.

One bright morning, as I stood at the window, tossing baby in my arms, my attention was attracted by a young man in sailor's dress, who was closely observing every house as he passed. I looked at him earnestly. Could it be my brother William? It must be he — and yet, how changed! I placed the baby safely, flew downstairs, opened the front door, beckoned to the sailor, and in less than a minute I was clasped in my brother's arms. How much we had to tell each other. How we laughed, and how we cried, over each other's adventures. I took him to Brooklyn, and again saw him with Ellen, the dear child whom he had loved and tended so carefully while I was shut up in my miserable den. He stayed in New York a week. His old feelings of affection for me and Ellen were as lively as ever. There are no bonds so strong as those which are formed by suffering together.

My young mistress, Miss Emily Flint, did not return any answer to my letter requesting her to consent to my being sold. But after a while, I received a reply, which purported to be written by her younger brother. In order rightly to enjoy the contents of this letter, the reader must bear in mind that the Flint family supposed I had been in the North many years. They had no idea that I knew of the doctor's three excursions to New York in search of me, that I had heard his voice, when he came to borrow five hundred dollars for that purpose, and that I had seen him pass on his way to the steamboat. Neither were they aware that all the particulars of Aunt Nancy's death and burial were conveyed to me at the time they occurred I have kept the letter, of which I herewith subjoin a copy:

Your letter to sister was received a few days ago. I gather from it that you are desirous of returning to your native place, among your friends and relatives. We were all gratified with the contents of your letter. Let me assure you that if any members of the family have had any feeling of resentment towards you, they feel it no longer. We all sympathize with you in your unfortunate condition, and are ready to do all in our power to make you contented and happy. It is difficult for you to return home as a free person. If you were purchased by your grandmother, it is doubtful whether you would be permitted to remain, although it would be lawful for you to do so. If a servant should be allowed to purchase herself, after absenting herself so long from her owners, and return free, it would have an injurious effect. From your letter, I think your situation must be hard and uncomfortable. Come home. You have it in your power to be reinstated in our affections. We would receive you with open arms and tears of joy. You need not apprehend any unkind treatment, as we have not put ourselves to any trouble or expense to get you. Had we done so, perhaps we should feel otherwise. You know my sister was always attached to you, and that you were never treated as a slave. You were never put to hard work, nor exposed to field labor. On the contrary, you were taken into the house and treated as one of us, and almost as free. We at least felt that you were above disgracing yourself by running away. Believing you may be induced to come home voluntarily has induced me to write for my sister. The family will be rejoiced to see you, and your poor old grandmother expressed a great desire to have you come, when she heard your letter read. In her old age she needs the consolation of having her children round her. Doubtless you have heard of the death of your aunt. She was a faithful servant, and a faithful member of the Episcopal church. In her Christian life she taught us how to live and, oh, too high the price of knowledge, she taught us how to die. Could you have seen us round her death bed, with her mother, all mingling our tears in one common stream, you would have thought the same heartfelt tie existed between a master and his servant, as between a mother and her child. But this subject is too painful to dwell upon. I must bring my letter to a close. If you are contented to stay away from your old grandmother, your child, and the friends who love you, stay where you are. We shall never trouble ourselves to apprehend you. But should you prefer to come home, we will do all that we can to make you happy. If you do not wish to remain in the family, I know that father, by our persuasion, will be induced to let you be purchased by any person you may choose in our community. You will please answer this as soon as possible, and let us know your decision. Sister sends much love to you. In the mean time, believe me your sincere friend and well wisher.

This letter was signed by Emily's brother, who was as yet a mere lad. I knew, by the style, that it was not written by a person of his age, and though the writing was disguised, I had been made too unhappy by it, in former years, not to recognize at once the hand of Dr. Flint. The hypocrisy of slaveholders! Did the old fox suppose I was goose enough to go into such a trap? Verily, he relied too much on "the stupidity of the African race."

I did not return the family of Flints any thanks for their cordial invitation — a remissness for which I was, no doubt, charged with base ingratitude. Not long afterwards I received a letter from one of my friends in the South, informing me that Dr. Flint was about to visit the North. The letter had been delayed, and I supposed he might be already on the way. Mrs. Bruce did not know I was a fugitive. I told her that important business called me to Boston, where my brother then was, and asked permission to bring a friend to take my place as nurse for a fortnight.

I started on my journey immediately. As soon as I arrived, I wrote to my grandmother that if Benny came, he must be sent to Boston. I knew she was only waiting for a good chance to send him North and, fortunately, she had the legal power to do so, without asking leave of anybody. She was a free woman, and when my children were purchased, Mr. Sands preferred to have the bill of sale drawn up in her name. It was conjectured that he advanced the money, but it was not known. In the South, a gentleman may have a shoal of colored children without any disgrace, but if he is known to purchase them, with the view of setting them free, the example is thought to be dangerous to their peculiar institution, and he becomes unpopular.

There was a good opportunity to send Benny in a vessel coming directly to New York. He was put on board with a letter to a friend who was requested to see him off to Boston. Early one morning, there was a loud knock at my door, and in rushed Benjamin, all out of breath.

"Mother," he exclaimed, "here I am. I run all the way, and I come all alone. How d'you do?"

Reader, can you imagine my joy? No, you cannot, unless you have been a slave mother.

Benjamin rattled away as fast as his tongue could go.

"Mother, why don't you bring Ellen here? I went over to Brooklyn to see her and she felt very bad when I bid her goodbye. She said, 'Ben, I wish I was going too.' I thought she'd know ever so much, but she don't know so much as I do, for I can read, and she can't. And, mother, I lost all my clothes coming. What can I do to get some more? I'spose free boys can get along here in the North as well as white boys."

I did not like to tell the sanguine, happy little fellow how much he was mistaken. I took him to a tailor and procured a change of clothes. The rest of the day was spent in mutual asking and answering of questions, with the wish constantly repeated that the good old grandmother was with us, and frequent injunctions from Benny to write to her immediately, and be sure to tell her everything about his voyage and his journey to Boston.

Dr. Flint made his visit to New York, and made every exertion to call upon me and invite me to return with him, but not being able to ascertain where I was, his hospitable intentions were frustrated, and the affectionate family, who were waiting for me with open arms, were doomed to disappointment.

As soon as I knew he was safely at home, I placed Benjamin in the care of my brother William, and returned to Mrs. Bruce. There I remained through the winter and spring, endeavoring to perform my duties faithfully, and finding a good degree of happiness in the attractions of baby Mary, the considerate kindness of her excellent mother, and occasional interviews with my darling daughter.

When summer came, the old feeling of insecurity haunted me. It was necessary for me to take little Mary out daily, for exercise and fresh air, and the city was swarming with Southerners, some of whom might recognize me. Hot weather brings out snakes and slaveholders, and I like one class of the venomous creatures as little as I do the other. What a comfort it is, to be free to say so.

It was a relief to my mind to see preparations for leaving the city. We went to Albany in the steamboat *Knickerbocker*. When the gong sounded for tea, Mrs. Bruce said, "Linda, it is late. You and baby had better come to the table with me."

I replied, "I know it is time baby had her supper, but I had rather not go with you, if you please. I am afraid of being insulted."

"No, not if you are with me," she said.

I saw several white nurses go with their ladies, and I
ventured to do the same. We were at the extreme end of the
table. I was no sooner seated, than a gruff voice said, "Get up!
You know you are not allowed to sit here."

I looked up and, to my astonishment and indignation, saw
that the speaker was a colored man. If his office required him to
enforce the by-laws of the boat, he might at least have done it
politely.

I replied, "I shall not get up, unless the captain comes and
takes me up."

No cup of tea was offered me, but Mrs. Bruce handed me
hers and called for another. I looked to see whether the other
nurses were treated in a similar manner. They were all properly
waited on.

Next morning, when we stopped for breakfast, everybody
was making a rush for the table. Mrs. Bruce said, "Take my
arm, Linda, and we'll go in together."

The landlord heard her and, said, "Madam, will you allow
your nurse and baby to take breakfast with my family?"

I knew this was to be attributed to my complexion, but he
spoke courteously, and therefore I did not mind it.

At Saratoga we found the United States Hotel crowded, and
Mr. Bruce took one of the cottages belonging to the hotel. I had
thought, with gladness, of going to the quiet of the country,
where I should meet few people, but here I found myself in the
midst of a swarm of Southerners. I looked round me with fear
and trembling, dreading to see someone who would recognize
me. I was rejoiced to find that we were to stay but a short time.

We soon returned to New York to make arrangements for
spending the remainder of the summer at Rockaway. While the
laundress was putting the clothes in order, I took an
opportunity to go over to Brooklyn to see Ellen. I met her going
to a grocery store. The first words she said, were, "Mother,
don't go to Mrs. Hobbs's. Her brother, Mr. Thorne, has come

from the South, and maybe he'll tell where you are."

I accepted the warning. I told her I was going away with Mrs. Bruce the next day and would try to see her when I came back.

Being in servitude to the Anglo-Saxon race, I was not put into a Jim Crow car on our way to Rockaway, neither was I invited to ride through the streets on the top of trunks in a truck, but everywhere I found the same manifestations of that cruel prejudice, which so discourages the feelings and represses the energies of the colored people. We reached Rockaway before dark, and put up at the Pavilion — a large hotel, beautifully situated by the seaside — a great resort of the fashionable world. Thirty or forty nurses were there, of a great variety of nations. Some of the ladies had colored waiting-maids and coachmen, but I was the only nurse tinged with the blood of Africa.

When the tea bell rang, I took little Mary and followed the other nurses. Supper was served in a long hall. A young man, who had the ordering of things, took the circuit of the table two or three times, and finally pointed me to a seat at the lower end of it. As there was but one chair, I sat down and took the child in my lap. Whereupon the young man came to me and said, in the blandest manner possible, "Will you please seat the little girl in the chair, and stand behind it and feed her? After they have done, you will be shown to the kitchen, where you will have a good supper."

This was the climax. I found it hard to preserve my self-control when I looked round and saw women who were nurses, as I was, and only one shade lighter in complexion, eyeing me with a defiant look, as if my presence were a contamination. However, I said nothing. I quietly took the child in my arms, went to our room, and refused to go to the table again. Mr. Bruce ordered meals to be sent to the room for little Mary and I. This was fine for a few days, but the waiters of the establishment were white, and they soon began to complain, saying they were not hired to wait on negroes. The landlord requested Mr. Bruce to send me down for my meals, because his servants rebelled against bringing them up, and the colored servants of other boarders were dissatisfied because all were not treated alike.

My answer was that the colored servants ought to be dissatisfied with themselves for not having too much self-respect to submit to such treatment, that there was no difference in the price of board for colored and white servants, and there was no justification for difference of treatment. I stayed a month after this, and finding I was resolved to stand up for my rights, they concluded to treat me well. Let every colored man and woman do this, and eventually we shall cease to be trampled under foot by our oppressors.

After we returned to New York, I took the earliest opportunity to go and see Ellen. I asked to have her called downstairs, for I supposed Mrs. Hobbs's Southern brother might still be there, and I was desirous to avoid seeing him, if possible. But Mrs. Hobbs came to the kitchen and insisted on my going upstairs.

"My brother wants to see you," said she, "and he is sorry you seem to shun him. He knows you are living in New York. He told me to say to you that he owes thanks to good old Aunt Martha for too many little acts of kindness for him to be base enough to betray her grandchild."

This Mr. Thorne had become poor and reckless long before he left the South, and such persons had much rather go to one of the faithful old slaves to borrow a dollar, or get a good dinner, than to go to one whom they consider an equal. It was such acts of kindness as these for which he professed to feel grateful to my grandmother. I wished he had kept at a distance, but as he was here, and knew where I was, I concluded there was nothing to be gained by trying to avoid him. On the contrary, it might be the means of exciting his ill will. I followed his sister upstairs. He met me in a very friendly manner, congratulated me on my escape from slavery, and hoped I had a good place, where I felt happy.

I continued to visit Ellen as often as I could. She, good thoughtful child, never forgot my hazardous situation, but always kept a vigilant lookout for my safety. She never made any complaint about her own inconveniences and troubles, but a mother's observing eye easily perceived that she was not happy. On the occasion of one of my visits I found her unusually serious. When I asked her what was the matter, she said nothing was the matter. But I insisted upon knowing what made her look so very grave. Finally, I ascertained that she felt troubled about the dissipation that was continually going on in the house. She was sent to the store very often for rum and brandy, and she felt ashamed to ask for it so often. Mr. Hobbs and Mr. Thorne drank a good deal, and their hands trembled so that they had to call her to pour out the liquid. Said she, "Mr. Hobbs is good to me, and I can't help liking him. I feel sorry for him."

I tried to comfort her by telling her that I had laid up a hundred dollars, and that before long I hoped to be able to give her and Benjamin a home, and send them to school. She was always desirous not to add to my troubles more than she could help, and I did not discover till years afterwards that Mr. Thorne's intemperance was not the only annoyance she suffered from him. Though he professed too much gratitude to my grandmother to injure any of her descendants, he had poured vile language into the ears of her innocent great-grandchild.

I usually went to Brooklyn to spend Sunday afternoon. One Sunday, I found Ellen anxiously waiting for me near the house. "Mother," said she, "I've been waiting for you this long time. I'm afraid Mr. Thorne has written to tell Dr. Flint where you are.

Make haste and come in. Mrs. Hobbs will tell you all about it."

The story was soon told. While the children were playing in the grapevine arbor, the day before, Mr. Thorne came out with a letter in his hand, which he tore up and scattered about. Ellen was sweeping the yard at the time, and having her mind full of suspicions of him, she picked up the pieces and carried them to the children, saying, "I wonder who Mr. Thorne has been writing to."

"I'm sure I don't know, and don't care," replied the oldest of the children, "and I don't see how it concerns you."

"But it does concern me," replied Ellen, "for I'm afraid he's been writing to the South about my mother."

They laughed at her and called her a silly thing, but good-naturedly put the fragments of writing together, in order to read them to her. They were no sooner arranged, than the little girl exclaimed, "I declare, Ellen, I believe you are right."

The contents of Mr. Thorne's letter, as nearly as I can remember, were as follows:

I have seen your slave, Linda, and conversed with her. She can be taken very easily, if you manage prudently. There are enough of us here to swear to her identity as your property. I am a patriot, a lover of my country, and I do this as an act of justice to the laws.

He concluded by informing the doctor of the street and number where I lived. The children carried the pieces to Mrs. Hobbs, who immediately went to her brother's room for an explanation. He was not to be found. The servant said they saw him go out with a letter in his hand, and they supposed he had gone to the post office. The natural inference was, that he had sent to Dr. Flint a copy of those fragments. When he returned, his sister accused him of it, and he did not deny the charge. He went immediately to his room, and the next morning he was missing. He had gone to New York, before any of the family were awake.

It was evident that I had no time to lose, and I hastened back to the city with a heavy heart. Again I was to be torn from a comfortable home, and all my plans for the welfare of my children were to be frustrated by that demon slavery. I now regretted that I never told Mrs. Bruce my story. I had not concealed it merely on account of being a fugitive, that would have made her anxious, but it would have excited sympathy in her kind heart. I valued her good opinion, and I was afraid of losing it if I told her all the particulars of my sad story. But now I felt that it was necessary for her to know how I was situated. I had once left her abruptly, without explaining the reason, and it would not be proper to do it again. I went home resolved to tell her in the morning. But the sadness of my face attracted her attention and, in answer to her kind inquiries, I poured out my full heart to her before bed time. She listened with true womanly sympathy, and told me she would do all she could to protect me. How my heart blessed her.

Early the next morning, Judge Vanderpool and Lawyer Hopper were consulted. They said I had better leave the city at once, as the risk would be great if the case came to trial. Mrs. Bruce took me in a carriage to the house of one of her friends, where she assured me I should be safe until my brother could arrive, which would be in a few days. In the interval my thoughts were much occupied with Ellen. She was mine by birth, and she was also mine by Southern law, since my grandmother held the bill of sale that made her so. I did not feel that she was safe unless I had her with me. Mrs. Hobbs, who felt badly about her brother's treachery, yielded to my entreaties, on condition that she should return in ten days. I avoided making any promise. She came to me clad in very thin garments, all outgrown, and with a school satchel on her arm, containing a few articles. It was late in October, and I knew the child would suffer. Not daring to go out in the streets to purchase anything, I took off my own flannel skirt and converted it into one for her. Kind Mrs. Bruce came to bid me goodbye, and when she saw that I had taken off my clothing for my child, the tears came to her eyes. She said, "Wait for me, Linda," and went out. She soon returned with a nice warm shawl and hood for Ellen. Truly, of such souls as hers are the kingdom of heaven.

My brother reached New York on Wednesday. Lawyer Hopper advised us to go to Boston by the Stonington route, as there was less Southern travel in that direction. Mrs. Bruce directed her servants to tell all inquirers that I formerly lived there, but had gone from the city.

We reached the steamboat *Rhode Island* in safety. That boat employed colored hands, but I knew that colored passengers were not admitted to the cabin. I was very desirous for the seclusion of the cabin, not only on account of exposure to the night air, but also to avoid observation. Lawyer Hopper was waiting on board for us. He spoke to the stewardess, and asked, as a particular favor, that she would treat us well. He said to me, "Go and speak to the captain yourself by and by. Take your little girl with you, and I am sure that he will not let her sleep on deck."

With these kind words and a shake of the hand he departed.

The boat was soon on her way, bearing me rapidly from the friendly home where I had hoped to find security and rest. My brother had left me to purchase the tickets, thinking that I might have better success than he would. When the stewardess came to me, I paid what she asked, and she gave me three tickets with clipped corners. In the most unsophisticated manner I said, "You have made a mistake, I asked you for cabin tickets. I cannot possibly consent to sleep on deck with my little daughter."

She assured me there was no mistake. She said on some of the routes colored people were allowed to sleep in the cabin, but not on this route, which was much travelled by the wealthy. I asked her to show me to the captain's office, and she said she would after tea. When the time came, I took Ellen by the hand and went to the captain, politely requesting him to change our tickets, as we should be very uncomfortable on deck. He said it was contrary to their custom, but he would see that we had berths below, he would also try to obtain comfortable seats for us in the cars, of that he was not certain, but he would speak to the conductor about it, when the boat arrived. I thanked him, and returned to the ladies' cabin. He came afterwards and told me that the conductor of the cars was on board, that he had spoken to him, and he had promised to take care of us. I was very much surprised at receiving so much kindness. I don't know whether the pleasing face of my little girl had won his heart, or whether the stewardess inferred from Lawyer Hopper's manner that I was a fugitive, and had pleaded with him on my behalf.

When the boat arrived at Stonington, the conductor kept his promise, and showed us to seats in the first car, nearest the engine. He asked us to take seats next to the door, but as he passed through, we ventured to move on toward the other end of the car. No incivility was offered us, and we reached Boston in safety.

The day after my arrival was one of the happiest of my life. I felt as if I was beyond the reach of the bloodhounds and, for the first time during many years, I had both my children together with me. They greatly enjoyed their reunion, and laughed and chatted merrily. I watched them with a swelling heart. Their every motion delighted me.

I could not feel safe in New York, and I accepted the offer of a friend that we should share expenses and keep house together. I represented to Mrs. Hobbs that Ellen must have some schooling, and must remain with me for that purpose. She felt ashamed of being unable to read or spell at her age, so instead of sending her to school with Benny, I instructed her myself till she was fitted to enter an intermediate school. The winter passed pleasantly, while I was busy with my needle, and my children with their books.

In the spring, sad news came to me. Mrs. Bruce was dead. Never again in this world should I see her gentle face, or hear her sympathizing voice. I had lost an excellent friend and little Mary had lost a tender mother. Mr. Bruce wished the child to visit some of her mother's relatives in England, and he was desirous that I should take charge of her. The little motherless one was accustomed to me, and attached to me, and I thought she would be happier in my care than in that of a stranger. I could also earn more in this way than I could by my needle. So I put Benny to a trade, and left Ellen to remain in the house with my friend and go to school.

We sailed from New York, and arrived in Liverpool after a pleasant voyage of twelve days. We proceeded directly to London, and took lodgings at the Adelaide Hotel. The supper seemed to me less luxurious than those I had seen in American hotels, but my situation was indescribably more pleasant. For the first time in my life I was in a place where I was treated according to my deportment, without reference to my complexion. I felt as if a great millstone had been lifted from my breast. Ensconced in a pleasant room, with my dear little charge, I laid my head on my pillow, for the first time, with the delightful consciousness of pure, unadulterated freedom.

As I had constant care of the child, I had little opportunity to see the wonders of that great city, but I watched the tide of life that flowed through the streets, and found it a strange contrast to the stagnation in our Southern towns. Mr. Bruce took his little daughter to spend some days with friends in Oxford Crescent, and of course it was necessary for me to accompany her. I had heard much of the systematic method of English education, and I was very desirous that my dear Mary should steer straight in the midst of so much propriety. I closely observed her little playmates and their nurses, being ready to take any lessons in the science of good management. The children were more rosy than American children, but I did not see that they differed materially in other respects. They were like all children — sometimes docile and sometimes wayward.

We next went to Steventon, in Berkshire. It was a small town, said to be the poorest in the county. I saw men working in the fields for six and seven shillings a week, and women for six and seven pence a day, out of which they boarded themselves. Of course they lived in the most primitive manner, it could not be otherwise, where a woman's wages for an entire day were not sufficient to buy a pound of meat. They paid very low rents and their clothes were made of the cheapest fabrics, though much better than could have been procured in the United States for the same money. I had heard much about the oppression of the poor in Europe. The people I saw around me were, many of them, among the poorest poor. But when I visited them in their little thatched cottages, I felt that the condition of even the meanest and most ignorant among them was vastly superior to the condition of the most favored slaves in America. They labored hard, but they were not ordered out to toil while the stars were in the sky, and driven and slashed by an overseer, through heat and cold, till the stars shone out again. Their homes were very humble, but they were protected by law. No insolent patrols could come, in the dead of night, and flog them at their pleasure. The father, when he closed his cottage door, felt safe with his family around him. No master or overseer could come and take from him his wife, or his daughter. They may separate to earn their living, but the parents knew where their children were going, and could communicate with them by letters. The relations of husband and wife, parent and child, were too sacred for the richest noble in the land to violate with impunity.

Much was being done to enlighten these poor people.

Schools were established among them, and benevolent societies were active in efforts to ameliorate their condition. There was no law forbidding them to learn to read and write, and if they helped each other in spelling out the Bible, they were in no danger of thirty-nine lashes, as was the case with myself and poor, pious, old Uncle Fred. I repeat that the most ignorant and the most destitute of these peasants was a thousand fold better off than the most pampered American slave.

I do not deny that the poor are oppressed in Europe. I am not disposed to paint their condition so rose-colored as the Hon. Miss Murray paints the condition of the slaves in the United States. A small portion of my experience would enable her to read her own pages with anointed eyes. If she were to lay aside her title and, instead of visiting among the fashionable, become domesticated, as a poor governess, on some plantation in Louisiana or Alabama, she would see and hear things that would make her tell quite a different story.

My visit to England is a memorable event in my life, from the fact of my having there received strong religious impressions. The contemptuous manner in which the communion had been administered to colored people, in my native place, the church membership of Dr. Flint and others like him, and the buying and selling of slaves, by professed ministers of the gospel, had given me a prejudice against the Episcopal church. The whole service seemed to me a mockery and a sham. But my home in Steventon was in the family of a clergyman who was a true disciple of Jesus. The beauty of his daily life inspired me with faith in the genuineness of Christian professions. Grace entered my heart, and I knelt at the communion table, I trust, in true humility of soul.

I remained abroad ten months, which was much longer than I had anticipated. During all that time, I never saw the slightest symptom of prejudice against color. Indeed, I entirely forgot it, till the time came for us to return to America.

We had a tedious winter passage, and from the distance specters seemed to rise up on the shores of the United States. It is a sad feeling to be afraid of one's native country. We arrived in New York safely, and I hastened to Boston to look after my children. I found Ellen well, and improving at her school, but Benny was not there to welcome me. He had been left at a good place to learn a trade, and for several months everything worked well. He was liked by the master and was a favorite with his fellow apprentices, but one day they accidentally discovered a fact: they had never before suspected that he was colored. This at once transformed him into a different being. Some of the apprentices were Americans, others American-born Irish, and it was offensive to their dignity to have a a nigger among them, once they had been told that he was a a nigger.

They began by treating him with silent scorn. Finding that he returned the same, they resorted to insults and abuse. He was too spirited a boy to stand that, and he went off. Being desirous to do something to support himself, and having no one to advise him, he shipped for a whaling voyage. When I received these tidings I shed many tears, and bitterly reproached myself for having left him so long. But I had done it for the best, and now all I could do was to pray to the heavenly Father to guide and protect him.

Not long after my return, I received the following letter from Miss Emily Flint, now Mrs. Dodge:

In this you will recognize the hand of your friend and mistress. Having heard that you had gone with a family to Europe, I have waited to hear of your return to write to you. I should have answered the letter you wrote to me long since, but as I could not then act independently of my father, I knew there could be nothing done satisfactory to you. There were persons here who were willing to buy you and run the risk of getting you. To this I would not consent. I

have always been attached to you, and would not like to see you the
slave of another, or have unkind treatment. I am married now, and can
protect you. My husband expects to move to Virginia this spring,
where we think of settling. I am very anxious that you should come
and live with me. If you are not willing to come, you may purchase
yourself, but I should prefer having you live with me. If you come, you
may, if you like, spend a month with your grandmother and friends,
then come to me in Norfolk, Virginia. Think this over, and write as
soon as possible, and let me know the conclusion. Hoping that your
children are well, I remain your friend and mistress.

Of course I did not write to return thanks for this cordial
invitation. I felt insulted to be thought stupid enough to be
caught by such professions.

> *'Come up into my parlor,' said the spider to the fly,*
> *'Tis the prettiest little parlor that ever you did spy.'*

It was plain that Dr. Flint's family were apprised of my
movements, since they knew of my voyage to Europe. I
expected to have further trouble from them, but having eluded
them thus far, I hoped to be as successful in future. The money
I had earned, I was desirous to devote to the education of my
children, and to secure a home for them. It seemed not only
hard, but unjust, to pay for myself. I could not possibly regard
myself as a piece of property. Moreover, I had worked many
years without wages, and during that time had been obliged to
depend on my grandmother for many comforts in food and
clothing. My children certainly belonged to me, but though Dr.
Flint had incurred no expense for their support, he had
received a large sum of money for them. I knew the law would
decide that I was his property, and would probably still give his
daughter a claim to my children, but I regarded such laws as
the regulations of robbers, who had no rights that I was bound

to respect.

The Fugitive Slave Law had not then passed. The judges of Massachusetts had not then stooped under chains to enter her courts of justice, so called. I knew my old master was rather skittish of Massachusetts. I relied on her love of freedom, and felt safe on her soil. I am now aware that I honored the old Commonwealth beyond her deserts.

For two years my daughter and I supported ourselves comfortably in Boston. At the end of that time, my brother William offered to send Ellen to a boarding school. It required a great effort for me to consent to part with her, for I had few near ties, it was her presence that made my two little rooms seem homely. But my judgment prevailed over my selfish feelings. I made preparations for her departure.

During the two years we had lived together I had often resolved to tell her something about her father, but I had never been able to muster sufficient courage. I had a shrinking dread of diminishing my child's love. I knew she must have curiosity on the subject, but she had never asked a question. She was always very careful not to say anything to remind me of my troubles. Now that she was going from me, I thought if I should die before she returned, she might hear my story from someone who did not understand the palliating circumstances, and that if she were entirely ignorant on the subject, her sensitive nature might receive a rude shock.

When we retired for the night, she said, "Mother, it is very hard to leave you alone. I am almost sorry I am going, though I do want to improve myself. But you will write to me often, won't you, mother?"

I did not throw my arms round her. I did not answer her. But in a calm, solemn way, for it cost me great effort, I said, "Listen to me, Ellen, I have something to tell you."

I recounted my early sufferings in slavery, and told her how nearly they had crushed me. I began to tell her how they had driven me into a great sin, when she clasped me in her arms, and exclaimed, "Don't, mother. Please don't tell me any more."

I said, "But, my child, I want you to know about your father."

"I know all about it, mother," she replied, "I am nothing to my father, and he is nothing to me. All my love is for you. I was with him five months in Washington, and he never cared for me. He never spoke to me as he did to his little Fanny. I knew all the time he was my father, for Fanny's nurse told me so, but she said I must never tell anybody, and I never did. I used to wish he would take me in his arms and kiss me, as he did Fanny, or that he would sometimes smile at me, as he did at her. I thought if he was my own father, he ought to love me. I was a little girl then, and didn't know any better. But now I never think anything about my father. All my love is for you."

She hugged me closer as she spoke. I thanked God that the knowledge I had so much dreaded to impart had not diminished the affection of my child. I had not the slightest idea she knew that portion of my history. If I had, I should have spoken to her long before, for my pent-up feelings had often longed to pour themselves out to someone I could trust. But I loved the dear girl better for the delicacy she had manifested towards her unfortunate mother.

The next morning, she and her uncle started on their journey to the village in New York, where she was to be placed at school. It seemed as if all the sunshine had gone away. My little room was dreadfully lonely. I was thankful when a message came from a lady, accustomed to employ me, requesting me to come and sew in her family for several weeks. On my return, I found a letter from brother William. He thought of opening an anti-slavery reading room in Rochester, and combining with it the sale of some books and stationery, and he wanted me to unite with him. We tried it, but it was not successful. We found warm anti-slavery friends there, but the feeling was not general enough to support such an establishment.

My brother, being disappointed in his project, concluded to go to California, and it was agreed that Benjamin should go with him.

Ellen liked her school, and was a great favorite there. They did not know her history, and she did not tell it, because she had no desire to make capital out of their sympathy. But when it was accidentally discovered that her mother was a fugitive slave, every method was used to increase her advantages and diminish her expenses.

I was alone again. It was necessary for me to be earning money, and I preferred that it should be among those who knew me. On my return from Rochester, I called at the house of Mr. Bruce, to see Mary, the darling little baby that had thawed my heart, when it was freezing into a cheerless distrust of all my fellow beings. She was growing a tall girl now, but I loved her always. Mr. Bruce had married again, and it was proposed that I should become nurse to a new infant. I had but one hesitation, and that was my feeling of insecurity in New York, now greatly increased by the passage of the Fugitive Slave Law. However, I resolved to try the experiment. I was again fortunate in my employer. The new Mrs. Bruce was an American, brought up under aristocratic influences, and still living in the midst of them, but if she had any prejudice against color, I was never made aware of it, and as for the system of slavery, she had a most hearty dislike of it. No sophistry of Southerners could blind her to its enormity. She was a person of excellent principles and a noble heart. To me, from that hour to the present, she has been a true and sympathizing friend. Blessings be with her and hers.

About the time that I re-entered the Bruce family, an event occurred of disastrous import to the colored people. The slave

Hamlin, the first fugitive that came under the new law, was given up by the bloodhounds of the North to the bloodhounds of the South. It was the beginning of a reign of terror to the colored population. The great city rushed on in its whirl of excitement, taking no note of the 'short and simple annals of the poor'. But while fashionables were listening to the thrilling voice of Jenny Lind in Metropolitan Hall, the thrilling voices of poor hunted colored people went up, in an agony of supplication, to the Lord, from Zion's church. Many families, who had lived in the city for twenty years, fled from it now.

Many a poor washerwoman who, by hard labor, had made herself a comfortable home, was obliged to sacrifice her furniture, bid a hurried farewell to friends, and seek her fortune among strangers in Canada. Many a wife discovered a secret she had never known before — that her husband was a fugitive, and must leave her to insure his own safety. Worse still, many a husband discovered that his wife had fled from slavery years ago, and as the child follows the condition of its mother, the children of his love were liable to be seized and carried into slavery. Everywhere, in those humble homes, there was consternation and anguish. But what cared the legislators of the dominant race for the blood they were crushing out of trampled hearts?

When my brother William spent his last evening with me, before he went to California, we talked nearly all the time of the distress brought on our oppressed people by the passage of this iniquitous law, and never had I seen him manifest such bitterness of spirit, such stern hostility to our oppressors. He was himself free from the operation of the law, for he did not run from any slaveholding State, being brought into the Free States by his master. But I was subject to it, and so were hundreds of intelligent and industrious people all around us. I seldom ventured into the streets, and when it was necessary to do an errand for Mrs. Bruce, or any of the family, I went as much as possible through back streets and by-ways. What a disgrace to a city calling itself free, that inhabitants, guiltless of offense, and seeking to perform their duties conscientiously, should be condemned to live in such incessant fear, and have nowhere to turn for protection. This state of things, of course, gave rise to many impromptu vigilance committees. Every colored person, and every friend of their persecuted race, kept their eyes wide open. Every evening I examined the newspapers carefully, to see what Southerners had put up at the hotels. I did this for my own sake, thinking my young mistress and her husband might be among the list, I wished also to give information to others, if necessary, for if many were running to and fro, I resolved that knowledge should be increased.

This brings up one of my Southern reminiscences, which I will here briefly relate. I was somewhat acquainted with a slave named Luke, who belonged to a wealthy man in our vicinity. His master died, leaving a son and daughter heirs to his large fortune. In the division of the slaves, Luke was included in the son's portion. This young man became a prey to the vices growing out of the patriarchal institution, and when he went to the North, to complete his education, he carried his vices with him. He was brought home, deprived of the use of his limbs, by excessive dissipation. Luke was appointed to wait upon his bed-ridden master, whose despotic habits were greatly increased by exasperation at his own helplessness. He kept a cowhide beside him and, for the most trivial occurrence, he would order his attendant to bare his back, and kneel beside the couch, while he whipped him till his strength was exhausted. Some days he was not allowed to wear anything but his shirt, in order to be in readiness to be flogged. A day seldom passed without his receiving more or less blows. If the slightest resistance was offered, the town constable was sent for to execute the punishment, and Luke learned from experience how much more the constable's strong arm was to be dreaded than the comparatively feeble one of his master. The arm of his tyrant grew weaker, and was finally palsied, and then the constable's services were in constant requisition. The fact that he was entirely dependent on Luke's care, and was obliged to be tended like an infant, instead of inspiring any gratitude or compassion towards his poor slave, seemed only to increase his irritability and cruelty. As he lay there on his bed, a mere degraded wreck of manhood, he took into his head the strangest freaks of despotism, and if Luke hesitated to submit to his orders, the constable was immediately sent for. Some of these freaks were of a nature too filthy to be repeated. When I fled from the house of bondage, I left poor Luke still chained to the bedside of this cruel and disgusting wretch.

One day, when I had been requested to do an errand for Mrs. Bruce, I was hurrying through back streets, as usual, when I saw a young man approaching, whose face was familiar to me. As he came nearer, I recognized Luke. I always rejoiced to see or hear of anyone who had escaped from the black pit, but, remembering this poor fellow's extreme hardships, I was peculiarly glad to see him on Northern soil, though I no longer called it free soil. I well remembered what a desolate feeling it was to be alone among strangers, and I went up to him and greeted him cordially. At first, he did not know me, but when I mentioned my name, he remembered all about me. I told him of the Fugitive Slave Law, and asked him if he did not know that New York was a city of kidnappers.

He replied, "The risk ain't so bad for me, as 'tis for you. 'Cause I runned away from the speculator, and you runned away from the massa. Dem speculators won't spend their money to come here for a runaway if they ain't sure to put their hands right on him. An I tell you I's took good care 'bout dat. I had too hard times down there, to let 'em ketch this nigger."

He then told me of the advice he had received, and the plans

he had laid. I asked if he had money enough to take him to
Canada.

" 'Pend upon it, I have," he replied. "I took care for dat. I'd
been workin all my days for dem cursed whites, an got no pay
but kicks and cuffs. So I thought this nigger had a right to
money nuff to bring him to the Free States. Massa Henry he
lived till everybody wish him dead, an when he did die, I
knowed the devil would have him, an wouldn't want him to
bring his money 'long, too. So I took some of his bills, and put
'em in the pocket of his old trousers. An when he was buried,
this nigger ask for dem old trousers, an they gave 'em to me."
With a low, chuckling laugh, he added, "You see, I didn't steal
it, they give it to me. I tell you, I had mighty hard time to keep
the speculator from findin' it."

This is a fair specimen of how the moral sense is educated
by slavery. When a man has his wages stolen from him, year
after year and the laws sanction and enforce the theft, how can
he be expected to have more regard to honesty than has the
man who robs him? I have become somewhat enlightened, but
I confess that, I agree with poor, ignorant, much-abused Luke,
in thinking he had a right to that money, as a portion of his
unpaid wages. He went to Canada forthwith, and I have not
since heard from him.

All that winter I lived in a state of anxiety. When I took the
children out to breathe the air, I closely observed the
countenances of all I met. I dreaded the approach of summer,
when snakes and slaveholders make their appearance. I was, in
fact, a slave in New York, as subject to slave laws as I had been
in a slave State. Strange incongruity in a State called free.

Spring returned, and I received warning from the South that
Dr. Flint knew of my return to my old place, and was making
preparations to have me caught. I learned afterwards that my
dress, and that of Mrs. Bruce's children, had been described to

him by some of the Northern tools, which slaveholders employ for their base purposes, and then indulge in sneers at their cupidity and mean servility.

I immediately informed Mrs. Bruce of my danger, and she took prompt measures for my safety. My place as nurse could not be replaced immediately, and this generous, sympathizing lady proposed that I should carry her baby away. It was a comfort to me to have the child with me, for the heart is reluctant to be torn away from every object it loves. But how few mothers would have consented to have one of their own babes become a fugitive, for the sake of a poor, hunted nurse, on whom the legislators of the country had let loose the bloodhounds. When I spoke of the sacrifice she was making, in depriving herself of her dear baby, she replied, "It is better for you to have baby with you, Linda, for if they get on your track, they will be obliged to bring the child to me, and then, if there is a possibility of saving you, you shall be saved."

This lady had a very wealthy relative, a benevolent gentleman in many respects, but aristocratic and pro-slavery. He remonstrated with her for harboring a fugitive slave, told her she was violating the laws of her country, and asked her if she was aware of the penalty.

She replied, "I am very well aware of it. It is imprisonment and one thousand dollars fine. Shame on my country that it is so. I am ready to incur the penalty. I will go to the State's prison rather than have any poor victim torn from my house, to be carried back to slavery."

The noble heart. The brave heart. The tears are in my eyes while I write of her. May the God of the helpless reward her for her sympathy with my persecuted people.

I was sent into New England, where I was sheltered by the wife of a senator, whom I shall always hold in grateful remembrance. This honorable gentleman would not have voted for the Fugitive Slave Law, as did the senator in *Uncle*

Tom's.Cabin. On the contrary, he was strongly opposed to it, but he was enough under its influence to be afraid of having me remain in his house many hours. So I was sent into the country, where I remained a month with the baby. When it was supposed that Dr. Flint's emissaries had lost track of me, and given up the pursuit for the present, I returned to New York.

Mrs. Bruce, and every member of her family, were exceedingly kind to me. I was thankful for the blessings of my lot, yet I could not always wear a cheerful countenance. I was doing harm to no one, on the contrary, I was doing all the good I could in my small way, yet I could never go out to breathe God's free air without trepidation at my heart. This seemed hard, and I could not think it was a right state of things in any civilized country.

From time to time I received news from my good old grandmother. She could not write, but she employed others to write for her. The following is an extract from one of her last letters:

Dear Daughter,

I cannot hope to see you again on Earth, but I pray to God to unite us above, where pain will no more rack this feeble body of mine, where sorrow and parting from my children will be no more. God has promised these things if we are faithful unto the end. My age and feeble health deprive me of going to church now, but God is with me here at home. Thank your brother for his kindness. Give much love to him, and tell him to remember the Creator in the days of his youth, and strive to meet me in the Father's kingdom. Love to Ellen and Benjamin. Don't neglect him. Tell him for me, to be a good boy. Strive, my child, to train them for God's children. May he protect and provide for you, is the prayer of your loving old mother.

These letters both cheered and saddened me. I was always glad to have tidings from the kind, faithful old friend of my

unhappy youth, but her messages of love made my heart yearn
to see her before she died. I mourned over the fact that it was
impossible. Some months after I returned from my flight to
New England, I received a letter from her, in which she wrote,
*Dr. Flint is dead. He has left a distressed family. Poor old man. I hope
he made his peace with God.*

I remembered how he had defrauded my grandmother of
the hard earnings she had loaned, how he had tried to cheat her
out of the freedom her mistress had promised her, and how he
had persecuted her children. I thought to myself that she was a
better Christian than I was, if she could entirely forgive him. I
cannot say, with truth, that the news of my old master's death
softened my feelings towards him. There are wrongs which
even the grave does not bury. The man was odious to me while
he lived, and his memory is odious now.

His departure from this world did not diminish my danger.
He had threatened my grandmother that his heirs should hold
me in slavery after he was gone, that I never should be free so
long as a child of his survived. As for Mrs. Flint, I had seen her
in deeper afflictions than I supposed the loss of her husband
would be, for she had buried several children, yet I never saw
any signs of softening in her heart. The doctor had died in
embarrassed circumstances, and had little to will to his heirs,
except such property as he was unable to grasp. I was well
aware what I had to expect from the family of Flints, and my
fears were confirmed by a letter from the South, warning me to
be on my guard, because Mrs. Flint openly declared that her
daughter could not afford to lose so valuable a slave as I was.

I kept close watch of the newspapers for arrivals, but one
Saturday night, being much occupied, I forgot to examine the
Evening Express as usual. I went down into the parlor for it,
early in the morning, and found the boy about to kindle a fire
with it. I took it from him and examined the list of arrivals.

Reader, if you have never been a slave, you cannot imagine

the acute sensation of suffering at my heart, when I read the names of Mr. and Mrs. Dodge, at a hotel in Courtland Street. It was a third-rate hotel, and that circumstance convinced me of the truth of what I had heard, that they were short of funds and had need of my value, as they valued me, and that was by dollars and cents. I hastened with the paper to Mrs. Bruce. Her heart and hand were always open to everyone in distress, and she always warmly sympathized with mine. It was impossible to tell how near the enemy was. He might have passed and repassed the house while we were sleeping. He might at that moment be waiting to pounce upon me if I ventured out of doors. I had never seen the husband of my young mistress, and therefore I could not distinguish him from any other stranger. A carriage was hastily ordered and, closely veiled, I followed Mrs. Bruce, taking the baby again with me into exile. After various turnings and crossings, and returnings, the carriage stopped at the house of one of Mrs. Bruce's friends, where I was kindly received. Mrs. Bruce returned immediately, to instruct the domestics what to say if anyone came to inquire for me.

It was lucky for me that the evening paper was not burned up before I had a chance to examine the list of arrivals. It was not long after Mrs. Bruce's return to her house, before several people came to inquire for me. One inquired for me, another asked for my daughter Ellen, and another said he had a letter from my grandmother, which he was requested to deliver in person.

They were told, "She has lived here, but she has left."

"How long ago?"

"I don't know, sir."

"Do you know where she went?"

"I do not, sir." And the door was closed.

This Mr. Dodge, who claimed me as his property, was originally a Yankee pedler in the South, then he became a merchant, and finally a slaveholder. He managed to get introduced into what was called the first society, and married Miss Emily Flint. A quarrel arose between him and her brother, and the brother cowhided him. This led to a family feud, and he proposed to remove to Virginia. Dr. Flint left him no property, and his own means had become circumscribed, while a wife and children depended upon him for support. Under these circumstances, it was very natural that he should make an effort to put me into his pocket.

I had a colored friend, a man from my native place, in whom I had the most implicit confidence. I sent for him, and told him that Mr. and Mrs. Dodge had arrived in New York. I proposed that he should call upon them to make inquiries about his friends in the South, with whom Dr. Flint's family were well acquainted. He thought there was no impropriety in his doing so, and he consented. He went to the hotel, and knocked at the door of Mr. Dodge's room, which was opened by the gentleman himself, who gruffly inquired, "What brought you here? How came you to know I was in the city?"

"Your arrival was published in the evening papers, sir, and I called to ask Mrs. Dodge about my friends at home. I didn't suppose it would give any offense."

"Where's that negro girl that belongs to my wife?"

"What girl, sir?"

"You know well enough. I mean Linda, that ran away from Dr. Flint's plantation, some years ago. I dare say you've seen her, and know where she is."

"Yes, sir, I've seen her, and know where she is. She is out of your reach, sir."

"Tell me where she is, or bring her to me and I will give her a chance to buy her freedom."

"I don't think it would be of any use, sir. I have heard her say she would go to the ends of the earth, rather than pay any man or woman for her freedom, because she thinks she has a right to it. Besides, she couldn't do it, if she would, for she has spent her earnings to educate her children."

This made Mr. Dodge very angry, and some high words passed between them. My friend was afraid to come where I was, but in the course of the day I received a note from him. I supposed they had not come from the South, in the winter, for a pleasure excursion, and now the nature of their business was very plain.

Mrs. Bruce came to me and entreated me to leave the city the next morning. She said her house was watched, and it was possible that some clue to me might be obtained. I refused to take her advice. She pleaded with an earnest tenderness that ought to have moved me, but I was in a bitter, disheartened mood. I was weary of flying from pillar to post. I had been chased during half my life, and it seemed as if the chase was never to end. There I sat, in that great city, guiltless of crime, yet not daring to worship God in any of the churches. I heard the bells ringing for afternoon service and, with contemptuous sarcasm, I said, "Will the preachers take for their text, *Proclaim liberty to the captive, and the opening of prison doors to them that are bound?* or will they preach from the text, *Do unto others as ye would they should do unto you?*" Oppressed Poles and Hungarians could find a safe refuge in that city, John Mitchell was free to proclaim in the City Hall his desire for "a plantation well stocked with slaves," but there I sat, an oppressed American, not daring to show my face. God forgive the black and bitter thoughts I indulged on that Sabbath day. The Scripture says, *Oppression makes even a wise man mad*, and I was not wise.

I had been told that Mr. Dodge said his wife had never signed away her right to my children, and if he could not get me, he would take them. This it was, more than anything else, that roused such a tempest in my soul. Benjamin was with his uncle William in California, but my innocent young daughter had come to spend a vacation with me. I thought of what I had suffered in slavery at her age, and my heart was like a tiger's when a hunter tries to seize her young.

Dear Mrs. Bruce, I seem to see the expression of her face as she turned away discouraged by my obstinate mood. Finding her expostulations unavailing, she sent Ellen to entreat me. When ten o'clock in the evening arrived and Ellen had not returned, this watchful and unwearied friend became anxious. She came to us in a carriage, bringing a well-filled trunk for my journey — trusting that by this time I would listen to reason. I yielded to her, as I ought to have done before.

The next day, baby and I set out in a heavy snow storm, bound for New England again. I received letters from the City of Iniquity, addressed to me under an assumed name. In a few days one came from Mrs. Bruce, informing me that my new master was still searching for me, and that she intended to put an end to this persecution by buying my freedom. I felt grateful for the kindness that prompted this offer, but the idea was not so pleasant to me as might have been expected. The more my mind had become enlightened, the more difficult it was for me to consider myself an article of property, and to pay money to those who had so grievously oppressed me seemed like taking from my sufferings the glory of triumph. I wrote to Mrs. Bruce, thanking her, but saying that being sold from one owner to another seemed too much like slavery, that such a great obligation could not be easily canceled, and that I preferred to go to my brother in California.

Without my knowledge, Mrs. Bruce employed a gentleman in New York to enter into negotiations with Mr. Dodge. He proposed to pay three hundred dollars down, if Mr. Dodge would sell me, and enter into obligations to relinquish all claim to me or my children forever after. He who called himself my master said he scorned so small an offer for such a valuable servant. The gentleman replied, "You can do as you choose, sir. If you reject this offer you will never get anything, for the woman has friends who will convey her and her children out of the country."

Mr. Dodge concluded that half a loaf is better than no bread, and he agreed to the proffered terms. By the next mail I received this brief letter from Mrs. Bruce:

I am rejoiced to tell you that the money for your freedom has been paid to Mr. Dodge. Come home tomorrow. I long to see you and my sweet baby.

My brain reeled as I read these lines. A gentleman near me said, "It's true, I have seen the bill of sale."

"The bill of sale!"

Those words struck me like a blow. So I was sold at last! A human being sold in the free city of New York. The bill of sale is on record, and future generations will learn from it that women were articles of traffic in New York, late in the nineteenth century of the Christian religion. It may hereafter prove a useful document to antiquaries, who are seeking to measure the progress of civilization in the United States. I well know the value of that bit of paper, but much as I love freedom, I do not like to look upon it. I am deeply grateful to the generous friend who procured it, but I despise the miscreant who demanded payment for what never rightfully belonged to him or his.

I had objected to having my freedom bought, yet I must confess that when it was done I felt as if a heavy load had been lifted from my weary shoulders. When I rode home in the cars I was no longer afraid to unveil my face and look at people as they passed. I should have been glad to have met Daniel Dodge himself, to have had him seen me and known me, that he might have mourned over the untoward circumstances which compelled him to sell me for three hundred dollars.

When I reached home, the arms of my benefactress were thrown round me, and our tears mingled. As soon as she could speak, she said, "Linda, I'm so glad it's all over. You wrote to me as if you thought you were going to be transferred from one owner to another. But I did not buy you for your services. I should have done just the same, if you had been going to sail for California tomorrow. I should, at least, have the satisfaction of knowing that you left me a free woman."

My heart was exceedingly full. I remembered how my poor father had tried to buy me when I was a small child, and how he had been disappointed. I hoped his spirit was rejoicing over me now. I remembered how my good old grandmother had laid up her earnings to purchase me in later years, and how often her plans had been frustrated. Now that faithful, loving old heart would leap for joy, if she could look on me and my children now that we were free. My relatives had been foiled in all their efforts, but God had raised me up a friend among strangers, who had bestowed on me the precious, long-desired boon. Friend. It is a common word, often lightly used. Like other good and beautiful things, it may be tarnished by careless handling, but when I speak of Mrs. Bruce as my friend, the word is sacred.

My grandmother lived to rejoice in my freedom, but not long after, a letter came with a black seal. She had gone 'where the wicked cease from troubling, and the weary are at rest'.

Time passed on, and a paper came to me from the South, containing an obituary notice of my uncle Phillip. It was the only case I ever knew of such an honor conferred upon a colored person. It was written by one of his friends, and contained these words:

Now that death has laid him low, they call him a good man and a useful citizen, but what are eulogies to the black man, when the world has faded from his vision? It does not require man's praise to obtain rest in God's kingdom.

So they called a colored man a citizen? Strange words to be uttered in that region.

Reader, my story ends with freedom, not in the usual way, with marriage. I and my children are now free. We are as free from the power of slaveholders as are the white people of the North. Though that, according to my ideas, is not saying a great deal, it is a vast improvement in my condition. The dream of my life is not yet realized. I do not sit with my children in a home of my own. I still long for a hearthstone of my own, however humble. I wish it for my children's sake far more than for my own. But God so orders circumstances as to keep me with my friend Mrs. Bruce. Love, duty, gratitude, also bind me to her side. It is a privilege to serve her who pities my oppressed people, and who has bestowed the inestimable boon of freedom on me and my children.

It has been painful to me, in many ways, to recall the dreary years I passed in bondage. I would gladly forget them if I could. Yet the retrospection is not altogether without solace, for with those gloomy recollections come tender memories of my good old grandmother, like light, fleecy clouds floating over a dark and troubled sea.